Praise for *Grant's Getaways – 101 Oregon*

"Grant has a way of capturing the Oregon experience i⸝
compelling. He leaves you feeling as if you'd just share⸝
as he reveals the secret details of an upcoming adventu⸝
writings capture this spirit of his personality and exud⸝
the outdoors. and all things Oregon."

—Todd Davidson, CEO, Travel Oregon

"Grant's new book of Oregon getaways offers a fine collection of places for some of the state's best fishing and wildlife viewing opportunities. His getaways will set you on the right track to enjoying Oregon's natural wonders. So, as Grant likes to say, 'Get out there and explore the Oregon outdoors' and be sure to grab a rod, binoculars, and this book before you go."

—Roy Elicker, Director, Oregon Department of Fish and Wildlife

"Every week, Grant McOmie thrills KGW's audience with his exciting outdoor stories. Now, this book gives readers that same opportunity to adventure with Grant!"

—Rick Jacobs, Executive News Director, KGW Media Group

"Grant's done it again! Oregon's outdoor ambassador, Grant McOmie, has compiled 101 Oregon getaways that are as diverse as they are enchanting, capturing every corner of this wonderful state in McOmie's trademark storytelling style. *Grant's Getaways* is the quintessential guide to discovering Oregon and its hidden wonders."

—Trey Carskadon, fifth-generation Oregonian and former Chairman, Oregon State Marine Board

"I've been a fan of Grant McOmie since his cub reporter days in Seattle. He is the voice of the great Pacific Northwest outdoors. Capturing not only the story of the destination, but sharing the legends, yarns, and accounts of the personalities that make Oregon this unique place we call home. Great read, makes me want to get outdoors even more!"

—John Williams, creator/host of *Wheelchair Destinations*

"Grant has long been a favorite of mine and now he's sharing the how, what, where, and when of his insightful outdoor adventures. Whether tree climbing, cooking up a crawfish boil, digging clams and fossils, kayaking, snowshoeing, or soaring skyward, Grant offers 101 concise vignettes that intrigue and encourage us to lace up our boots and get out there. As Grant so aptly puts, 'Why live here if you don't go searching for those singular moments which set Oregon apart.' Amen."

—MJ Cody, coeditor of *Wild in the City*

Grant's Getaways
101 Oregon Adventures

Grant McOmie

WESTWINDS
PRESS®

Text © 2013 by Grant McOmie
Photography © 2013 by Jeff Kastner, Courtesy of Travel Oregon

All rights reserved. No part of this book may be reproduced or
transmitted in any form or by any means, electronic or mechanical,
including photocopying, recording, or by any information storage
and retrieval system, without written permission of the publisher.

Library of Congress Cataloging-in-Publication Data

McOmie, Grant.
  Grant's getaways : 101 Oregon adventures / Grant McOmie.
    pages cm
  Includes bibliographical references and index.
  ISBN 978-0-88240-861-3 (pbk.)
  ISBN 978-0-88240-947-4 (epub)
  1. Oregon—Guidebooks. 2. Outdoor recreation—Oregon—
Guidebooks. I. Title.
  F874.3.M4 2013
  917.9504—dc23
                              2013001610

Cover photo by Don Best
Designer: Vicki Knapton
Map: Gray Mouse Graphics

Published by WestWinds Press®
An imprint of Graphic Arts Books

GRAPHIC ARTS
BOOKS®

GraphicArtsBooks.com

For my father, Grant McOmie Sr., who showed me which end of a fishing rod catches the big ones. And for my wife, Christine, my finest and favorite travel companion.

Contents

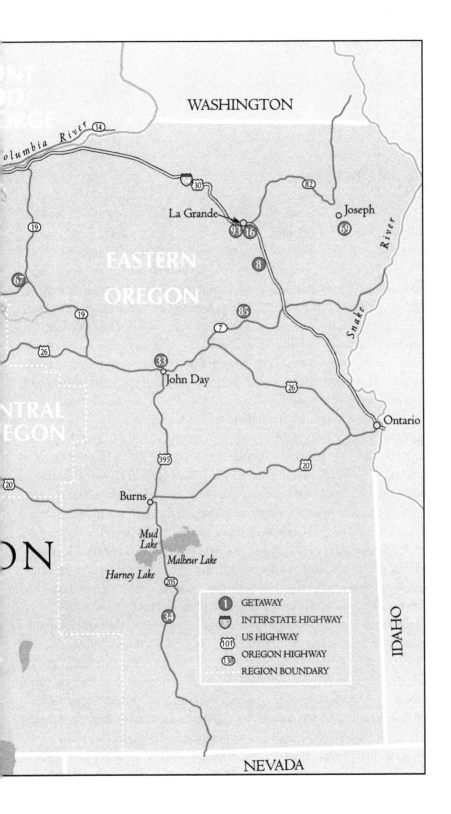

WASHINGTON

Columbia River (14)

(19)

(84) (30)

(82)

La Grande

Joseph

(93)(16)

(69)

EASTERN

(67)

Snake River

(8)

OREGON

(19)

(85)

(7)

(26)

(33)

John Day

(26)

NTRAL
EGON

Ontario

(395)

(20)

(20)

Burns

Mud
Lake

Malheur Lake

Harney Lake

(205)

①	GETAWAY
	INTERSTATE HIGHWAY
(101)	US HIGHWAY
(138)	OREGON HIGHWAY
	REGION BOUNDARY

IDAHO

(34)

ON

NEVADA

Acknowledgments

R eporters are like stones skipping across a pond of water, zipping from story to story each day of the week, but I've been very lucky in that my assignments always seem to get me good and wet and thoroughly immersed in some timely issue or alongside fascinating people, or visiting intriguing places and enjoying exciting outdoor activities. By my calculations, I have written and produced thousands of segments and programs on the great Oregon outdoors over the past three decades. I've spent countless hours on the road traveling across the region for each one of them and here's a little secret—I've loved every minute of it! Mostly because the beauty of travel is the unexpected treasure I've often found along the way; treasures that are measured in the memories of the varied sights and sounds that have connected this small town kid to his home state in ways that I only dreamed about as a boy.

Fortunately, many of my television partners have enjoyed our dream jobs too. So thanks to my partners and colleagues, who helped to capture the images that became the foundations of the stories in this fine collection: Photographers Tom Agosti, Kevin Eyres, Bryon Garvin, Bob Jaundalderis, Mark Plut, Eric Spolar, Mike Rosborough, and Tom Turner. I most especially thank my photography partner, Jeff Kastner, who has worked exclusively on the "Grant's Getaways" segments and programs for the past four years. His keen eye for capturing just the right scene and his remarkable editing skills make me proud to be associated with him. In fact, his skills are shown off in the still images in this book and I sincerely hope you enjoy his work! Without their collective help none of these stories would have been shown or told.

My sincere thanks to the Travel Oregon management team for their trust and confidence in me to represent Oregon—including CEO Todd Davidson, Mo Sherifdeen, Kevin Wright, and Emily Forsha. I also thank these key individuals: David Lane of the Oregon Department of Fish and Wildlife, Ashley Massey of the Oregon State Marine Board, and Chris Havel of the Oregon Parks and Recreation Department. I appreciate their insights, advice, and story suggestions. Further, I extend my sincere appreciation to the KGW-TV management team including DJ Wilson, Brenda Buratti, Rick Jacobs, and Rich Kurz and especially, former News Director Rod Gramer. Each continues to embrace and encourage our work at every turn. In fact, all of these folks support the "Grant's Getaways" endeavors and allow me the privilege of travel across the region.

Thanks to the folks at Graphic Arts Books for the chance to renew friendships and partnerships and share my stories in the new downloadable e-book format, including Doug Pfeiffer, Tim Frew, Vicki Knapton, and Angie Zbornik. Special thanks to Kathy Howard at Graphic Arts Books. She is a wonderfully patient editor who corrected and improved this text a thousandfold and then some.

I also thank my longtime friend and one of the best fellows you'd ever want to join on a fishing trip, Trey Carskadon. He was the conduit for many of the "Grant's Getaways" partners and helped breathe life into the idea that the program could become an ambassador of sorts for the state of Oregon. I will always be indebted to him for his support and encouragement.

I also thank Jan Smith. She was a Professor of Communications at the University of Portland in 1980 and she cajoled, prodded, and encouraged me to pursue my idea of outdoor storytelling with video. She made certain that I landed a news internship at KGW and it is safe to say that I would not be here—now—doing this—had it not been for her encouragement.

Scores of folks donated goodwill, time for an interview, and maybe a tip or two about a new wayside or feature just around the bend, and I thank you all for your time. Finally, to my many KGW and Travel Oregon viewers who continue to enjoy our travels on the road in a little bit of heaven called Oregon, my sincere thanks to you too.

—Grant McOmie
Forest Grove, Oregon

Introduction

Heeey kid! Yes, YOU—McOmie—get in here. I'll give ya five minutes—starting NOW!" Alan Goldberg's shrill and demanding voice shot across the crowded newsroom—just twenty minutes before air time on a hectic news day. I reacted to my boss's call-out with both surprise and relief. Relief that I'd finally have a chance to pitch my kernel of an idea for a new approach to my storytelling assignments, and at the same time I was struck with considerable shock because we were just minutes away from the start of the daily newscast. It was the time of day when news managers seldom wanted to talk about new ideas unless the ideas directly affected the day's most important and culminating event—the 5 o'clock news.

I scrambled into his cramped corner office and quickly began to pitch an idea that I'd been mulling over since the airing of a recent series of stories on Hells Canyon—a region that I thoroughly relished and work which included segments that I'd taken great pains to produce—because the series not only contained stories about adventure in the deepest river canyon in the country, but the interesting folks who managed to carve out a living in a remote and dangerous place along the Snake River Canyon. I explained to Alan that after three years of his leadership I'd enjoyed covering the great outdoors with my weekly reports and special programs, but I really wanted a franchise name and a small corner of the regular news broadcast that I could call my own; a handful of minutes each week when we could show viewers what's "right" with their world.

"What do you want to call it?" he shot back—his teeth firmly locked on a well-chewed cigar. (Yes, a cigar. And yes, smoking in the newsroom was allowed in those days.) I offered a number of possibilities where the station's logo was firmly waved across the top—but he would have none of it. "Why not name it after what you do, eh? You're never around here much, eh? Seems to me you're always getting away from it all, eh? So, Grant Gets-A-Way? No . . . Grant Goes Away? No . . . Grant's . . . uhh . . . Getaways? I like that—it's easy to remember and we will run it each Thursday." The second part of my request was a bit more problematic. You see, all I really needed from Alan, who had brought me back to Portland from our Seattle sister station to fill a niche of outdoor reporting in a state prized for recreation, travel, and environmental concerns—what I really needed to launch "Grant's Getaways" was the dual promise of a photographer who would be assigned to work with me on the outdoor beat and also that I be entrusted with one of the prized newsroom credit cards. I yearned to travel the open road and reach into each and every nook and cranny and corner of the Pacific Northwest for my stories, especially to produce stories about my home state of Oregon.

If I could pull it off, each of my requests would be true prizes for a young reporter who'd started his career only six years earlier. At the same time, if approved, my requests would mark that I had really proven myself of value to the operation. In fact, I had—through a handful of projects (including the delivery of a ten-part series and a one-hour special program that we produced in Southeast Alaska, where photographer Mark Plut and I had boated and flown in every conceivable aircraft and watercraft imaginable across thousands of miles in one short week). I'd shown that I could deliver what I promised, that I was reliable at handling the station's money and did not exceed my budget, and critically, that the programs continued to attract viewers and sponsors as measured by the all-important Nielsen ratings. It helped that our programs also kept the station's sales staff happy. I felt I was in good stead on all counts!

"Well, it will be tight, but I can swing a photographer if we can keep your production output up to a certain level but about that credit card . . ." I really don't recall Alan's exact words but they included something about his great confidence in me and how I must shoulder more responsibilities and finally—yes, he concluded, he could make the newsroom credit card—my golden ticket to freedom and travel—happen, but just "don't screw anything up" and "stay in touch with us about your comings and goings. Now get outta here—I've a news room to run."

And so, "Grant's Getaways" was born twenty-six years ago and what a run it's been. Over the years and after thousands of stories, I have often wondered during the early years of my storytelling career, whether I was getting away from the rush and grind and responsibility of the daily news schedule? Was I shirking the nagging journalistic responsibilities we reporters feel are owed to our viewers or did I truly find more interesting stories about Oregon's people, places, and outdoor activities "out there" somewhere in quiet remote corners of the state where folks went about their daily routines—where I still think the good stories just wait to be told. I suspect it was probably a bit of both.

After all, most of my news colleagues really enjoyed—in some cases savored—covering the day-to-day news about the latest crimes, notable political machinations, or the bad doings behind the doors of the rich or powerful people. Truth was, I didn't care much for chasing ambulances and preferred the wide-open spaces that Oregon offered. Early on, I was mentored by a real pro—Charles Kuralt—(yes, the man who made travel and a life "On the Road" an American television phenomenon) who told me that TV reporting can be a "fine way to paint an empty canvas with pictures, just don't mess it up by letting your words get in the way." That was my mantra from the start. It still is and I have worked very hard at it for a very long time.

It has always been my hope that "Grant's Getaways" makes people smile or even swell a bit with pride for all that there is in this part of the world. I also hope that viewers learn something about Oregon that they didn't know before. For gosh sakes, why live here if you don't go searching for those singular moments which set Oregon apart from just about everywhere else? I have described many times how we work to show off Oregon in our programs—my partners and I have paddled, soared, hiked, biked, climbed, flown, dived, swum, crawled, and—yes—driven tens of thousands of miles in trucks, jeeps, and vans, on motorcycles, and inside buses and RVs across a region reaching east to the Snake River and south through the Siskiyous. For the most part, my story assignments put me face to face with interesting characters, intriguing destinations, and a menagerie of wildlife from eagles to whales, salmon to elk, and even to cave-dwelling bats. Most of us rarely see such a wide array of critters and only dream about such wild adventures. Mine has been a dream job, akin to a year-round Adventures 101, where class is always in session and the homework chronicles spectacular places and amazing activities.

Grant's Getaways: 101 Oregon Adventures spans the varied geophysical regions of Oregon and includes a number of adventures for each month of the year. I hope you consider this book both a playground and a classroom, for in it we'll journey to a little-known corner of Oregon where you can stroll through a lush rain forest marked by a rare and towering stand of ancient giant fir trees. We'll cast baits to catch and release a dinosaur of a fish species from the mighty Columbia River. We'll saddle up and join a horseback trip into the little-known Santiam State Park in Oregon's Cascade Mountains. I'll take you where wildlife rules the grounds and the visitors are in cages of a sort at the unique drive-through wildlife viewing experience of Wildlife Safari. Your kids will love finding buried treasure in the form of ancient fossils they can dig for keeps. We'll tour Oregon snow country on snowshoes, speed across forest trails aboard an ATV, and dip paddles into an estuary on a trip that provides up close views to wildlife. We'll put on swimsuits and dive into a cool, refreshing stream on a sweltering summer's day and gather crawfish—and then I'll show you how to prepare them in a feast fit for kings.

Speaking of feasts, readers have encouraged me to offer more recipes, and in this book I have. Not only will you learn about a premier place to pick baskets of huckleberries, but I'll also share a favorite recipe for huckleberry cobbler that is out of this world! In addition, I've included lip-smacking salmon, crab, and razor clam recipes that will impress your friends with true Oregon taste and flair.

My getaway selections are a start for your own family adventures. They offer some standout features, such as an inspiring viewpoint, a unique hike to a secluded campground, or a spectacular wildlife moment. Many are accessible on a tank of gas, though others do require more planning and time. I also describe many interesting side trips that include activities or people or programs you should know more about that are adjacent to the primary getaway destination. I mention wheelchair accessibility where available, though there is almost always a path or trail nearby that can be navigated in a wheelchair. Each getaway concludes with contact names, phone numbers, and websites for further information.

The point of all this, as I like to tell folks in person, on the air, or in writing, is just to get out there, enjoy Oregon any time of year, and make some memories of your own. So lace up your hiking boots and buckle up your seat belts too. We're traveling toward adventures that make Oregon so special. I hope *Grant's Getaways: 101 Oregon Adventures* helps guide your way.

So Easy Anyone Can Try

Adventures Without Limits

GETAWAY #1 – MOUNT HOOD / THE GORGE

A hike in Oregon snow country means finding the "right fit" for a snowshoe, but there's more according to Keith Mussallem, lead guide for the Washington County based nonprofit called Adventures Without Limits (AWL). This group that specializes in finding the right fit for folks who rarely get to go. "Our programs are geared toward working with anyone who has a known disadvantage—physical, developmental, financial—and they come to us because they know they're going to be taken care of. They show up and we'll handle it all."

Recently, it was "all handled" at the popular White River West Sno-Park near Mount Hood—the starting point of a two-mile hike for folks who'd never done anything like it before. Since 1995, Adventures Without Limits has taken folks where they want to go, whether kayaking, white-water rafting, rock climbing, cave exploring, camping, or many other types of year-round recreation adventures. Kris Williams, AWL's executive director, said the nonprofit group refuses to say "no" to anyone who has an appetite for adventure. Whether it's lack of skill, experience, or money, they make certain everyone gets a chance to explore Oregon.

"I can't tell you how many times we've taken people from Portland out to mountains like Mount Hood or over to the coast—teenagers or adults—who've never been to any of those places before. So, for the first time they're experiencing something that can be a real eye-opener for them—an amazing and empowering experience."

Out on the White River snow trail, AWL's "companions" helped guide many newcomers who were challenged by the snow, the slope, and the new feel of ungainly snowshoes. "Many of our participants come to do the activities but can use an extra set of hands due to varying ranges of disabilities," noted guide Devan Schwartz. "Our companion comes along and just stays there—attentive to the personal needs

Folks come for the convenience of fresh snowfall at White River Sno-Park near Mount Hood.

of the client and that gives everyone a chance to try something new and have a good experience."

Each step up the trail brought each person closer to a mountain of new confidence where their successes were measured by broad smiles from new accomplishments, plus an eagerness for more adventure. "We want them to have a complete experience, a little bit more awareness, but also a lot of joy in what they do," added Keith. Kris agreed, "So they'll feel safe and empowered and feel confidant to get out there and do it on their own."

For More Information

Where: 1341 Pacific Avenue, Forest Grove, OR 97116
Web: www.awloutdoors.com
Phone: 503-359-2568; Fax: 503-359-4671
Watch the Episode: www.traveloregon.com/nolimits

Reduce, Reuse, and Recycle
Hopworks Brewpub

When I heard there was a "new kid on the brew block" in Portland at a unique eco-pub where sustainability is king and where reduce, reuse, and recycle provide the foundation of a thriving new business, I jumped at the chance to see what makes the HUB, or Hopworks Urban Brewery, work so well.

The HUB is a neighborhood hit where standing room only is the rule on most nights. Folks come from all over to Southeast Portland's 29th and Powell to sip a brew, dine with friends, and relax in the knowledge that things are different in the newest neighborhood eco-pub. Keri Rose, a neighbor and regular customer, explained: "It's amazing beer that's organically brewed, plus really friendly people and I think you get something uniquely Portland. I think the HUB speaks to all of us who are really oriented toward that way of life." The HUB is an eco-pub and it's a first on the Southeast Portland brew scene that's built upon the practices of sustainability, organic ingredients, and eco-friendly ideas. The business is the brainchild of Christian Ettinger, the HUB's brewmaster with fourteen years of experience brewing beer, and alongside his dad, Roy Ettinger, a veteran architect with forty years of experience, the team codesigned the nearly seventeen-thousand-square-foot eco-pub.

Both agree, the 1948 building that they selected for the HUB, once a diesel fuel depot and a former Caterpillar Tractor showroom, wasn't always warm or inviting. "Oh no, not at all," noted the elder Ettinger. "It was full of dust, you couldn't lean on anything because you'd get black soot on you. There were tons of wires strung on the ceiling . . . just forty-three years of decay and dust and it was that greasy, grime."

Christian quickly added, "We turned what was sixty years of a business into piles of material that were to be either recycled or shredded into fuel or reused." The deconstruction took over a year and a half to complete—but they salvaged every bit of mate-

There are no strangers, just friends that haven't met yet, at Southeast Portland's Hopworks Urban Brewery.

rial from the old building—the first step in walking the talk of creating a sustainable brewery and restaurant where reduce, reuse, and recycle is an everyday business.

Christian noted that the bones of the building, the old-growth Doug fir posts, beams, and planks were solid, substantial, and deserved new life. The old wood became the booths, bar, and other varied pieces of furnishings in the HUB. And then there is Christian's signature statement; scores of bike frames and old wheel rims that were incorporated above the bar and the booths of his pub. "Every one of these frames was recycled and I'm only about three hundred bucks into this—and it really sets the bar apart from anyplace around."

Downstairs, you could say the same thing about the HUB's brewery where pesticide-free and fertilizer-free ingredients are staples of the ten crafted organic beers that the HUB produces each week. In the kitchen, organic ingredients take center stage too—from pizza dough to the sauces to the sandwiches with all the trimmings and more. In fact, even the heat from the pizza oven is recycled and circulated to heat the pub's water. "That's free heat," said Christian. "Free heat is free energy and lowers our bills but it also lowers our needs to bring in fossil fuels."

Lionne Decker, the HUB's general manager, is quick to point out that the entire HUB team walks the talk of taking care of the environment and making customers smile at the same time. "It starts with a commitment to the environment, a commitment to what you're putting on the plate, what you're putting in the pint. Really, it's a commitment to leaving the world a better place than we found it. It's amazing! It really is."

It's amazing adventure that may keep you coming back for more—built upon a philosophy worth living. The HUB is one of just three Oregon breweries—out of eighty statewide—that have made the move to produce all organic beer. The folks who work at the HUB are eager to share and explain all of the different ways that they walk the talk of sustainability. So, stop in and enjoy a beer and strike up a conversation! The folks at the HUB will be pleased to tell their story—it's that sort of a friendly, neighborhood place.

For More Information

Where: 2944 SE Powell Boulevard, Portland, OR 97202

Web: www.hopworksbeer.com

Phone: 503-232-HOPS (4677); Fax: 503-232-4676

Watch the Episode: www.traveloregon.com/ecopub

Solitary Sentinels
Oregon's Heritage Trees

When you've a Heritage Tree in your line of sight—and a camera in hand—you better have the object of your passion in clear focus. Steve Dierckx and Michael Horodyski are landscape photographers who say their eyes are open wide with wonder and pride when a real giant comes into view, like the giant sequoias that line the walkway to the Washington County Courthouse in Hillsboro. Steve noted, "They act like sentinels, very scenic, picturesque." Michael added as he took a quick photo, "These century-old trees are not only unusual—they are in rare company across the state too." He's right! They join more than fifty other trees called Oregon's Heritage Trees.

I learned long ago about the value of Oregon's significant trees during an encounter with Maynard Drawson, one of the most interesting and enthusiastic documenters of regional history. I had known of Maynard's efforts to identify and protect Oregon's really old and really big trees for many years, yet surprisingly our paths never crossed until 1999, when the Oregon Travel Council published a new brochure, largely a result of Maynard's work, showcasing fifteen Oregon Heritage Trees.

They are part of a unique program sponsored by the Oregon Travel Information Council that was established in 1995 to recognize Oregon's special trees and to increase public awareness of the important contribution of trees to Oregon's history and the significant role they still play in the quality of life. It is the only state-sponsored program of its kind in the nation.

Maynard was a fine, gracious gentleman and purveyor of facts about our past who had a passion for holding on to heritage trees as though they were members of his family. In fact, I'll never forget his remark to me about the friendships you can make through Oregon's big old trees: "If you find someone who really cares about trees, why then, Grant, you've found someone who's probably worth knowing!" Despite being seventy-something years old, Maynard was as sharp and active as a person half his age and his enthusiasm was infectious. He could recite historical facts, places, and names of people, places, and trees at the drop of a hat. In those days, many called him Oregon's "Ambassador of Trees," a spokesperson for the magnificent, stately, and significant trees that have survived through the years.

You may have seen some of Oregon's finest examples, like the Hager Pear Tree at the hectic junction of I-5 and State Highway 22 in Salem. Planted in 1848, the old tree was part of a huge orchard that supplied fruit across the state. It's the only one left. Or Waldo Park in downtown Salem: although small in acreage, it is a huge park in stature that's located right next to the Capitol Building. Or inside Willamette Mission State Park, home to the oldest cottonwood tree in the country.

Paul Ries, the Oregon Department of Forestry representative to the Heritage Tree Committee, said, "This tree is not only old—225 years or more—but you or I could not get our arms around this tree—we'd need five, six, seven more of us just to do that." Paul added that Oregon's Heritage Trees are living legacies, often planted by pioneer ancestors and they are links to Oregon's rural roots. "We really take trees for granted," said Paul. "They provide us so many benefits: clean air, clean water, lumber products, places to recreate, but there is also that personal connection we have with trees—their stories help make that connection to the things that have happened in our past and help us understand the present."

Stories like the Nyberg English Chestnut located at the Nyberg Road exit off I-5 in Tualatin, Oregon. John Nyberg was a man who said "no" to progress so as to save a very old and very significant chestnut tree. He was a simple but brave farmer at the turn of the twentieth century. In 1903, he planted an orchard of more than 150 trees that grew tall and gorgeous—the orchard included several stately English chestnut trees.

But in 1954, bulldozers were building the interstate highway and the big old trees were in the right of way and they were coming down at breakneck speed. One hundred and fifty had fallen on the Nyberg farm—many were planted in the nineteenth century. Grandson Arne Nyberg told me that most had fallen and there was just one tree left—this one—when his granddad said "No more."

"The D-9 cat was pushing them over right and left and that's where he took his stand—he literally stood in front of the cat and stopped it from bulldozing down the last chestnut tree. Imagine that! He was a small but brave man and what a rare Oregon story about how a citizen can save a tree."

Heritage Trees don't have to be the oldest or the biggest or even a native tree but the candidate for consideration sure needs to have a good story. Like the story behind the Student Planters' Grove in the Tillamook State Forest, a grove of Doug firs planted by children nearly sixty years ago. Paul explained: "The story of the Tillamook State

You'd need four more friends to link arms to surround the oldest cottonwood tree in the country at Willamette Mission State Park.

Forest is a story of rebirth and renewal and that grove signifies that. Many of the trees were planted by schoolkids following several devastating fires that burned much of the forest to the ground. It's an amazing story."

The Valley of the Giants is an amazing heritage deep in the Oregon Coast Range, where you can walk among five-hundred-year-old Doug fir trees. "For those that make the effort to get there it is an amazing remnant of what was once here throughout much of Oregon," noted Paul. "It's a small valley of giant trees and you feel very small against some of the big trees that grow in the place."

Back at the Washington County Courthouse, Steve and Michael agreed the giant sequoias are not only super models—but the stories in the trees will teach you much about our state. "I love trees," said Michael. "I mean that's one of the great things we've got in this state; so many trees and so many varieties and so many great stories."

Note: To read more about the Valley of the Giants, see chapter 39, "It Will Make You Feel Small/Valley of the Giants."

For More Information

Where: Oregon Travel Experience, 1500 Liberty Street SE, Suite 150, Salem, OR 97302-4609

Web: www.ortravelexperience.com

Phone: 1-800-574-9397; Fax: 503-378-6282

Watch the Episode: www.traveloregon.com/heritagetrees

A Friend to the Critters
Wildlife Images

Dave Siddon has walked the talk of helping sick and injured wildlife for more than thirty years. He owns and manages Wildlife Images near Grants Pass in Southern Oregon. Throughout his lifetime of study and hands-on practice, Dave has come to know hawks and eagles and vultures and scores of other sharp-eyed birds of prey very well.

For many years he was a fixture at the Oregon Zoo—even started their raptor program. Twelve years later he decided to go home to Wildlife Images and follow his father's life's work rehabilitating sick or injured animals and educating folks. His father, Dave Siddon Sr., was a well-known figure in the wildlife rehabilitation world. He opened the clinic in 1981 following his own passion for helping cougars and eagles and bears get well and get back to the wild. Dave Sr. passed away in 1996 following a battle with cancer, and his son promised to dedicate his life to the center's most important mission. "When my father was dying of cancer he came to me and said, 'Would you consider leaving the zoo and making sure my place doesn't die along with me?' and how do you say no to that? So I came down here and dedicated my life to making sure this place continues to do the good work it does."

Dave Siddon Jr. was well prepared for the challenge. He worked for Sea World where he trained sea lions and dolphins, he worked at the Oregon Zoo, and he has blazed his own trail into the world of wildlife rehabilitation. Wildlife Images offers wildlife viewing opportunities at every turn: perhaps a fox, a bobcat, a large brown bear, and especially the wildlife that fly.

Dave noted that some animals come to Wildlife Images from would-be pet owners who realize too late that some critters just don't make good house pets. The center receives and treats over 2,500 animals annually, and approximately 90 percent of those that survive their initial injuries are returned to the wild. The organization's clinic, nature center, and animal holding facilities are located on twenty-four acres of natural habitat adjacent to Oregon's famous Wild and Scenic Rogue River, which serves as an excellent location for wildlife release.

Each year thousands of visitors tour the center to see animals ranging from grizzly bears to mountain lions to small arctic foxes and even tiny hummingbirds. As we strolled past display cages containing coyotes, a badger, porcupines, red foxes, and others, Dave pointed out with pride the close-up opportunities that visitors enjoy at an open-air exhibit for bald eagles, turkey vultures, and ravens. As we walked into the small building, Dave reached over and lifted a large metal window. The opening looked out to a grassy area, dotted with many small native plants and towering trees jutting to the sky.

Backyard Bird Resorts

When is a birdhouse a "home?" Oh, that's easy! It's when feathered residents move in and build a nest.

Birding is a popular outdoor recreational activity for many Oregonians—whether it's watching for varied species, filling a feeder, or even building the songbirds a home! But some Oregonians go the extra mile to make sure native songbirds get more than a simple roof over their heads: they get a backyard resort for a home.

Spectacular shows are easy to come by in winter; not just the huge flocks of waterfowl or solo raptors like hawks and eagles, but also the smaller songbird species. In fact, consider attracting wildlife species like songbirds into your own backyard. Hillsboro resident Dennis Frame loves the sights and sounds of the wild—so he builds feeders and houses for native songbirds.

Dennis's structures aren't really homes but his elaborate wooden abodes are more akin to—well, bird resorts. Washington County resident Irene Dickson has two of Dennis's beautiful yet functional feeders and each is firmly planted in the ground on fence posts six feet off the ground in her yard. She said that they "really work."

"They add such pleasure and peace," said the avid bird fan. "They're real de-stressors too. Plus, the resort detail is fabulous and impressive with the little rock walls, benches, and other details. It looks like a little cabin by a lake."

Dennis is a builder of human homes by trade, but in his cozy and well organized carpentry shop, he said his greatest pleasure comes from crafting the elaborate bird

Dave Siddon Jr. holds one of his prized wild friends, a golden eagle that's a popular ambassador for Wildlife Images.

resorts. "This is my little getaway and I can come in here and get away from it all and get creative too."

He's always been a fan of simple, rustic log cabin homes and will often scour the countryside for "models" that he can reproduce on a small scale for the birds. "I'll drive and spot one and 'Oh, that's cool.' Maybe snap a photo or make a mental note and then re-create it in a bird house." Dennis has been "chipping away" at his hobby for fifteen years and said it's the tiny details that impress most people.

The resorts sport stone and mortar chimneys, decks with handrails, and small pieces of character that set them apart from ordinary store-bought models—including a wooden front door. "The door actually opens. I do that because you must clean out the resort following each nesting year. In fact, the birds seldom return the following year unless you do that. I try to make it an easier job." Dennis also trades, barters, and salvages for everything—recycling for the birds!

On top of that, he rarely sells a house; instead, through the years he has given them away to nonprofits like his local Rotary Club and the Jackson Bottom Wetlands Education Center. The groups then sell Dennis's bird resorts and raise hundreds of dollars to support their educational programs. "This is my way of giving back to the community. I believe in community; they help me out, so I help them out. And getting people out of their houses and learning more about the outdoors is a positive way to go in my book."

You can reach Dennis Frame via e-mail: hackum@comcast.net.

A fine mesh net draped over the entire scene and prevented the birds from leaving the grounds. "Perfect perches," I noted as I admired the very natural setting. Dave then shared more of his father's vision and passion. "It was my father's real dream to put together a facility for the bald eagles and other raptors where people can see them without wire and obstructions. They're such beautiful and majestic birds, you'd like to see them in some sort of situation that mimics what you'd see in the wild." Wildlife Images offers unique educational opportunities to schools, organizations, and the general public and conducts tours six days a week year-round. Reservations are required, and the facility is closed most national holidays. You can visit, wander with a tour, and learn more about the remarkable people that help Oregon wildlife, motivated by Dave Siddon Sr.'s simple yet powerful belief: "If you don't have wildlife, it's not a good place to be."

For More Information

Where: 11845 Lower River Road, Grants Pass, OR 97526-9613
Web: www.wildlifeimages.org
Phone: 541-476-0222
Watch the Episode: www.traveloregon.com/friendtocritters

Monument to History
Fort Yamhill State Heritage Area

I f you know where to look, Oregon's history books come to life in the great out-doors—including one of the oldest and more controversial chapters that even predates Oregon statehood. It is history that's open for you to explore at a military outpost that's also one of Oregon's newest state parks—a trail to new understanding about Oregon's past at Fort Yamhill State Heritage Area near Grand Ronde, Oregon.

A stroll across the Fort Yamhill State Heritage Area with Oregon State Parks Ranger Ryan Sparks is a bit like time travel—back 150 years to the time of pioneers, Native Americans, and US soldiers. Ryan says Fort Yamhill was the "blue line" provided by more than one hundred US soldiers above the Grand Ronde Valley. The soldiers provided protection for five hundred Native Americans from thirty different tribes who were forced to the Grand Ronde Reservation in 1856.

"The soldiers would have con-gregated on the large grassy area—drilling in formation all of the time," said Ryan. "There were six officers' quarters at the highest end of the fort—white-washed build-

Information kiosks explain Fort Yamhill's compel-ling story of the US military presence in Oregon during the 1850s.

ings with wide porches. The officers would sit out on the front porch and watch the soldiers down below on the parade grounds."

Today, you can still see signs from those times inside one of the original and intact officers' homes. Although undergoing a painstaking restoration, the old home is remarkably well preserved. "There are original hand-hewn beams," noted Ryan. "Upstairs, the roof has no nails, but wooden pins that hold the rafters together. Actually, the weight of the roof holds it all in place."

Oregon State Parks and Recreation Department considers the house a treasure chest because it may have been the residence for then Lt. Phil Sheridan who was fresh from West Point Academy and commanded Fort Yamhill years before the Civil War led him to fame and glory. Fort Yamhill's story isn't always pleasant. After all, the US Army was there for a purpose: in the 1850s as new emigrants arrived from back east, westward expansion approached a peak, and more land was developed by Oregon pioneers.

The army was there to protect the remaining Native Americans in the wilderness, but it was a symbol of the government's "big stick" of power and authority. That power was specifically symbolized by the heavy timbered "blockhouse": a military defensive structure and a presence that couldn't be denied. "I am not a Native American," said Ryan, "so, I can only imagine that if you lived on the reservation, and looked up at the blockhouse each day, it would be intimidating; it definitely had a dominant position on this side of the hill facing the reservation."

The original blockhouse survives in Dayton, Oregon, where it's being restored as the centerpiece of a city park and you can visit it anytime in the heart of downtown Dayton. It's a wonderfully wooded area and the park resonates with Oregon history. It is also the central gathering place for Dayton's community and worth a side trip.

Even three generations later, Confederated Tribes spokesman Eirik Thorsgard said Fort Yamhill provides a memory that remains strong. "The fort is not just a place of subtle hostility for us, but it's also a line of protection." Eirik said that the irony of Fort Yamhill is that the military presence was despised and yet without it, the people who were brought so long ago might not have survived. "Reservations are probably the biggest detriment to the Indian people," noted Eirik. "But they were also our saving grace for if we hadn't been placed on reservations we may have gone the way of the dinosaurs."

In fact, the Grand Ronde Tribes partnered with Oregon State Parks so that all of the stories from those days—stories that connect all of us to enduring Oregon history—will continue to be told at this historic parkland. "The history of Fort Yamhill is not just the tribe's history," said Eirik. "It is the state of Oregon's and really part of the nation's history, so it is important for everyone who calls Oregon home today to fully understand and appreciate the past."

For More Information

Where: Drive east of Salem on Oregon State Highway 22 to the park entrance 1 mile north of Valley Junction.

Web: www.oregonstateparks.org

Phone: 800-551-6949 or 503-393-1172

Watch the Episode: www.traveloregon.com/fortyamhill

Hot Shot for a Cold Spell
Belknap Hot Springs

The McKenzie River Scenic Byway may leave you slack-jawed and spellbound. State Highway 126 is a timeless transition on the western approach into Oregon's Cascade Mountains. "It is scenic and it is beautiful," noted local travel expert Meg Trendler. "You are driving along the river and you get these glimpses of an absolutely crystal clear river all along the way and lots of greenery too."

Like century-old drawing cards along the way, Lane County's covered bridges including Goodpasture Covered Bridge, at 165 feet it's Oregon's second longest, and Belknap Bridge, a river crossover since 1890. "The bridges were generally made of wood back in the '20s and '30s but if you covered them, the timbers would last twice or three times longer in Oregon's wet weather."

Wet may be what you'll get when you reach the plunge pool world of Sahalie Falls and Koosah Falls—the trail is always open and easily reached off the highway. "The water just comes shooting out like a fire hydrant," said Meg with a smile. "It's a huge wall of

A soak at Belknap Hot Springs will refresh your mind, body, and soul as it has for more than a century.

water any time of year and then there's a great path you can walk from Sahalie to Koosah falls so it's not even five minutes from your car to the falls."

The McKenzie River Valley is a year-round recreation destination and the centerpiece for many is the McKenzie River National Recreation Trail. The trail is twenty-six miles long and about half that distance is below the snow line, so you've good opportunities for hiking and biking anytime. People have long enjoyed the McKenzie River, often called Oregon's first fishing and boating playground.

Roger Fletcher, a local historian and owner of River's Touch, said that drift boating was spawned on the McKenzie River; the birthplace for the all-Oregon boat with its unique style of riding atop the rapids. "The McKenzie boats evolved in the 1920s as fishing guides searched for boats with maneuverability and capacity . . . it made water previously inaccessible, accessible. Of course, that was a two-edged sword . . . because as people discovered the opportunities, more and more people came to the river."

When they came, many visitors also found a distinct way to warm up after a long day on the water. Belknap Hot Springs has been a hot shot for a wintertime cold spell since the 1850s and you can even see the water bubbling out of the ground.

It's 200°F at the source, according to Marlene Watson, the Belknap resort manager, who noted that at that temperature, you could cook an egg. A series of underground pipes cool the water so by the time it reaches the nearby pool, it's a warm and relaxing environment.

"We have family groups who get together here because it is so relaxing," added Marlene, "They can swim, hike, read, and relax and they love it." Belknap Hot Springs Resort offers full-service accommodations including overnight camping for RV, tent, or trailer—even rental cabins and a full-service lodge. Marlene added that the McKenzie River draws visitors back along a scenic drive that is "steady and serene." "You hear the river go by and it's just a wonderful place to get away and forget all your troubles—relax!"

Note: To read more on drift boats, see chapter 91, "Rowing Through History/The All-Oregon Boat."

For More Information

Where: Belknap Lodge, 59296 Belknap Springs Road, Blue River, OR 97413
Web: www.belknaphotsprings.com
Phone: 541-822-3512
Watch the Episode: www.traveloregon.com/belknaphotsprings

Mush Puppies!
Dog Sledding at Mount Bachelor

Jerry Scdoris has twelve of the most faithful friends one mountain of a man could ever hope to have in a lifetime. Consider what they do for him: Whenever Jerry hollers "Hey," these dedicated buddies of his rise to their feet and go. Actually they run and run and run anywhere he tells them to go. They will pull hundreds of pounds while enduring deep snow or slippery ice and a biting wind that would send most of us indoors for rest and relaxation beside the nearest toasty warm woodstove.

And get this: They never, ever complain. In fact, they love to be outdoors when winter is its roughest: downright mean and nasty. Jerry's best friends are huskies.

"These huskies been doing this for thousands of years. It's like—why do birds fly, why do fish swim—my dogs just got to run." They're not big or brawny either. Rather, they're medium-sized pooches about twenty pounds each, but they are huge when it comes to desire and energy and enthusiasm to please people.

During a visit to Jerry's Iditarod training camp near Mount Bachelor, I asked him how he trains dogs for the kind of pure commitment it takes to run and pull through the snow. He told me his dogs "are 110 percent go-power. They just have to run out of pure joy." Jerry explained, "It all starts out fast and exhilarating. I think it surprises people how fast and how powerful these little dogs are. A lot of folks have sled dog dreams—they've read Jack London novels as youngsters and have just had it in their brain to go for a sled dog ride—that's how I started—decades ago."

Jerry is in his twenty-first season at Mount Bachelor, but he has been a professional musher for over thirty years. He also takes passengers on a thrilling dogsled ride across a three-mile course. He's covered 100,000 Alaska wilderness miles with his dog teams and he likes to say the dogs are "experts in motion." Watching Jerry work with his dogs, you witness an incredible transformation when he attaches the huskies to their traces individually and they become a team.

The older, veteran lead dog is generally calm in comparison to the younger huskies. The excitement and energy build among these youngsters, who bark and yelp for joy until the musher releases the drag brake and steps onto the back runners. No longer do you hear a dozen whining individuals, because the dogs' eagerness settles into a determination to pull hard and fast no matter the weight in the attached sled basket.

It's a heart-pounding thrill when you join Jerry Scdoris's "sled of dreams" in the Deschutes National Forest.

Dave Sims, a longtime partner in Jerry's business, designs and builds all of the equipment including the toboggan-style sleds that carry up to six hundred pounds—plenty of room for mom, dad, and a couple of kids. "The sleds are safe, they're sturdy, and they're comfortable for people to sit in. You can fill them up heaping to the top so you can haul a lot of gear in them." I was intrigued with so much energy about to be let loose, so my wife, Christine, and I didn't hesitate to accept Jerry's invitation to sit in the comfy sled. Actually, Chris sat while I was invited to stand on the runners. With that, we were off in a moment of madness, down a slope into a wooded stand, leaving a snowy wake flying up behind us. The loop trail's first part follows a narrow Forest Service trail flanked by Douglas fir and ponderosa pine. As we slip-slid along, it was a bit like a combination sled and rollicking roller-coaster ride. Jerry reminded me the dogs are bred for only one reason: "to run, run, and keep on runnin'."

Then he surprised me and asked, "Would you like to try running the team, Grant?" "You bet! What do I need to know—besides hanging on?"

"Keep your knees slightly bent, take your right foot off the brake, and put it on the runner," he replied. "Then say 'Okay.'"

"Okay," I whispered, uncertain what I should expect from the eager dog team.

"Nooo—you gotta mean it," Jerry gently scolded, then shouted to his team in a commanding tone, "Okay, okay!" And we were off again! The feeling was exhilarating and surprisingly quiet. We cruised silently at nearly twenty miles an hour. Suddenly I found time to admire the surrounding mountains that peek through the forest.

Whether you stand or sit, hold on to your hat when you enjoy the exhilarating dog sled ride near Mount Bachelor.

The deep powder is a storybook landscape for speeding through narrow trails in a dense pine forest with boughs bent low from a fresh powdery blanket. According to Jerry, "half of the visitors come up with a Sergeant Preston of the Yukon fantasy. They are not real sure what to expect—perhaps bigger dogs, and then they're amazed with my guys' speed and enthusiasm. You know, Grant, these animals just don't want to stop."

You'll want to stop in, though, and make Jerry Scdoris and his best friends part of your Oregon snow-country adventures. The training camp and rides open with the first fall of snow in November and continue into spring. There's a certain peaceful feeling out on the trail, a feeling that—even for an hour or so—all is right with the world.

For More Information

Where: Mount Bachelor, 13000 SW Century Drive, Bend, OR 97702

Web: www.mtbachelor.com

Phone: 800-829-2442

Watch the Episode: www.traveloregon.com/mushpuppies

A Front Row Seat to Wildlife
Elkhorn Wildlife Area

Here's a lesson that thirty years of covering wildlife stories has taught me: Always expect the unexpected! For one thing, critters never keep appointments. They can be the most daunting story subjects to capture on tape, and I've plenty of photography partners in the TV news business who will testify to that frustration. We have spent countless hours—no, make that days—traveling across hundreds of miles, often in the worst of weather, hoping to capture just the right moment when a wild animal will display some unique behavior. Be it salmon jumping a waterfall; sage grouse strutting across their springtime desert leks or breeding grounds; or hiking into distant, craggy mountains searching for cougar or bear dens, I have learned that when it comes to encountering wildlife, it pays to be a lucky rather than an accomplished journalist.

Winter rules the distant Elkhorn Mountains where the ice floes stack streamside and snowdrifts line roadways and a sea of white spans the horizon—it is snow country near Baker City and you can make an appointment to go along for the ride of a lifetime and help feed hundreds of wild Rocky Mountain elk at Oregon's Elkhorn Wildlife Area.

It is bone-chilling cold that shows little sign of thawing! But at Anthony Creek in Baker County, a Saturday morning warming fire chases the 20°F chill away before you step aboard T&T Wildlife Tours. Alice Trindle shares the reins of the operation with partner Susan Triplett while local horseman Mike Moore lends a hand. "For twenty years," noted Mike, "they've been taking people up and down this hill and get you up as close to Rocky Mountain elk as you will ever get in your life—a unique experience." It is the only horse-drawn wildlife tour in Oregon . . . and Jed and Waylen, a pair of Percheron draft horses, are the heavy pullers.

"This is their third winter they've been here helping us out," said Alice. "Part of it is their temperament; they are probably the most petted horses in the county. They are our equal partners." Each weekend, all of the partners pitch in to feed the elk that make Anthony Creek a winter home from mid-December through February; they will spread up to a dozen alfalfa bales to feed 150 elk. "Scoop-loop is our biggest elk, a bull elk and he's a seven by seven. That means he has seven points [the antler points] on one side and seven points on the other. Antlers are quite amazing—the fastest growing bone in the animal kingdom. . . . They can grow as much as an inch in a day and weigh up to thirty-five pounds on these Rocky Mountain elk."

T&T Wildlife Tours is an asset to Oregon's Fish and Wildlife Department that maintains nine other feeding stations across the twelve thousand acres that make up the Elkhorn Wildlife Area. For Ed Miguez and the other state wildlife area staff members it means traveling 145 miles each day. The Elkhorn winter feeding program started in 1971 and today the feeding crew keeps 1,200 hungry elk up in the forest rather than down on nearby ranch-lands that are scattered across the valley floor. Ed is the Wildlife Area manager and said that they will feed 850 tons of alfalfa hay each winter and the elk must be fed each day. "We don't miss a day! These elk know that there's feed available on ranches for feeding the cattle in winter, so if we miss a day, there's a good chance we'll lose them. If that happens, it's extremely hard for us to get them back, so we don't miss a day."

Some bull elk sport massive antlers called racks that can weigh more than forty pounds.

Most of the Elkhorn Wildlife Area is closed to the public in winter except Anthony Creek, so it's a rare and wonderful learning opportunity. An open viewing area allows you a chance to see the herd anytime or bring the family and spend a few bucks to see Oregon's largest game animal—up close. "The younger bulls start some play fighting," said Alice. "Some sparring—but really isn't too serious . . . pushing and pulling on each other really hard. They'll also make that noise you just heard—that 'mewing' sort of sound. That's kind of his signal that 'I'll give up and you've won this round this time, but just wait until next time and another round.'"

The morning hay wagon at the Elkhorn Wildlife Area is the best spot to view the parade of elk, which seem close enough to touch.

Susan added that after twenty years, they continue to learn as much as the visitors. "I think it's being able to do something you really enjoy. Alice and I joke that we're going to call it quits when it's not fun, but here it is twenty years later—we're still having fun!"

"There's always something to be observed with these elk," added Alice. "To be this close to these magnificent animals and to learn more about them is a real treat for everyone. That's a real special thing that we can offer folks who visit."

For More Information

Where: 61846 North Powder River Lane, North Powder, OR 97867

Web: www.tnthorsemanship.com

Phone: Office: 541-856-3356; Cell: 541-519-7234

Watch the Episode: www.traveloregon.com/elkhornwildlife

A Gem of a Museum

Rice Northwest Museum

GETAWAY #9 – GREATER PORTLAND

There's geologic drama based at one of the most interesting historic homes of the Portland area, a home that houses one of the most magnificent collection of rocks and minerals in the region. The Rice Northwest Museum of Rocks and Minerals has been a drawing card for rock hounds for more than forty years—it provides even the casual visitor a stunning visual treat. Traffic speeds by at a shattering pace on Highway 26 in Washington County, while tucked away in the woods, just off Helvetia Road, time slows down.

It's a home where an Oregonian's spirit of independence lives, and Linda Kepford, the museum's assistant director, can tell you much about the man who lived there. "Dick Rice liked the quality of the materials he chose and this home was built to last—the construction was very good—he wanted only the best." Rice was a self-made timber man who made himself a fortune in the forest and also built a home in the woods that staggers the imagination. Rice cleared the land, dug out the dirt, poured the foundation, and then built a sprawling 7,500-square-foot ranch-style home in 1951. It was a gift to his wife, Helen—and a statement that hard work and self-reliance pay off.

The museum's curator, Rudy Tschernich, explained that Rice built the home to house an amazing array of valuable gemstones and minerals that Dick and Helen collected from across the country. "They built the basement so they could house their collection. They were very active collectors in both purchasing and going out in the field . . . their collection became world famous because of some of the very finest specimens that they have."

The ranch-style home that Rice built over half a century ago was recently selected as the first of its kind to make the National Registry of Historic Places. A stroll down a hallway can show you why the home is so special. Rare Oregon myrtlewood was used

Rare and unusual mark the massive gemstone collection inside the sprawling Rice Northwest Museum.

everywhere: the baseboards, the doorjambs, the window trim, the doors, the cabinets. "It's a very hard wood, substantial," noted Linda. "It's absolutely gorgeous and the patterns in it are beautiful—and it is a durable wood and something that would last a long time."

Rice traded his Doug fir logs for rafts of myrtlewood logs from timber owners in Coos Bay. But there's more—in the kitchen you'll see cabinetry built from "quilted maple," a unique and stunning wood that came from nearby Vernonia. While Dick and Helen Rice passed away in 1997, after sixty-three years of marriage, Chester Epperson, a visitor and member of the Tualatin Valley Gem Club, said that the Rices' legacy gives so much pleasure to so many people who walk through their home. "The Rice Northwest Museum of Rocks and Minerals has always been a hidden treasure. The energy of the people who dug the rocks, built the displays, it's so perfect and you're just in awe—it's in the top three museums of the West Coast."

For More Information

Where: 26385 NW Groveland Drive, Hillsboro, OR 97124

Web: www.ricenorthwestmuseum.org

Phone: 503-647-2418; Fax: 503-647-5207

Watch the Episode: www.traveloregon.com/gemmuseum

Romance of Waterfalls
Oregon Waterfalls in Winter

While the Columbia River Gorge has long impressed us with its gigantic size, I cherish its nooks and crannies even more—especially where the water flows and famous falls whirl and shimmer and ripple and where you can leave all distractions behind. "This really is a place where you can shut your cell phone off, turn the laptop off, and reconnect with each other and with the past," noted Diane McClay, Oregon State Parks' ranger.

At 125 feet, Shepperd's Dell is small in size as Gorge falls go. It rolls out of Young's Creek to become a foamy moment that resembles a bowtie turned on its side. The water boils and roils, then slips and slides down forty feet of smooth rock face before it twists and shoots up high to celebrate its freedom and falls into a rocky cradle. George Shepperd opened Shepperd's Dell to the public in 1915 as a tribute to his wife. What a romantic!

One mile east of Shepperd's Dell is Bridal Veil Falls State Park, a day-use site for a picnic or a stroll down a half-mile trail to a stairway and viewing platform. The park's namesake drops in two tiers and it is best enjoyed with someone special. You'll see why when you stand on the viewing platform and gaze up at the 160-foot waterfall plunging twice in a wide, steep slide. Diane added, "It looks the veil of a bride's gown coming down and across the back. In fact, a lot of people get their wedding invitations stamped at the Bridal Veil Post Office, so there is a lot of nostalgia and a connection to history."

If time is of the essence and you're ready to head back toward Portland, travel west on the scenic highway past Shepperd's Dell Falls a mile and a half to Latourell Falls, where an incredible show speaks for itself. Really! Latourell Falls hisses and bellows and shouts for attention as it falls 249 feet. It's the second-highest falls in the Gorge and seems to take on a life of its own you can't help but appreciate.

The falls was named for Joseph Latourell, an early settler of the area, and donated to the state of Oregon in 1929 by Guy W. Talbot. A paved trail allows you to hike to the base of this falls and continues across a bridge to a picnic area. Diane cautioned to keep safety close to heart when you trek this way: "One can get lost in the beauty of this area and we strongly suggest that people have their feet grounded when they start looking around—you can get overwhelmed with both the height and the massive nature of the rocks in the area."

Ninety miles to the west, photographer Don Best likes to say he hasn't met a waterfall he doesn't love: "to shoot with a camera." Don is a lifelong local in Tillamook County—his grandfather arrived by horse and wagon and his father told tales of old-

Bridal Veil Falls is the sort of place that invites hugs and kisses along this waterfall tour.

growth timber, giant elk, and waterfalls galore. So Don looked up at Munson Falls, the tallest waterfall in the Oregon Coast Range, with a nostalgic nod to a somewhat romanticized past and offered us a tip or two that might help you capture the best that falling water offers. "The secret to shooting a waterfall is to get as slow a shutter speed as you can so that the water looks silky. To do that, dial the shutter speed to twenty-fifth of a second or even fifteenth of a second. All of that water will have a real silky look to it."

Don added that there are many waterfalls in the Tillamook State Forest that go unvisited and are underappreciated. He called it a "treasure hunt for nature's beauty" and he added: "The fun part of it all is discovering them, but I always tell people that God is better at the posing part than I am at taking pictures. Waterfalls are spectacular."

You've many spectacular waterfalls to choose from when you visit the nine-thousand-acre state parkland called Silver Falls State Park. It offers a gorgeous Trail of Ten Falls plus the rustic South Falls Lodge that stands large from rock and timber construction. Dorothy Brown-Kwaiser, a park ranger at Silver Falls noted that, "The lodge is gorgeous and I think it's one of the highlights in Oregon. They used natural materials, timbers, big stonework, and a huge, open room with big beams and a rustic feeling. There's a fire going and it has that smell; just feels like a lodge, like you're in a wilderness feeling surrounded by nature."

Campers can let the romance last longer inside rental cabins that offer many of the comforts of home. (Reservations are advised.) Remember—rain gear and hiking boots will make your hiking adventures more comfortable in winter. "It's a bit quieter this time of year," noted Dorothy. "You experience things differently—more on your own without the crowds and so the sounds in the park are different. There are so many reasons to be here—but really, the waterfalls are at the center of everything at Silver Falls State Park."

For More Information

Columbia River Gorge National Scenic Area
Where: 902 Wasco Street, Suite 200, Hood River, OR 97031
Web: www.fs.usda.gov
Phone: 541-308-1700

Tillamook Forest Center
Where: 45500 Wilson River Highway, Tillamook, OR 97141
Web: www.tillamookforestcenter.org
Phone 503-815-6800 or 866-930-4646

Silver Falls State Park
Where: State Highway 214, 26 miles east of Salem
Web: www.oregonstateparks.org
Phone: 503-873-8682, ext. 31

Watch the Episode: www.traveloregon.com/waterfallromance

Frozen in Time
Erratic Rock State Natural Site

Imagine a time—not so long ago—a turbulent and tumultuous chapter of geologic history, when gigantic icebergs carried by floodwater that was more than four hundred feet deep floated across the broad-shouldered Willamette Valley.

Rick Thompson is a detective—not a crime detective but of Oregon geologic history. This winter, he's on the trail of one of the region's oldest mysteries: how hundreds of Montana granite stones ended up in farm fields in Oregon's Willamette Valley. "They've been in the ground a very long time," noted Rick on a recent field trip into western Washington County. "Farmers usually plow or till them up and they're often just sitting where the icebergs left them as they melted."

It may be hard to believe, but it's true! In the blink of a geologic eye, a series of tremendous floods occurred every fifty years for two thousand years—beginning nearly fourteen thousand years ago near the end of the Ice Age. Gigantic, glacial Missoula Lake (in what is now Montana), backed up by an ice dam several miles wide and half a mile high, burst through its western wall and raced across the plains and valleys between Montana and the Pacific Ocean.

Geologists say some five hundred cubic miles of floodwater and icebergs roared across the Northwest, carrying away anything and everything in their path. As the ice flowed, it broke into thousands of pieces, and many of the pieces ended up stranded along the flood route. Like ticker tape from a spent parade, the icebergs scattered, then melted and deposited what was trapped inside: granite rocks! These "erratics"—a geological term that describes a rock found a considerable distance from its place of origin—range from pebble- to baseball- to car-sized boulders that still dot the Willamette Valley.

Icebergs in Oregon's farm country? "It's true!" said Rick, a member of the Lower Columbia Chapter of the Ice Age Floods Institute. "The icebergs just floated around and then reached a certain area and sat there, melted, and these rocks fell out," he added. The evidence of icebergs is all around the metro area too, like the hiking trail at Fields Bridge Park along the Tualatin River in West Linn.

Three granite rocks totaling forty-six thousand pounds rest along the trail. Rick's group, Ice Age Floods Institute, designed the paved, wheelchair-accessible trail, complete with several information kiosks. As you stroll, you learn much about the remarkable events that occurred fifteen thousand years ago.

In fact, one kiosk offers a colorful map that Rick created of the Willamette Valley that shows off the ancient Lake Allison, a four-hundred-foot-deep lake that stretched from Kalama, Washington, to Eugene, Oregon. The ancient lake was created when the massive Lake Missoula burst through an ice dam and flooded the region. "I used a topographic map and traced the four-hundred-foot-depth level all the way down to Eugene. I drew all the nooks and crannies where the valleys would have filled with water and then I went back and put in all the major cities, towns, and highways so people can have a sense and appreciation for how much water there was in the valley."

Rick is a self-proclaimed "flood nut" and said that the huge floods roared through the Columbia River Gorge with water lapping at the ridgetops. He said that the flood events occurred perhaps a hundred times. The floods carried giant granite boulders called erratics deep into the Willamette Valley across Lake Allison.

In fact, not long ago we flew with Roger Anderson and his Vista Balloon Adventures over the valley floor and saw the lasting impressions of the flood events. It was a breathtaking ride to be sure, but it was also quite revealing for we could easily make out Lake Allison's marks on the valley floor.

We could see the rise and fall of the river and lake bottom that was created during the Ice Age floods. In addition, you don't have to travel far to see and touch ancient history too. There's a huge erratic rock near Sheridan, Oregon, at Erratic Rock State Natural Site. At ninety tons, it's the biggest in the state and you can visit and touch the rock anytime. Not far from that site is another huge erratic that you can visit and perhaps enjoy a glass of pinot too. Pull into Left Coast Cellars winery and see the second largest erratic in Oregon.

What makes erratics so special? "Oh, the distance from the source," noted Rick, "Montana—plus it's all granite and to imagine the size of the iceberg that carried a ninety-ton rock so far from its source is just amazing." The icebergs floated across Lake Allison for a time and most were pushed west by prevailing winds. When the water dropped and the bergs melted, the granite chunks were left behind—like a ring around the bathtub. "It affected the entire Northwest and shaped the Willamette Valley," said Rick.

Moreover, the Lake Missoula Floods eventually brought pioneers to Oregon in a roundabout way. It's true! You see, the floods of rock, ice, and other debris scoured the Eastern Washington landscape of all its rich topsoil and then deposited it in the Willamette Valley. It was the same rich topsoil from which early Oregon pioneers built a thriving agricultural economy in the mid-nineteenth century.

Rick speculated, "It's interesting because if the flood and erratic events had not happened, Oregon agriculture might never have developed either." It is such a powerful and compelling story that nearby Tualatin, Oregon, has embraced it too. In 2011, Yvonne Addington, president of the Tualatin Historical Society, helped arrange the delivery of two giant erratics that are now displayed at the Tualatin Heritage Center.

She said that local folks are betting the erratic story is something people will want to see and know better. Put simply, she believes that "if you display the ancient rocks, people will come."

"We have a strong interest in the Ice Age here," said Yvonne. "A local man discovered a mastodon skeleton in 1962 [it is displayed in the Tualatin City Library] and that has led into erratics conveying the power of nature that shaped our community. It's something that visitors and residents can enjoy and it has a special quality that no other city really offers." Back out in Washington County, Rick continues to track down more erratics across farmland as he develops an "Ice Age Trail." He wants travelers to someday journey to the region and learn more about the powerful forces that shaped the Oregon we know today. "It's a detective story," he said. "And I love mysteries!"

For More Information

Fields Bridge Park
Where: 821 Willamette Falls Drive, West Linn, OR 97068
Web: www.westlinnoregon.gov
Phone: 503-557-4700

Erratic Rock State Natural Site
Where: State Highway 18, 6 miles east of Sheridan, along Oldsville Road
Web: www.oregonstateparks.org
Phone: 800-551-6949

Tualatin Heritage Center
Where: 8700 SW Sweek Drive, Tualatin, OR 97062
Web: www.tualatinhistoricalsociety.org
Phone: 503-885-1926

Watch the Episode: www.traveloregon.com/erraticrocks

Feels Like Floatin' on a Cloud
Mount Hood Snowshoeing

I f you can walk, you can snowshoe"; it's an easy sport that's close at hand in the Mount Hood National Forest near Trillium Lake. Jeff and Emmi Nishimura love to play in the snow: it keeps them feeling young and active in winter—plus it's a fun adventure to explore someplace new like the Trillium Lake Trail in the Mount Hood National Forest. The couple recently discovered that snowshoes don't slow them down but have opened up the outdoors to new adventures in the winter months.

Whether rain, snow, or shine, Trillium Lake's expansive view of Mount Hood makes this popular destination well worth a visit.

Emmi noted, "They're so easy to walk in, they're not heavy at all and it's really beautiful out here in the winter. I often feel like I am floatin' on a cloud when fresh powder covers the ground. I never knew it could be so much fun to hike in the snow—

or rather, on top of the snow." They're not alone—thousands of folks have discovered that Oregon's winter landscape is inviting and easy to travel through with a pair of snowshoes strapped to their boots.

Drew and Emiko Hall decided to get away from it all on a daylong adventure to Trillium Trail because it's easy to reach just past Government Camp along State Highway 26.

Lightweight aluminum alloy snowshoes are a far cry from the early days of leather and wood snowshoes.

"We love to hike but we're not really into skiing or snowboarding," noted Drew. "We figured get out here during the winter months. It's the fresh air, the scenery, and fewer people out on the trails." His wife, Emiko, added, "If you're a true Oregonian, a little rain or winter mix won't throw you off—just go do it."

If you've never done it before—you might stop in and chat with an expert before you go—someone like Erin Harri at REI in Hillsboro. Erin really knows snowshoes—she's been enjoying the sport the past decade and said that the shoes you choose have come a long way over the years: "Lightweight aluminum has made all the difference. Plus, the latest flexible plastics have made the uppers and the bindings fairly malleable and yet they withstand frigid temperatures." Erin advised that you look for a "one step" binding system that allows you simply to step in and pull one strap to tighten your boot into the shoe.

A word about those boots—think waterproof! You will be in snow after all, so keeping dry is critically important. "If you are doing recreational light hiking, wear light hiking boots," added Erin. "If you're running and racing in your snowshoes, wear waterproof running shoes. But above all, it's critical to keep the water out." Clothing is critical too! Erin advised layering with synthetic-based clothing that wicks moisture away from your body—never wear cotton but wear a synthetic base layer, then an insulating layer of fleece or down and then top it off with a waterproof or windproof jacket. "Layering is all the difference because you're working up a sweat while you walk so as you get warmer, you can remove a layer, then add it back when you stop for a break." She added that many local outdoor stores including REI offer snowshoe

Allow yourself three to four hours to make the round-trip snowshoe hike at Trillium Lake.

clinics that will teach you more about the shoe styles, proper fit, clothing options, and places to go.

That brings us back to Trillium Lake—according to Erin it is one of the best beginner sites around: "The trail is a five-mile loop around the lake. It's a pretty good decline as you're heading in (about two miles) so a bit of elevation on the way out but around the lake it is fairly flat and wide all the way around. Tracks on the inside of the loop are for cross-country skiers and those on the outside are for snowshoers. If you are a beginner, allow a full day for your hike into Trillium Lake. Bring a lunch, energy food, and lots of water—as aerobic as it is, you lose a lot of water—it is important to remain hydrated."

There are many places for newcomers to try beyond the Trillium Trail in the Mount Hood National Forest. Consider Frog Lake, White River Sno-Park, and the Tilly Jane District at Cooper Spur on the north side of Mount Hood. Something else to keep in mind—Erin noted that winter can be called "weather fickle!" That is, the snow level rises up and falls down thousands of feet each week, so check on the snow conditions and the weather forecast before you go.

For More Information

Trillium Lake Trail

Where: Travel east on US Highway 26, past Government Camp, to the Forest Road 2656 parking area. During the winter, an Oregon Sno-Park permit is required.

Web: www.fs.usda.gov

Phone: 503-668-1700

Watch the Episode: www.traveloregon.com/trilliumlake

Off-Roading

Tillamook State Forest

I t's a cool and cloudy morning at Roger's Camp in the Tillamook State Forest, key staging area for folks who like to travel off-road. I've traveled into the heart of the forest at the invitation of a familiar face and avid off-roader: my brother, Mark McOmie. My brother's off-road recreation is more than a hobby—it's a passion that has shaped much of his outdoor travel and recreation plans. It's also been something that he's shared with his entire family for nearly twenty years.

"ATV-ing is a great family sport," Mark explained. "It's a super opportunity to get together and explore the outdoors. I think most of the fellows in our party probably have multiple uses for their machines—part workhorse, part recreation vehicle. In fact, I started riding in the early '90s while on hunting trips and it's taken off from there." Recently, several of Mark's friends joined him for a ride across designated trails in the state forest. They certainly have plenty of trails to choose from for our day's adventure.

Jahmaal Rebb, ATV specialist with the Oregon Department of Forestry, said that there are more than 130 miles of trails across the Tillamook State Forest. Jahmaal manages the trails and the riders who travel in the forest and he noted that there's a "dedicated following" of riders who come to play on the state forestland. "This is a community that's been very active since the 1930s—really, since the first Tillamook Burn. Motorized recreation is a big deal here and the folks still come here, put in time on varied projects to improve trails and improve access—they really have a passion for play."

There are three primary off-highway vehicle (OHV) riding areas available in the forest including Browns Camp, Jordan Creek, and Diamond Mill. A wide variety of trails provide access into some of the more remote and scenic parts of the forest and provide challenge and excitement for both beginners and experts. "We offer a very extensive network of trails," said Jahmaal. "Scores of off-road trails are a part of a multiuse recreation system. So, you must expect to encounter quads, motor bikes, and full-sized four-wheel drives out here." So, what's it like to climb aboard and grab on

Mark McOmie enjoys making the mud fly while off-roading across the designated off-road motorized vehicle trails of the Tillamook State Forest.

to the steering of a powerful ATV four-wheel-drive quad? In a word—amazing! They are quick to respond, easy to steer, and surprisingly comfortable too.

Steve Lewis, a veteran rider with close to thirty years of riding experience in the state forest, said, "For those who like to go to an amusement park and ride a roller coaster—well, that's what it's like only you are in the woods and you're in total control of the machine." It is also recreation where risk and danger wait at every turn, so safety and common sense and controlling your speed are critical. That's where recently adopted rules come in. For example, young riders must carry an ATV Safety Education card that shows the rider has passed a mandatory on-line test.

The Oregon Department of Parks and Recreation (OPRD) manages the ATV On-Line Safety Education Course and John Lane, OPRD ATV safety program manager, said that by 2014, every ATV rider in Oregon must pass the test and carry the card. "It's free . . . takes just a couple of hours to complete, and when you're all done we'll send you a safety education card that's required to be with you when you go out and ride."

There are more changes coming to enhance the safety aspects of Oregon's off-road riding: a new Hands-On ATV Training class is now required for all riders aged fifteen and under. John added that thirty-five-thousand Oregon youth riders will have to take the course, so now is the time to do it."

"If you have kids that are thinking about getting into the sport or are already in the sport—get them into a training class right away. Get them in now—don't wait for the last minute rush!"

For More Information

Where: Tillamook Forest Center (Trail Maps) 45500 Wilson River Highway, Tillamook, OR 97141

Web: www.tillamookforestcenter.org

Phone: 503-815-6800 or 866-930-4646

Watch the Episode: www.traveloregon.com/offroadriders

The Rugged Edge of Oregon
Cape Perpetua Scenic Area

Some call it the "rugged edge of the Oregon coast'" where the sun and surf meet to leave you spellbound and breathless: Cape Perpetua Scenic Area, where in winter, except for surf and wind, the coast slows down. That's easy to understand—few distractions, few folks around . . . especially along Oregon's rugged edge of life.

It's more than forty miles of central Oregon coastline beginning at Waldport and continuing along a southerly stretch of Coastal Highway 101 marked by steep headlands, jagged volcanic outcrops, and jaw-dropping scenic drama. Oregon State Parks Ranger David Weisenback said that the sheer beauty of the place surprises many first timers: "It is such a beautiful and unique area—you can hike to the overlooks, the viewpoints, across the rocky shorelines. No matter where you travel in the world, this is still one of the most scenic areas."

In fact, it is so significant and prized a place that 2,700 acres of massive Cape Perpetua is designated a National Scenic Area. Two miles south of Yachats, Oregon, you will find the Cape Perpetua Visitor Center and it is open daily.

US Forest Service Manager David Thompson noted that atop Cape Perpetua you can turn in any direction for views that simply amaze: "Certainly the coast is the most dramatic, the part that captures your attention first," said David. "And yet if you turn and look the other way, you've got this unbelievably green Sitka spruce forest with a wealth of moss and ferns and giant trees—it's all special."

The visitor center provides a wealth of hiking choices too: over eleven different trails for a total of twenty-seven miles and the wonderful thing is that at one point or another many of the trails interconnect with one another. The Captain Cook Trail is wheelchair accessible, and leads you from the visitor center to skirt the shoreline.

At low tide, the trail puts on quite a show as waves crash into rocky crevices and cracks at a place called Spouting Horn.

If you wish to wander longer consider the astounding collection of Oregon State Park Waysides with names like Neptune, Ponsler, or Strawberry Hill, where tide pools invite closer inspection during the ebbing tide. Nearby, Washburne State Park Campground invites you for an overnight stay where winter campers are welcome in a tent, trailer, or RV. For those who love to camp, but lack the right gear, Park Ranger Deborah Edwards said to consider renting a yurt: "Camping in winter can be just as exciting as the summertime; you just have to deal with a bit more rain and a yurt is perfect. You get a bunk bed which sleeps two on the bottom and one on the top, a futon, table, and a couple of chairs, plus heat and light."

Little more than five miles away, another site requires you to take a short stroll on a paved trail and then a quick ride in an elevator down the face of a cliff for 208 feet to reach Sea Lion Caves. This natural wonder has been an Oregon coastal icon as far back as many folks remember; more than one hundred acres of the adjacent land has been in private ownership since 1887. "It's been a drawing card for the curious," said

The low tide spray seems to explode at Cape Perpetua's Spouting Horn so don't forget your rain gear!

manager Boomer Wright. He explained that the massive cave is the largest along the West Coast and where 250 Steller sea lions are a raucous, rowdy crowd.

"They are very social animals with their barking, crawling over each other, and even nipping one another." Boomer added that up to one thousand Steller sea lions use the cave from November through late summer: They are often seen lounging, loafing, or just plain sacked out on the rocky interior cliffs or boulders. "Of course, there is the large center rock that we call 'King of the Hill,'" noted Boomer, "and there is usually quite a bit of fighting between sea lions to see who gets to rest atop it."

The Steller sea lions are not the only wildlife species that are easy to spy at Sea Lion Caves. Back atop, keep eyes out for soaring raptors like hawks and eagles that are often seen on the hunt—or flocks of shorebirds that dance and dazzle and skirt the surf. David Thompson said that it is a remarkable scene and one that is often overlooked in winter: "Without a doubt, it's the most gorgeous stretch of the Oregon coast with the collection of rocky shores. So, the geology, the geography, and certainly the forest add up to a wonderful place to relax and wonder and wander if you want a place to decompress."

For More Information

Cape Perpetua Scenic Area
Where: 2400 US Highway 101, Yachats, OR 97498
Phone: 541-547-3289

Sea Lion Caves
Where: 91560 US Highway 101 North, Florence, OR 97439
Web: www.sealioncaves.com
Phone: 541-547-3111

Watch the Episode: www.traveloregon.com/capeperpetua

Dawn Patrol
Klamath Basin Bald Eagles

S tillness at daybreak accompanies the arctic air that plummets the early morning to subfreezing. It's a lonely time as the only headlamps for miles—ours—pierce the darkness on a back road in Oregon's Klamath Basin. Despite the bone-chilling cold, wildlife expert Dave Hewitt says there is no better time to tally the dawn fly-out of the largest gathering of bald eagles in America. We have come to Bear Valley Wildlife Refuge (part of the Klamath Basin National Wildlife Refuges Complex), a large forest of old-growth timber that provides the eagles with protection from the wind and cold.

It is the staging area for the eagles' daily fly-out as the birds take wing and search for food. "There's one," said Dave. "Right over your head, Grant! It's coming right over the road. Yeah, it's fantastic! As the sun is coming up, just starting to get light, you can see forty, fifty, sixty eagles get up, swoop and soar and glide right over the top of you. It's pretty impressive to watch when you have several hundred eagles and you just can't count fast enough."

I could not—twenty, thirty, forty—soon I was dazzled and dizzied by the birds appearing in front

Some bald eagles travel from as far away as Alaska to winter at the many Klamath Wildlife Refuges.

Scores of eagles gather across private grain fields and pastures where they hunt for small rodents.

of us, then disappearing across a distant ridgeline. I simply could not keep track of them all. Finally I gave up my count and enjoyed the show with the small group of birders who had joined us. We gazed across to the eastern horizon, toward a soft shade of rose that marked the approaching sunrise.

Darryl Samuels noted, "It's the thrill of the hunt without the gun—you have your binoculars and you might see sixty bald eagles and you might see ten—it varies and one may just fly right over our heads." His wife, Diana Samuels, eagerly agreed and added, "It's just great to come out here early and watch them as they go out to feed at the refuge."

Over a thousand eagles arrive at Klamath Basin each winter from Canada and Alaska, following their food supply of ducks, geese, and other birds. Despite the frigid conditions during much of the winter, large bodies of water such as Upper Klamath Lake often remain unfrozen, and large flocks of ducks help prevent some of the smaller ponds from freezing over as they paddle about.

David Menke, staff member at the US Fish and Wildlife's Klamath Refuge Headquarters, guided us across miles of intersecting roadways that checkerboard the Lower Klamath Refuge. David suddenly stopped, brought his binoculars up, and gazed across an otherwise flat, drab-brown grain field (wheat harvest had occurred months earlier) with scores of black dots with white heads on the distant horizon.

"Is this a buffet table for the eagles?" I asked with a chuckle. "Absolutely! A real smorgasbord—or whatever—and this field—I guarantee you—will not be this way a week from now—the birds will be in another field. You see, they are hunting field mice and other rodents. It's really something to sit and watch the birds hunt here."

David said there are many awesome sights to see across nearly 170,000 acres of both state and federal wildlife refuges in the Klamath Basin. Multiple auto tour routes make the travel easy, so be sure to stop in at the Klamath Refuge Headquarters where free maps and brochures will set you on the right trail to enjoy the show. While each season offers some new species to see, Dave Hewitt added that winter is the best time to see the most raptors, including the largest concentrations of eagles.

"We may get a period when it freezes in December and then we might get open water in January and February and the eagles respond accordingly: They'll stand on the ice and feed on waterfowl. Eagles on telephone poles, eagles on irrigation equipment, eagles on farm fields—mostly they just stand around a lot, so there's endless opportunities to observe wildlife."

Visitors to Klamath Wildlife Refuge who wish to explore the Klamath Birding Trail have a wonderful educational opportunity just around the corner at the annual Winter Wings Festival in mid-February. Diana said that it draws hundreds of people from across the country who have a real passion for birding—and especially for bald eagles. "The Winter Wings Festival celebrates the return of all the migratory birds to the Klamath Basin in the wintertime. Bird-watching is a hobby and pastime that's growing and our festival has really benefited from the increased interest. We are one of the premier destinations for bird-watching on the West Coast."

Audubon member Dave Hewitt said that the Klamath Basin Audubon Society produces the three-day event with more than one hundred volunteers from the local community who give thousands of hours to help people learn and understand more about Oregon's wildlife heritage. "There are many activities designed for families and kids and you don't really have to know anything about birds, just have a passing interest in nature and we'll show you some pretty exciting things."

For More Information

Where: Klamath Basin National Wildlife Refuge Complex
Web: www.fws.gov/klamathbasinrefuges
Phone: 916-667-2231
Watch the Episode: www.traveloregon.com/klamathbirding

Visit the Valley of Peace
Hot Lake Springs

Outdoor moments in Northeast Oregon's Grande Ronde Valley are stunning and spacious with scenery that takes your breath away, and when you step inside David Manuel's art studio, it's clear that it's the little things that keep the past alive. David is an artist who owns a love affair with Oregon's past—like his latest sculpture that depicts the William Price Hunt expedition.

Hunt led a group of rugged explorers through this part of Oregon two hundred years ago. They were on assignment for John Astor and determined to bring an American presence to the British-dominated region at the mouth of the Columbia River. "I want to make sure everything that I do tells a story—it's so important that way—that's what keeps me interested." For David, the journey's truth is etched in short strokes with a sharp blade across soft clay. "I spend a lot of time on each buffalo hair too. I don't like the sharp edges because you can cut your hand on some bronzes with sharp edges. So I create them to overlap and it'll really shine that way too."

You may have seen David's work before—at Portland's Chapman Square where *The Promised Land* shines as a monumental bronze statue. Now, his new gallery and studio provide a glimpse to his genius as one of America's finest artists. "I love history and that's what keeps me going! That is why it's so hard to go home at night too, because I get so involved in these pieces."

But David doesn't have to go far when he goes home. That's because he works where he and his family have lived for nearly a decade: Hot Lake Springs. It is a sixty-thousand-square-foot hospital turned hotel that rose above the Grande Ronde Valley floor more than a century ago. In fact, at one time Hot Lake was the center of a "good health movement" that drew people from across the country. They came by train seeking cures for what ailed them in the mineral hot springs that bubbled up from deep in the earth. But the place hit hard times—capped by a devastating fire in the spring of 1934.

By the turn of the last century, the building was ready to fall. Holes in ceilings reached to where there should have been a roof. All but 2 of the 350 windows were broken out and floors were falling down. The locals thought it was only a matter of time until the building collapsed: "Everybody thought it was dead," said John Lamoreau, a former Union County commissioner. "There was no hope, no chance and some people were skeptical because so many had tried to restore it before and failed. To me, the Manuel family looked like the best hope."

It wasn't just a mess: it was dangerous and bulldozers waited in the wings to tear it all down. It was against this dramatic backdrop that the Manuel family bought Hot Lake in 2003. Despite a personal cost that would rise to more than $10 million, the Manuel family was all-in for the enterprise. David's wife, Lee Manuel, explained that they risked everything because "holding on to Oregon history" was something they could not let go. "It was as though this ol' lady, this ol' building, this history rose from the ground and spoke to us," she said. "It took on a life of its own. We were drawn into that."

Today the transformation is nothing short of magnificent! The successful Hot Lake Springs Bed and Breakfast boasts twenty-two stunning rooms, a restaurant, and the new Restore Spa that is sure to please anyone interested in rest and relaxation. Plus, there's David's gallery and the bronze foundry—where you can watch artisans transform his work into lasting bronze art—and David's uniquely impressive collection of American Indian artifacts and US military memorabilia that date to the War of 1812.

Still for many people it is the promise of rest and relaxation in the "Valley of Peace" while enjoying the mineral hot springs. It is all so hard to resist. John observed that it is a place to soak up one of the most remarkable Oregon pioneering stories of the twenty-first century. "Not only do we in Union County give thanks to Dave and Lee, but I think the whole state needs to give thanks for what they did here. They brought this place back to life."

For More Information

Where: 66172 State Highway 203, La Grande, OR 97850

Web: www.hotlakesprings.com

Phone: 541-963-4685; Fax: 541-963-4876

Watch the Episode: www.traveloregon.com/hotlake

MARCH

The Forest in Our Backyard
Magness Tree Farm

GETAWAY #17 – GREATER PORTLAND

As the suburbs grow larger and our pace of life goes faster, it's good to know that some Oregon places provide an outdoor escape into a bit of the backwoods where you can learn more about Oregon's forests too. When spring has returned to Oregon's forests, you can see the splendor in showy ways. Not just the blossoms or the fresh greenery, but brilliant sunshine on a day too nice to stay indoors. If you follow Bill Wood's lead, there's a good chance you'll learn something new too.

Bill is chief guide and the man in charge at the Magness Tree Farm and he will teach you much about life in his forest. Magness Tree Farm is an eighty-acre parcel tucked into the hills just a handful of miles between Wilsonville and Sherwood, Oregon. In 1977, Howard and Pansy Magness donated the land to be used for purposes of environmental education. The site boasts more than two miles of trail; most of it is a fairly gentle grade and as you hike, you will often have Corral Creek by your side. Down close to the ground, you will also enjoy the first signs of spring: white-faced trilliums light up the scene and they are prime at this time of year. "Most of the spring flowers are beginning to show," noted Bill. "We'll have all kinds of color here in the next four or five weeks. But right now is trillium time and we have hundreds."

Magness is just part of the outdoor education story because it is owned by the nearby World Forestry Center (WFC), located in Portland's west hills adjacent to the Oregon Zoo. If you travel to the WFC, step indoors and explore the Discovery Museum for a hands-on education that complements the outdoor experience. The museum offers more than one hundred exhibits that will open your eyes and perhaps capture your imagination.

You can go aboard a white-water raft, climb into a tree lift that soars more than fifty feet high for a bird's-eye view into a tree canopy, or you can buckle up in a four-

62

wheel drive vehicle to tour an African rain forest. "We really want the experiences to be enjoyed by the family; not just for kids, not just for adults," noted spokesperson Mark Reid. "We have things for every member of the family and at every age level."

Laurie Hale hadn't been to the World Forestry Center since she was a kid. On this trip, she wanted her three young children to see what the museum experience is all about. "I was here in sixth grade and it was awesome then," she said. "Now, it's even better with a lot of interactive things for the kids to do. They can pretend they're at a log mill, ride a parachute like a smoke jumper and the best part is that they're actually doing those things."

Back in the forest at the Magness Tree Farm, be sure to check out the

The learning never stops at the Magness Tree Farm—the site is open year-round to visitors who like to hike or perhaps camp for a night in their rustic cabins.

three rustic cabins that you can rent for a longer stay. Each cabin sleeps up to twelve people and offers electricity, but no heat—so if you spend the night, you want to prepare for colder nights. Reservations are required. Bill said that once folks discover the Magness landscape, they seldom want to leave: "When they first come here, they are awe-inspired by the creek and the serenity of the surroundings. They hear the birds, see the squirrels, and relax with their kids. When we see them a second time, they usually bring another family and so our circle expands. It's really a wonderful place to be and yet you don't have to travel far to get here."

For More Information

Where: 31195 SW Ladd Hill Road, Sherwood, OR 97140
Web: www.worldforestry.org
Phone: 503-228-1367
Watch the Episode: www.traveloregon.com/treefarm

Pack-Rat Prizes
Three Mile Museum

S hortcuts are meant to get you where you're going a whole lot faster, but there are some back road rest stops where you'll want to put on the brakes, catch your breath, and savor a unique perspective on Oregon's past. So it is at a word-of-mouth museum in Washington County where a local man hangs on to history for your enjoyment at the one and only Three Mile Museum.

Winter's hold seems firm and lasting across Oregon on a March morning that is marked by fresh snowfall. The snow lights up the scene across the Coast Range mountain foothills, while across rural Tualatin Valley, these are cold, quiet times and the farming life is mostly indoors.

Tom Meier is a lifelong learner and self-proclaimed "protector" of Oregon's past at a place you've likely missed. His farmstead home is resting site for one of a kind farm tools that got the jobs done when ingenuity was born of necessity; items that were once upon a time headed for the landfill and irreverent death.

For decades, Tom has scoured old homesteads and family estate sales and gathered items that can leave you scratching your head.

Three large barns house Tom Meier's remarkable collection of unique Oregon memorabilia that includes everything from the prized to the practical.

His rescued items include cowboy spurs, old film projectors, and even older telephones. He said that the adventure of it all has left him eager for more: "When you see an original and authentic antique or artifact that says 'Oregon,' believe me, you will know it—it jumps out at you." Tom said his collectibles are better preserved at his museum than the local landfill. "I bought one collection from a farmer as he was heading to the dump and I said, 'No, this stuff has value.' And he added, 'Well you get it out of here then and I'll value you.' I swear if it weren't for me, this would be buried a hundred feet in the ground and lost forever."

There are really old political buttons and fishing stuff to catch the big ones included in Tom's massive collection of fourteen thousand items spread across three large outbuildings on his rural property. It is a collection that continues to grow each day at a place that just makes you feel good to see that someone cares this much about our past. Tom's friends frequently stop in at the Three Mile Museum; sometimes they show up offering donations. A neighbor and longtime friend, Jim Shores, has admired Tom's museum for decades. He recently offered Tom a unique device that had been in Jim's family as long as he could remember: a small wooden "butter printer" that was at least a century old.

Tom was excited to see the rare item: "I'll be honest with folks—especially if it's got little value—but every once in a while we get lucky. This is a real treasure, believe me; that's something you just can't buy today." Jim offered, "We've become such a throwaway society—buy it, use it for awhile, and then throw it away. But back in the early days of Oregon, the family kept so many things and we used them until they were extremely worn out and had no value anymore."

Tom admitted to forty years of selectively pack ratting Oregon memorabilia. The former grade school teacher is adamant that we risk losing ourselves when we lose touch with where we've come from. His Three Mile Museum is a tie that binds us with our stuff and with Oregon's past and keeps it on hand for folks who live in the present. "I have things here that no one else has," boasted Tom with a hearty laugh. "How many people have a museum in the backyard? Why have these things if I can't show them off?"

For More Information

Where: Western Washington County/Near Banks, OR

Contact: Tom's word-of-mouth Three Mile Museum welcomes visitors and doesn't require an admission fee, but it does require a reservation to visit, especially for small groups of people. Tom asks visitors to contact him in advance via e-mail at Thomasmeier@frontier.com.

Watch the Episode: www.traveloregon.com/3milemuseum

A Perfect Paddle
Netarts Bay

When spring break is just around the calendar corner and you're yearning for vacation time that's close to home but offers an escape that feels a million miles away—all you need is a paddle, a PFD (personal flotation device), and a spirit of adventure to enjoy "A Perfect Paddle" on Netarts Bay.

A clear sky plus brilliant sunshine added up to a March surprise on a recent weekend along the Oregon coast. It was a perfect time to dive into new adventure on the quiet side of coastal life with Kayak Tillamook's lead guide, Paul Peterson. Paul has been a skipper aboard large fishing boats from Oregon to Alaska, but these days he shows newcomers the perfect paddle strokes that will keep them safe. Before we got our boat bottoms wet, he demonstrated the forward paddle stroke during our land-based prep session: "So in it goes," said Paul, who reached forward with the paddle, "and then it's a push-pull move inside that imaginary strike zone of baseball."

Our small troop of paddlers prepped for a trip on Netarts Bay, a small Tillamook County estuary. Marc Hinz co-owns and operates Kayak Tillamook with Paul and he said that the business grew out of a college class. He added that kayaking tours "just happened" because he was in the right place at the right time and owned the right passion for water. His business has grown to fill a recreation niche that was missing in the Tillamook coastal communities. He added that the twelve-foot-long kayaks are akin to "beginner's dream boats."

"You need to know nothing about kayaking because the majority of our tours are built for beginners. If you have ever paddled a canoe, this kayak has similar stability; it's a bit wider and more stable than oceangoing kayaks too."

Once the half hour shore-based session wrapped up, we dropped in at near-ebb tide at the Netarts Bay public marina to enjoy a winter's day that was too nice to believe. Tucked into the comfortable and stable kayak, I followed Paul and Marc's lessons. Soon, I became the master of my boat as I caught on to the basic forward, backward, and sweeper strokes. We wore PFDs as Paul shepherded us along the edge of the bay; the beauty of the craft is that it can float and maneuver in just inches of water. Paul carried proper safety gear that included a VHF radio and a first aid kit, and he kept us a safe distance away from the estuary's rough bar.

It is critical for newcomers to this sport to join experienced professionals like Paul who know the water well, because conditions on the water can change in a heart-beat and inexperienced boaters can get into unexpected trouble. Paul also noted that all nonmotorized boats longer than ten feet are required to have a ten-dollar Aquatic Invasive Species Permit. The money from the permit helps to develop and manage programs that keep nonnative plants and animals out of Oregon's waterways.

At 2,700 acres, Netarts Bay is relatively small in size with no major rivers, but several small creeks that feed into it. Paul and Marc agreed that the bay's high water quality is largely due to its remoteness, small size, and more: "There is no industry on this bay," noted Paul. "So, there's nothing polluting it and it's all natural. In the wintertime when we have the heavy runoff you'll see some turbidity, but primarily it's a clean bay."

"Netarts Bay is one of the most pristine bays on the Oregon coastline," added Marc. "It is shallow throughout, no more than fifteen feet deep, and the water is so clear you can see right to the bottom. You can see Dungeness crabs crawling across the bottom of the bay, so visibility makes this a nice waterway to paddle and it is a very popular clamming destination too."

All you need is a paddle, a PFD (personal flotation device), and a spirit of adventure for a day on Netarts Bay.

Mila Le and John Vella traveled from their Portland home to join us for a day of paddling on Netarts Bay. It was just the second time each had tried kayaking recreation. Yet, each felt right at home in the cozy confines of their boats. "I think most anyone can do it," said John. "It's amazing how easy and comfortable it feels. It's pretty natural—as long as you remain calm when the little waves come up and splash you." Mila agreed that the wet suited her just fine too: "It's about as close as you can get to the water without being in the water. It also feels really different from a typical motorboat where you are perched up and looking down into the water. In a kayak you're so much closer to the water and I like that closeness."

Kayak Tillamook's tours reach across six Tillamook County estuaries for a total of eighty miles on bays, rivers, sloughs, and backwater areas. "That's about eight-hundred square miles of flat water paddling opportunities," noted Marc. "Most of which are tidal influenced—but we also have lakes—freshwater lakes and intimate little sloughs that wander up into coastal forests—there's a lot for us to see and do in a kayak."

There's even more too! Marc offered me a copy of the new Nehalem Estuary Water Trail Map, a hands-on guide produced and published by the Tillamook Estuaries Partnership. The guide is free and available to kayakers and other boaters. It is the first in a series of water trail maps that will eventually detail all of the Tillamook estuaries including Netarts Bay. If you wish to make Netarts Bay a longer stay, consider nearby Cape Lookout State Park, located a few miles from the bay. Park manager Pate Marvin said that the parkland offers 225 sites including rental cabins and thirteen yurts. "You can walk to your heart's content on the beach," said Pate. "Once you get away from the campground, a mile or two—you're not going to see a whole lot of people as you hike Netarts Spit—even in the busy summer season—so you can really find peace and solitude and enjoy the outdoors."

Mila and John agreed that Netarts Bay is a special place and kayaking offers intimate moments where nature's touch restores the soul: "The mountains, the water—you can even hear the ocean in the distance," noted John. "There's so much variety and we're so fortunate to be able to enjoy all of this anytime because it is so close to Portland." Mila smiled and added, "When you hit it just right, it's awesome. Everyone should try it."

For More Information

Where: Kayak Tillamook, PO Box 1270, Tillamook, OR 97141
Web: www.kayaktillamook.com
Phone: 503-866-4808
Watch the Episode: www.traveloregon.com/perfectpaddle

Oregon Waterways Alert!

The morning sun rises above the unusually quiet waters of Clatsop County's Cullaby Lake. That is, until sirens blare and the lights flash and suddenly a high-speed chase erupts in the middle of the lake. It's a fast-tracking, high-powered jet boat, but there's no crime for the officer to chase down—instead, this event is jet boat training, where speed and agility earn passing grades at Oregon's Marine Patrol Academy.

The Oregon State Marine Board sponsors the annual academy that recently drew thirty-five officers from thirty-one counties and the Oregon State Police to the small coastal fresh-water lake. The officers participate in two weeks of training; some classroom, some in a swimming pool, but much of it in boats that rotate through a dozen "scenario stations" where the officers face real life situations.

"The role players are all scripted," said Dale Flowers, Oregon State Marine Board staff member. "They face probable cause, stop and consent issues in varied situations that are drawn from real life. The officer has to think on his feet and work with his partner." They are the men and the women who risk their lives to save yours when you get into water-based situations that are over your head."

It's the sort of training that drew Deputy Joe Reeves from distant Wallowa County: "We're dealing with people who are out trying to have a good time," noted Joe. "They are out on the water to have fun and so we approach every situation like that by making sure they have the right safety equipment on board. We check to make sure they have the right personal flotation devices, fire extinguisher, and those kinds of things for safety."

Joe added that the instruction comes from experienced officers who guide the new-comers through the varied exercises—even simply coming alongside another boat—and this helps me prepare for summer duty at Wallowa Lake. The students move their boats through a series of complex boating exercises; moving forward then backing up into tight quarters, towing another boat, and the proper way to come alongside another boat.

In 2011, Oregon marine patrol officers made over fifty thousand contacts on the state's varied waterways and they issued little more than 2,400 citations. The single greatest citation-worthy problem centered on PFDs (personal flotation devices) because people don't wear them, or worse, they don't carry them. "We do a lot of hands on," added Dale. "But basically the real work for them is going to begin when they go back to their home waters and put what they've learned here into practice there. And it's a team—really, marine law enforcement is a family in this state." This year, the "family" will grow larger as law enforcement officers join a new environmental war against aquatic invasives. While it hasn't happened yet, tiny mussels called quagga and zebra could be in Oregon soon. And other invasives called New Zealand mud snails are already here.

At Henry Hagg Lake in Washington County, state fishery biologist Rick Boatner spearheads a volunteer boat inspection station. He leads five teams of two inspectors each who will fan out across Oregon this spring to inspect boats and many locations. He reached into a small plastic container and pulled out a handful of small, drab-gray, quagga mussel shells. "This bunch came off one side of one prop at Lake Mead last summer. And as you can see, they cluster each other, so you get smaller ones on top of the bigger ones, so they grow on top of each other."

The invasive mussels could arrive in Oregon by way of Nevada where the most recent infestation was discovered four years ago. Rick said that the invasives have cost state governments in the Great Lakes area hundreds of millions of dollars over the past three decades. In that part of the country, the zebra mussel invasions have collapsed fisheries, taken over beaches, and clogged miles of pipelines. Each mussel filters a liter of water a day and removes nutrition from the water that in turn starves the fish that live in the area too. Rick added, "It is the last thing we ever want to see happen in Oregon. They will be looking for signs of the mussels and snails that can hitchhike into Oregon's waterways on boats' motors, trailers—really, just about any marine surface. It's not just the boats, but the boots that anglers wear—especially the anglers that cast lures or baits in rivers and lakes across the United States.

He said that the cure is easy enough: "Scrub! It's that simple. After you get out of the water and before you get to another water body. A small brush will take care of 90 percent of the problem right there." So, how big is the risk of aquatic invasives coming to Oregon? Oregon State Marine Board Aquatic Invasives expert Glenn Dolphin said: "They (Oregonians) should be very alarmed by the risk. It's serious because it will affect everything in our water-rich region."

Glenn said that the mussels threaten more than recreation because they can live on practically any surface, so they can easily infest drinking water pipelines, agricultural water lines, and hydroelectric production facilities too. "This is really the first program in Oregon that's been focused on the aquatic invasives. We are trying to get ahead of the curve and be proactive and preventative. This is really an aggressive first step that the state is taking on the aquatic invaders themselves."

Serious business indeed, for it has already hit too close for comfort, noted Glenn. Washington officials recently came across a boat for sale in the Spokane area that had a bilge full of quagga mussels. The boat had traveled to Spokane from Lake Mead, and fortunately it hadn't touched any Oregon waters. Glenn noted that if it had, water-based recreation would change forever.

The new Aquatic Invasive Species (AIS) inspection program is paid for through a five-dollar permit for both motorized and nonmotorized boats alike. Motorized boat owners will see the increase in their boat registration. But if you paddle a canoe or a kayak or row down a white-water river in a watercraft that's ten feet or longer, you'll need to buy the new Aquatic Invasives Permit for each boat that goes in the water. You must carry the AIS permit on your person when you are in the boat on an Oregon waterway. "We're asking people to look past the five dollar bill that you have to pay and look to where the money is going and what we're doing with that money. This money doesn't get lost in the general fund; it's dedicated money that goes back into a direct benefit to the boaters that pay into it."

Recreation managers are posting new signs at many boat ramps across Oregon too. The posters ask boat owners to inspect their watercrafts and thoroughly drain and clean them. Meanwhile, Rick noted that the battle lines are drawn—now is the time to make certain the aquatic invasives don't land in Oregon waterways. "The simplest means and cheapest means is to deal with them right now, because once they become established, then we're going to deal with containment just to protect what we take for granted today: fresh water and electricity at a cheap rate. Everything will change."

For More Information

Where: Oregon State Marine Board, 435 Commercial Street NE, #400, Salem, OR 97309-5065

Contacts: 503-378-8587; Fax: 503-378-4597

This Creek Will Carry You Away
Drift Creek

If you spend enough time in the Oregon outdoors, you realize that when it comes to winter weather, luck is a good partner to have by your side. So it was on a recent streamside stroll into a watershed where the rain is often measured in feet rather than inches but where huge surprises waited at the end of the trail.

Drift Creek will carry you away—perhaps where imagination travels—on a wonderful trail alongside a classic "pool and drop" Oregon stream. Flanked by ferns, alder trees, and vine maple, Drift Creek Trail winds through the rain-drenched Siuslaw National Forest. "You can come out and hike this trail pretty much all year as it's a pretty gentle downhill with a lot of switchbacks," noted US Forest Service (USFS) Manager George Buckingham. "It's only three miles round-trip and a fairly easy grade so you can bring small children and they do just fine."

George and USFS Recreation Specialist J. W. Cleveland were our trail guides for an amazing adventure into a unique area of the forest—one characterized by a marvelous payoff for our time and efforts. But J. W. cautioned, "Rain gear is a necessity this time of year! Be sure to have it in your vehicle and then make the call about taking it when you get to the trailhead. It can get really wet in here so you could need the gear. You want to make sure you've got a camera too, because you're going to see some pretty amazing things."

The Drift Creek Trail is amazing until you arrive at something even better and bigger that will take your breath away: a 240-foot-long cable suspension bridge!

"The feeling that you have is really a bit like being suspended off the ground—a hundred feet off the ground," noted George. "There's a stream down below you and a waterfall flooding in so it really triggers your auditory senses too. It's quite a neat experience."

Anchored by cables and ties that are cemented into opposing bluffs, the bridge holds more than 150,000 pounds, so it's not going anywhere anytime soon. While the bridge does offer a bit of a bounce, the thirty-inch wide tread is perfectly safe and the bird's-eye view will leave you spellbound. As does Drift Creek Falls, a seventy-five-foot free-fall, whopper of a waterfall that's located immediately below you. George said something "really big happened here last summer."

"The entire rock face of the falls tumbled into the stream below and the stream is actually under the rock now—it goes underground where as there used to be a pool." That's right—after millions of years of standing tall, more than 150 feet of basalt rock wall fell into Drift Creek.

Drift Creek winds and wends through a coastal rain forest in the Siuslaw National Forest.

"There's one boulder down there that would fill up most of the parking lot in front of my office," noted George with a chuckle. "As you can see columnar basalt has strongly vertical joints and the water worked in there over time—probably over thousands of years in this wet climate and eventually gravity took over and 'boom'— just slipped off."

The sound of the crashing rock wall must have been deafening—perhaps even terrifying—but fortunately, no one was in the area when it happened in August of 2010. Nevertheless, it is a thrill to see from way up high and it's the sort of hiking experience best enjoyed this time of year. "Now is the time to get out and view the falls," added J. W. "That's especially true after a large rain event. If you come here in the summertime when the water flow is lighter, it just isn't the same."

The suspension bridge offers a bit of a bounce but the reward includes a spectacular aerial view of Drift Creek.

"People do love to come here," added George. "It is fantastic to provide unique places like this for people to recreate in, get close to a rugged outdoor setting, and get some exercise at the same time. It's well worth your time for a visit."

For More Information

Where: Off of US Highway 101, South of Lincoln City, Lincoln City, OR 97367
Phone: USFS/ Siuslaw National Forest: 541-750-7000
Watch the Episode: www.traveloregon.com/driftcreek

A Sneak Peek at Nature
White River Wildlife Area

Back road byways are the best when they lead you down trails toward Oregon's secret hideaways. The east side of Mount Hood offers two hideaways for the price of one and each feels a million miles away from city hubbub and noise.

It's little more than a ninety-minute drive from Portland to explore the White River Wildlife Area. It's a place where you may soon discover that back-road adventures are the very best when they let you enjoy a sneak peek at nature.

There are nearly thirty thousand acres of refuge that reach across more than twenty miles of terrain that provides an eastern point of view to the mountain.

Josh Moulton, manager of the White River Wildlife Area said, "We're a bit off the beaten path for sure, tucked out here in the oaks and pines at about 2,100 feet in elevation. You soon see, it's a different sort of wildlife area."

The White River Wildlife Area was established in the 1950s to keep wintering deer and a growing elk herd up in the Cascade Mountain foothills rather than down on neighboring farmlands. "A winter feeding program continues to serve the wildlife, both deer and elk," added Josh. "We begin feeding in early December at designated stations throughout the refuge and the animals pretty much tell us by their behavior when to stop. That is usually about now. We planted an alfalfa field last year and the deer love that. It's giving visitors a bit more reliable opportunity for viewing the deer herds—which can reach several hundred strong in winter."

Josh said that the eastside view to Mount Hood is a surprise for visitors too: "We're less than twenty miles as the crow flies and while many of my friends in the valley say, 'You should see our view of Mount Hood,' I have to chuckle because you really should see it from this side too. It really shines from up here."

Above the nearby burg of Tygh Valley, an overlook provides a peek to the namesake White River and marks a route that pioneers followed in the great migration across Oregon to reach the Willamette Valley. There are several lakes and ponds but a short cast away where boating and fishing can be enjoyed: "Many folks have weekend or summer homes at Pine Hollow Reservoir and nearby Rock Creek Reservoir," said Josh. "People come for the fishing—trout fishing. It's easy access for the kids too—no steep banks."

From Tygh Valley, you may wish to strike out farther east on a short four-mile drive along State Highway 216 to another secret hideaway where the White River plunges over a basalt shelf. White River Falls State Park offers a sprawling greenway with scattered picnic tables at a day-use site that opens each spring.

You'll be drawn to explore the rugged quarter-mile trail that takes you river-side where you discover something more: A complicated system of pipes and flumes diverted water from above the falls down into a powerhouse and where electricity-producing turbines generated power for the region from 1910 to 1960.

The Dalles Dam construction and completion led to the White River project's demise and it shut down in the '60s. For obvious safety reasons, Oregon State Parks does not want visitors inside the old powerhouse building that is falling in upon itself. "Keep Out" signs on the shuttered building make that message clear, so observe the signs as you explore the riverside scenery.

Do not forget a camera when you hike this path for the photo ops are numerous and stunning—of the river, the canyon, and the powerful White River Falls where two plunge pool falls drop more than ninety feet in dramatic fashion at this time of year. The park is a popular picnicking, hiking, and fishing retreat for visitors who wish to dip their toes in this corner of the greater Deschutes River corridor. White River Wildlife Area and White River Falls State Park offer easy-to-reach high desert escapes—for scenery, history, and relaxation.

For More Information

Where: 78430 Dodson Road, Tygh Valley, OR 97063
Phone: 541-544-2126
Watch the Episode: www.traveloregon.com/whiteriver

Passages Through Time
Covered Bridges of Linn County

S cenic back roads close to home—those rural roadways you have to spend a bit more time to experience—have long been my favorite. Perhaps through chance, but more often with a county road map and curiosity, I have found some of my most interesting stories just wandering where the pavement leads. As Charles Kuralt described in his autobiography, "I am one who fell in love with the little roads, the ones without names or numbers." Put me in his camp, for it's often where you'll find me searching for adventures.

Oregonians can be pretty pleased with themselves and this little-known fact: We have more covered bridges than anywhere else in the western United States, fifty-three to be exact. While many bridges have been retired (cars and heavy trucks and time do exact a toll), most are open to cyclists and hikers. That's just fine: the slower, the better for admiring the workmanship and artistry of a covered bridge. Although built to protect their wooden platforms from the abundant rainfall, covered bridges also became known for protecting couples in search of a little privacy. I've heard them referred to in some circles as "kissing bridges."

Flanked by the western Cascade foothills, Linn County in the spacious northeast corner of the Willamette Valley serves up a scattering of wistful, romantic reminders of a horse-and-buggy past. More than a dozen of these curious river crossings show off their original rough-hewn posts and beams and sometimes these roadways let you set your clock back too—on a journey into unexpected bliss!

Bill Cockerell, president of the Covered Bridge Society of Oregon, recently joined me for an afternoon tour across Linn County to see and admire some of the county's historic covered bridges. "You think of a covered bridge," noted Bill, "and you think of horses and buggies! You just want to relive that period of a hundred years ago...

Let Shimanek Bridge be your gateway to a simpler era across the quiet countryside of Linn County.

when times were slower. A romantic time, even if it is only in our minds—may not have been true, but it sure feels like it."

It feels like a Huck Finn sort-of-world at Shimanek Covered Bridge—a gorgeous beauty decked out in "Navajo Red" colored paint and it spans Thomas Creek. It is one of eight covered bridges in Linn County according to Bill, who said that most of the covered bridges were built in the 1930s when big timber was abundant and affordable. "That 'Navajo Red' is the only one in Linn County of that color," added Bill. "While inside this bridge it is painted white, plus light coming through the louvered windows makes for better visibility and so it is safer."

Safety is important these days because traffic roars past at a shattering pace—a far cry from slower days of the past century. Still, there are other covered bridges that are off the beaten path and hint of bygone times. For example, Hannah Covered Bridge is picture-postcard perfect! This stunning whitewashed covered bridge was built in 1936 and offers a bit of a Norman Rockwell kind of American moment. Bill said, "People just love this type of bridge because you can look out of it—you can see the fishermen downstream or people swimming too. It really is nearly like walking across any uncovered bridge."

Hannah Bridge may have you wondering, why did they cover the bridges in the first place? Bill said it was simple economics! "An uncovered bridge will last eight, ten years tops. But a covered bridge with a cedar roof could last forty or fifty years with proper maintenance."

As you will see, there is plenty of water running under the covered bridges of Linn County, so don't be surprised if you end up at Oregon Department of Fish and Wildlife's Roaring River Hatchery. This is a place that raises real whoppers—the kind with fins. Seventy percent of Oregon's catchable hatchery trout are raised at Roaring River Hatchery. Tim Schamber, the Roaring River Hatchery manager, provided a tour and explained the state's program: "The fun part of my job is making them aware and getting people involved in what we do here. So we try for interactive displays and exhibits . . . we try to put as much energy as possible toward that type of education."

Not far from the Roaring River Hatchery, you'll enjoy a chance to relax at Larwood Wayside—the only site in the state where a river flows into a creek. It's called Crabtree Creek and it is where you will find Larwood Covered Bridge, built more than seventy years ago. Bill said that he believes the covered bridges of Linn County will last even longer. "I think they're here to stay—for another hundred years at least—at least I hope so!" They are distinct and special and all Oregonians should be proud that we still have so many to enjoy.

For More Information

Where: 3010 Ferry Street SW, Albany, OR
Phone: Linn County Roads Department: 541-967-3919

Covered Bridge Society of Oregon
Where: c/o Bill Cockrell 3940 Courtney Lane South East, Salem, OR 97302
Web: www.covered-bridges.org
Phone: 503-399-0436

Roaring River Hatchery
Where: 42279 Fish Hatchery Drive, Scio, OR 97374
Web: www.dfw.state.or.us
Phone: 503-394-2496

Watch the Episode: www.traveloregon.com/linncounty

Two-Wheeled Adventure
Covered Bridges Scenic Bikeway

When the weather warms, it seems far too many Oregon byways can be busy blurs that just don't allow you enough time to slow down, get out of the race, and set your own pace for travel across the state. In the southern Willamette Valley, you will slow down and savor the spirit of cycling adventure along the new Covered Bridges Scenic Bikeway, near Cottage Grove.

There's a certain pride to your pedaling when your hometown offers the "best of the best," said Travis Palmer, Cottage Grove resident. Travis boasted that his community's recent recognition by the Oregon Parks and Recreation Department for the new scenic bikeway was a capstone for a rail-to-trail conversion project that offers so much: "It's the scenery, it's the quiet, it's the wildlife, and there's no doubt in your mind you're on one of the best pieces of trail in the state."

You'll love rolling through six bridges on a thirty-six-mile stretch of flat, paved bikeway along the new Covered Bridges Scenic Bikeway as you glide past scenery that takes your breath away. Longtime resident Greg Lee said, "It adds to everything that's already here: we have the nearby mountains with rivers and Dorena Lake for boating, fishing, camping, and hiking, so the bikeway adds to the flavor of the place."

Travis added that the crown jewel of the varied bridges is the recently restored Chambers Bridge, the only covered railroad bridge west of the Mississippi. "These covered bridges were torn down by the thousands across the country and only a handful of communities really recognized how great and important they were—Cottage Grove is one of those places."

Built in the 1920s, Chambers Bridge had hit on hard times and was on the brink of collapse a couple of years ago when the community decided they couldn't let that happen. They raised millions of dollars to fund the restoration in 2010 and soon began to take the old bridge apart piece-by-piece. "If we're the covered bridge capital of Oregon," said Travis, "how could we let the biggest, the best, the most historic fall into the river? It was important to save this bridge and we're glad we did."

The rebuilding of Chambers Bridge went on the fast track. They used 30 percent of the old bridge materials and rebuilt a connection with history that reopened to cyclists and hikers in December 2011. "We saved a structure that defined us and sets us apart from every other town in America!" said Travis. It is also a reflection of the larger Cottage Grove dedication to hold on to history: "We are a classic small-town-in-America downtown," added Travis. "If you walk downtown, see all these great old shops and yet we've got modern businesses tucked right next to it. We fancy ourselves as the melting pot of the Pacific Northwest."

Blair Winter showed up a couple years ago and added a key ingredient to the Cottage Grove pot when he bought Rainy Peak Bicycles, the town's only bike shop. Blair is an ambassador of sorts for the fast growing two-wheeled recreation and said the new Covered Bridge Bikeway is a perfect fit for the southern end of the Willamette Valley: "It's family friendly and really easy to ride with little traffic, and of course, the mountain bike community has discovered some of our great mountain trails as well." He is right! Oakridge, Oregon, is little more than an hour away and boasts over five hundred miles of Cascade Mountain trails that offer a challenge and fine complement to the new scenic bikeway. If you don't normally travel with your bike—not to worry—Rainy Peak also rents bikes, so you can cruise in, rent a bike, and get on the new bikeway in a matter of minutes.

For More Information

Covered Bridges Scenic Bikeway
Where: Cottage Grove, OR
Phone: 503-986-0631

Rainy Peak Bicycles
Where: 711 East Main Street, Cottage Grove, OR 97424
Web: www.rainypeak.com
Phone: 541-942-8712

Watch the Episode: www.traveloregon.com/coveredbridgebikeway

Lions, Tigers, and Bears. Oh My!
Wildlife Safari

GETAWAY #24 – SOUTHERN OREGON

Spring vacations always put a little extra spring in my step! It's the anticipation of a new adventure—and when my sons lived at home, it was a special chance to experience the outdoors through their eyes. Those childhood adventures motivated me to pack up a bit of our household and take our home on the road. I'm sure the same holds true today for many parents who are eager to explore unique Oregon destinations with their kids that will teach them more about wildlife.

For more than thirty-five years, Wildlife Safari in a unique Southern Oregon setting has provided plenty of adventures for tens of thousands of families. The wildlife park spans more than six hundred acres of rolling, oak-studded hills and savanna-like grasslands near the small burg of Winston. As you travel through Winston, you cannot miss the centerpiece of the town: a life-size bronze sculpture of the rare cheetah, an endangered species that numbers but a few thousand in the wild. The statue serves as a symbol of the continuing efforts that Wildlife Safari established many years ago to help wildlife.

There are lions, tigers, and bears—plus another one thousand animals that roam free while visitors are in the cages at Wildlife Safari. It's like a zoo except you are in the cage.

Wildlife curator Sarah Roy said, "It's the opposite of a zoo because you drive through in your car, and a giraffe can walk right up to your car, rhinos can walk right up to your car, the zebra herd will run across the road. It's amazing!" Sarah is right! Just like that— our interview came to a halt as J. T., a towering twelve-year-old giraffe stopped, stooped, and zoomed in for a closer look. Actually, there were many similar incidents and that's not surprising when you consider there are three hundred different species . . . close to one thousand animals "in charge" at a park that's unlike any you've visited before.

Our visit offered something new that visitors can experience called Wildlife Encounters. It's a new program that puts you in closer proximity to many species—a bit of what Roy called, "behind the scenes opportunities." We visited the brown bear area and found ourselves just feet away from a trio of six-year-old brown bears—separated by half a dozen electrically charged so-called "hot wires." Sarah explained, "The boys just woke up from hibernation a week ago and now we come out here several times a day for training purposes. Bears are so smart and mentally active so we give

It's an adrenaline rush when you're eye to eye with the grizzly bears at Wildlife Safari.

them simple fruit juices that are frozen and the bears treat them like popsicles—we also offer fruit trays and nuts—hide berries in boxes—so they get a chance to rip the boxes apart and play a little bit. We scatter treats around the area, throw frozen fruit in the pond, and they love it."

There's nearly four miles of roadway that wind through the complex on a route that takes you through several distinct animal communities including Asia, Africa, and the Americas. Each area is home to scores of species you rarely get to see this close. Flamingos, cougars, emus, tigers—and each is fascinating. We stopped in for a rare encounter with a pair of animals that have grown up together. Ellie is an Anatolian shepherd dog and her enclosure friend is a cheetah named Sonora. Each is four years old and they have grown up together. "The dog breed is quite protective, loyal, and dedicated to whatever they are raised with," explained Sarah, "so basically Sonora is Ellie's herd of sheep. We wanted to bring this breed in as a companion

The visitors are "in the cages" while the wildlife range across Wildlife Safari's six hundred acres.

animal to teach more about saving cheetahs in the wild."

In fact, that remains the number one conservation mission for Wildlife Safari—one that began in 1973 when the park opened to the public. The cheetah captive-breeding program has been a fixture at Wildlife Safari for nearly forty years. In fact, we met two newcomers to that program: Chimba and Mohawk are two male cubs born in September 2010 to Liz, a fourteen-year-old cheetah, and they will stay with their mom for one year. Sarah noted that in the wild, cheetahs remain critically endangered; there are less than ten thousand cheetahs living in the wild worldwide.

But it's the king of the animal kingdom that you may remember the most. I will certainly remember our "encounter" with Tao, a three-year-old African lion. You see, we played tug of war with Tao. "It's great exercise," said Sarah. "It's also good enrichment that keeps him and the other three lions mentally stimulated, so we do this each day and we thought it would be fun and educational to pull our visitors into the game too."

Two towering fences separate the lion from humans—each grabs hold of the forty-foot-long rope—humans with their hands, Tao with claws and powerful jaws and sharp teeth. We then pulled back and forth on the long rope—or rather we held our ground while Tao pulled on us—it was a remarkable experience as the four-hundred-pound lion showed his amazing strength and easily pulled on the rope that six of us held on to. "It is good exercise and the animals seem to have fun. So do the people," noted Sarah. "Each looks forward to this exercise—in fact, our lions come running over anytime it is rope time. It's pretty impressive when you feel him pulling—you can really feel that power in the rope—it's amazing!"

It is all of that and more and contributes to a remarkable outdoor experience across fascinating parkland that will entertain and teach you much about wildlife across the planet. After an hour or so, we arrived back at the Safari Village, near the park's entrance, where you may stroll around the manicured lawns, neatly trimmed hedges, masses of blooming daylilies, and carefully trimmed shade trees of Safari Village Gardens. The Safari Village offers a restaurant where you can get a fine meal, a snack bar for your favorite soft drink and light lunch, a gift shop for memorabilia, and regular educational animal shows. It's so comfortable and so inviting, you may not wish to leave, but you'll miss more interesting parts of the parkland.

If the village is not to your liking, a number of benches are strategically located next to ponds of water where you can watch the pink flamingos. Ah yes, the pink flamingo, practically an icon in America's landscape, except that these are not plastic: they are very real and happy to pose for you in front of bright yellow daylilies and a shimmering pool.

The cheetah has been the park's symbol from the beginning because the graceful cats face such terrible odds against their survival in the wild. According to the Smithsonian Institute, there are between 8,000 to 10,000 cheetahs living in the wild. The Cheetah Conservation Fund reports that Namibia has the world's largest population of cheetahs and less than 2,400 remain in the wild there. The plight of cheetahs symbolizes the problems that many predators face throughout the world. As Sarah explained, people fear predators, especially big cats like the lion, cheetah, and leopard. "Our attitudes and misconceptions have led to their endangerment because what people fear they often choose to destroy." Wildlife Safari tries to change that attitude by helping you to understand and care about wildlife. Perhaps that will improve their chance of survival in the wild.

For More Information

Where: 1790 Safari Road, Winston, OR 97496
Web: www.wildlifesafari.net
Phone: 541-679-6761
Watch the Episode: www.traveloregon.com/wildlifesafari

Trail of Ten Falls

Silver Falls State Park

R ain, rain, go away, come again another day." Have you ever found yourself humming this well-known ditty on a gray March afternoon? Never? Yeah, right! Fact is, endless spring showers that are splintered only by occasional slices of sunshine are the way of life in the northwest corner of the West from March through May. And if you're new to this country, here's my best advice: "Get used to it!"

Since there's little to do about it, why not find the beauty—no, make that the delight—in the Oregon outdoors when the rain seems to fall from above in buckets. I suggest you scoot into the hills near Silverton to a state park guaranteed to deliver huge, powerful, surging natural events that captivate your eyes, your ears, and perhaps your soul.

At Silver Falls State Park, fourteen foamy white curtains whirl and ripple and tumble and shimmer at one of the most delightful parklands in Oregon. Adam Bacher, an Oregon resident and noted landscape photographer, says he's lucky enough to capture the falls from every angle. "To me, Silver Falls State Park is like a miniature Columbia River Gorge," noted Adam. The two of us paused just yards away from the full force of the majestic and loud South Falls. "In one afternoon, on foot, you can see three major waterfalls and several smaller ones in less than a mile and a half of easy hiking."

We held tight to the steel guardrail alongside the ten-foot-wide trail and were just about to duck behind the famous whopper waterfall that's on the Trail of Ten Falls at Silver Falls State Park. Adam's a pro who finds the walking is pure pleasure inside Oregon's largest state parkland. In fact, across more than nine thousand acres, you will find many waterfalls that boom and seem to shout for your attention. As we hiked, Adam explained that mountain snowmelt accompanying the annual spring rains builds the south and north forks of Silver Creek to swollen threads of white water that race down canyon drainages all across the vast forest parkland.

Thundering and roaring from recent downpours, the many cascading falls inside the park are immense spectacles to behold. Nestled in the lower elevation of Oregon's Cascade Mountains, Silver Falls is blessed to be located in a temperate rain forest. "They come in all shapes and sizes, Grant—we have a little over seven miles of canyon trail in this park, with three different access points and several different hiking loops. You can choose how far you want to go and which falls to visit, so if you're looking for waterfalls, you can get the whole package right here—and we owe it all to prehistoric volcanoes."

South Falls shimmers and swirls as it drops 177 feet into the South Fork of Silver Creek at Silver Falls State Park.

The geologic history behind so many falls in one location is impressive. It seems millions of years ago, successive and destructive lava flows covered the entire western region of Oregon. But over time within this parkland, the wind, rain, and ice eroded or cut through the lava to create tributary creeks and their falls—plus the main stem of Silver Creek. So much beauty from long-ago devastation is worth pausing to consider!

Down the Trail of Ten Falls, Adam offered a photo tip: let each waterfall guide you to their larger scenes. "Each item in nature is in its own unique context and so the more of that kind of foreground that I can show, I think the more it enhances the photo . . . I mean those cracks are literally layers of lava and who knows, a million years apart, a couple hundred thousand years apart . . . the geology here is just fascinating."

"The park's recent history is fascinating too," explained Silver Falls State Park Ranger Dorothy Brown-Kwaiser. She said that the Civilian Conservation Corps constructed South Falls Lodge in the 1930s. "The lodge is gorgeous and I think it's one of the highlights," said Dorothy. "You can see all the stonework—all the places where they drilled the stone in order to split it apart. Look at the beams up above and you see the hand-hewed marks. It's gorgeous."

Deemed a "recreation demonstration site," and guarding the pathway entrance to South Falls, the rustic lodge is a scaled-down version of Mount Hood's Timberline Lodge. It stands large in the park, complete with rugged rock and timber construction. Following a recent remodel, it is now an interpretive center, equipped with a food vendor and a very welcome fireplace. "There's a fire going and it has that wonderful woodsy smell," said Dorothy. "It just feels like a lodge, like you're in a wilderness feeling; like you're in nature."

Campers who come for a longer stay can enjoy campsites that are open year-round. You will find unique group camping areas like the Old and New Ranch buildings, the Silver Creek Youth Camp, the North Falls trailer and tent areas, and RV, cabin, and tent camping in the overnight campground (fifty-four electrical sites, fifty-one tent sites, and showers, closed October 31 to April 15; fourteen rental cabins open year-round.) Additional cabin rentals and complete group accommodations can be found at the Silver Falls Conference Center. Guided daytime horse trail rides for people of all abilities are available from Memorial Day to Labor Day for a fee.

Back on the trail, Adam pointed out the slow but certain descent along the trail to reach each falls. "That's important to keep in mind for the return trip, which is all uphill," he offered as we came to an intersection with a pathway leading to Frenchie Falls. This falls is tiny and hidden in comparison to most of the obviously gigantic falls in the park, but its seclusion is at the heart of its charm. The next, Lower South Falls, also offers a hike behind a wall-of-water feature that gives you a unique perspective for enjoying the ninety-three-foot free fall. Lower North Falls requires a 1.5-mile hike to reach; it's more akin to a thirty-foot block or wedge of water, rather than the more typical long, cascading drop characteristic of most of the park's falls.

Nearby Winter Falls is just the opposite: long and delicate at 140 feet from its base to its top. Middle North Falls is next in the lineup along the Canyon Trail; it's distinguished by another walk behind the falls, although it's on a side route that dead-ends just beyond the falls. Soon you'll come face to face with Drake Falls, which is the smallest of the entire park at just twenty-seven feet; here's a great photo opportunity because of the contrast between surging white water and black bedrock and river rock just visible under the surface. It's 2.4 miles from South Falls to Double Falls, which is the only two-tiered falls in the park. One mile farther is Twin Falls, which takes a sharp ninety-degree turn on a bend in the creek and then splits into two falls around a protruding rock face.

It's nearly another mile to powerful and hypnotic North Falls, which explodes out of a small slice in the bedrock and falls 180 feet into the canyon below; it's so loud that it's difficult to hold a conversation here with your travel companions! You can also walk behind North Falls. Upper North Falls (about a half mile beyond North Falls) is a sixty-five-foot drop that offers a wide curtainlike affair that drops into a beautiful pool below.

Adam insists that you will slow down at Silver Falls State Park—the trails, the scenery, the wonder of it all—gives you little choice. "I count my blessings that I have access to something this beautiful an hour and a half from Portland. It's all pretty incredible!" Another incredible way to enjoy this part of Oregon is the Silver Falls Tour Route. Consider it an old-fashioned Sunday drive through this corner of the Willamette Valley and make it a daylong affair. It's a tour once taken, you'll never forget!

For More Information

Where: On State Highway 214, 26 miles east of Salem.
Web: www.oregonstateparks.org
Phone: 503-873-8681, ext. 31 or 800-551-6949
Watch the Episode: www.traveloregon.com/trailoftenfalls

Like Wings of an Eagle
Soaring Over Washington County

GETAWAY #26 – GREATER PORTLAND

Oregon by air is a marvel! Our getaways have taken you to wonderful places that take the breath away: from a helicopter crossing the Cascades Mountains to a hot air balloon ride over wine country, or even a special delivery "trout drop" above a mountain pond. Rather than imagine the many faces of Oregon from four thousand feet up, why not try a unique airplane ride that offers peace, quiet, and a thrilling experience.

It's an aircraft minus a motor called a sailplane and they take off each week from the Willamette Valley Soaring Club (WVSC) to soar over Washington County. Pilots agree that Oregon's landscape provides spectacular and stunning points of view. "It's really peaceful and quiet up there," said flight instructor Bruce Pearson. Bruce is also the flight manager for the WVSC and added that the motorless, high-flying recreation is an addiction. "It is a passion! Once you try it, you can't live without it and it's something anyone can do."

The Willamette Valley Soaring Club has operated for more than fifty years near North Plains. It is the largest club in the country with over two hundred members and a dozen planes in the club's fleet. WVSC offers anyone a chance to ride aboard a "perfectly good airplane that doesn't have a motor."

"Well, that just makes it safer," chuckled Bruce. "Our planes don't have engines so we're always prepared to land at any given time. It's the safest flying there is."

Sailplanes were once made exclusively of wood, but aluminum, fiberglass, and carbon fiber technology have made modern sailplanes incredibly light. When matched with the latest electronics, the planes can stay aloft for hours and cover hundreds of miles. "It is all about flying efficiently and cutting through the air without disturbing it anymore than you have to," said Bruce. "These days we fly higher, farther, and stay up longer than ever before."

Fifteen-year-old Holly Dotson got hooked on soaring after just one summertime ride. Since then she has logged thirty-six flights and plans to become a licensed pilot. "It's a thrilling, once in a lifetime experience that I just had to do lots more," said the young flier. "Some of my friends think I'm crazy, but others think it's cool and ask, 'When will you take me up?'"

"Birds have been doing it for millions of years," added Bruce with a laugh. "We do the same thing but with one handicap: we don't flap our wings." Holly is the student and Bruce is her instructor and the two meet two or three times each week to review her bookwork and prep for the next flight. "Anyone can start learning to fly a sailplane," said Bruce. "You can qualify to solo when fourteen and it is rare that someone cannot learn how to do this."

Holly's parents, Sean and Shannon Dotson, agreed that their daughter's path was set after she took her first flight: "It's a minimum of two hours a day of studying the books," noted her mom. "So she's given up a lot and really sacrificed time with her friends, soccer, and things like that because she's constantly studying—but she loves it."

"She's grown in confidence too," added her dad. "She needs to take command of a plane and needs that confidence and ability to be in control at all times." As the tow plane rises to four thousand feet, Holly said that the best flying time is after the towline's released and she's on her own, soaring with nature's wind and updrafts called thermals.

She added that the experience is "quiet and breathtaking," but she remains alert at all times: "You have to watch everything—other planes and birds—and you have to find the thermals just like a bird does. That's where the hot air rises from the ground to give the plane more lift. Thermals allow you to stay up longer and travel further, sometimes hundreds of miles in a day. It's so much fun and anyone can go—come on out and try!"

For More Information

Where: Willamette Valley Soaring Club, 11870 NW Dersham Road, North Plains, OR 97133

Web: www.wvsc.org

Phone: 503-647-0913

Watch the Episode: www.traveloregon.com/likeaneagle

A Playground in the Trees
Tree to Tree Adventure Park

Sixty-feet off the ground is a point of view that will take your breath away and it's found in Oregon's only aerial parkland, Tree to Tree Adventure Park set in the foothills of the Oregon Coast Range in western Washington County. The fifty-seven-acre forested parkland is unlike anything you've ever experienced off the ground. In fact, you might consider it a playground in the trees.

Marissa Doyle, comanager of the unique park, said, "You will feel like a kid again when going through this course. We have tunnels and bridges and Tarzan-like ropes . . . all sorts of fun stuff built for adults to play up in the trees." Instructor George Bidiman guides folks across the four different tree-to-tree courses—each course is progressively more challenging and he helps people find steady steps on a shaky trail or across a swinging, swaying wobbly way. George said, "It is flat-out freedom up in the air and probably the closest thing you can get to flying outside of an airplane."

Each climber must wear a safety harness that connects with two lanyards that sport lobster claw–type clips that link you to thick wire cables. Each cable can hold up to ten thousand pounds, so once you're clipped in—you're not going anywhere except across the aerial trail.

The new Tree to Tree Adventure Park is a family-owned business that is the brainchild of co-owners and managers Marissa Doyle and Molly Beres. Molly hopes that the park's location (a short drive from Scoggins Valley Park and Henry Hagg Lake) will attract a following once they have discovered the park's unique features. "Portland is the best place for this sort of thing because there are so many outdoorsy people here. Everyone likes to be outside doing active things and extreme sports and this will fit in just fine."

Marissa added, "People come to Hagg Lake to hike, to bike, to rent boats—to be outside and just enjoy nature. We're an extension for those kinds of activities and yet we offer a unique experience outside of the normal fishing, boating, and hiking activities that are that so popular at the lake." Marissa said that the new business also offers a course for youngsters, one that offers the same elements as the adult version but is much closer to the ground. The course admission isn't based on age—but on height—that is, with your arms extended overhead you must be able to reach six feet, six inches, to play on the full-sized course after you've passed the basic training course. If a youngster is unable to reach six feet, six inches but can reach at least five feet with their arms extended, he or she can play on the smaller course.

The park's many course features are called "elements" and range from simple swaying bridges to horizontal rock walls and tunnels that you must climb across or climb through to continue the course. Many participants agreed that the climbing experience felt safe despite the fifty-foot elevation and that it is an experience full of surprises: First-timer Leah Perkins noted, "I was worried at first that I'd be a little too old and out of shape to make it—but I must say that I felt like I really got something done out here—I made it through and didn't fall once."

Perkins's friend Mary Higley noted that each element is unique, challenging, and left her with a distinct feeling of accomplishment: "A couple of times I had my feet get out in front of me a little bit, so I really had to use my arm strength to get back up—plus, the sway of the platforms can be a little frightening, but I'd definitely do it again. It was a lot of fun."

Instructor George added that everyone who has completed the course since it opened this spring has left with a huge smile: "Everyone's having a great time—they come for the challenge but also the fun of feeling like a kid again and it doesn't get any better than that."

That feeling never lets up on the course either—it's surpassed only by the thrilling payoff that waits for each climber at the end. "We end every course with a zip line and so it's the payoff for your hard work because everybody loves a zip," noted a smiling Molly. "Our whole purpose is to be outdoors, enjoy nature, and enjoy being in Oregon—just to love where you are—it's the best!"

For More Information

Where: 2975 SW Nelson Road, Gaston, OR 97119
Web: www.treetotreeadventurepark.com
Phone: 503-357-0109
Watch the Episode: www.traveloregon.com/treetotree

A Governor's Legacy
Rowena Crest

I t's a view that's never twice the same down a trail to a timeless place. The Historic Columbia River Highway provides a "moving" experience in more than one twist of the word. You wriggle along the old roadway—never more than at twenty-five to thirty miles per hour.

The expansive views to the ancient and eroded Columbia Basin basalt flows stir something inside that speaks of what pioneers must have felt upon the sight of steep rock ridges and deep defiles. Their great journeys and sacrifices nearly at an end, perhaps their experiences appeared more worthwhile to them in the presence of such magnificence.

The Tom McCall Preserve atop Rowena Crest is in the heart of the Columbia River Gorge where April is the prime time for spring wildflowers. Steve Terrill, a native Oregonian and noted landscape photographer, said Rowena Crest is a "slice of heaven on Earth."

"The first word that comes to my mind is 'diversity,'" noted Steve on a recent field shoot. He strolled through a section of trail that stretched toward the glorious Columbia River and he stopped every few yards to admire the incredible riot of color that had broken out. "There is an explosion of color that's almost surreal," he said. "I just love this—I almost feel like I'm the only person out here!"

There is great drama in the heart of the gorge at Rowena Crest. Gaze to the Washington side and observe the geologic drama found in the vertical rock spikes called the Ortley Pinnacles. Here a dozen basalt flows, dating back ten to sixteen million years, jut over one another. Geology plays an obvious and significant defining role in the Gorge from ancient lava flows to the impact of catastrophic Ice Age floods, and even more recently and regularly from volcanic ash deposits from the not-so-friendly

Mount St. Helens. Yes, the view of Gorge geology from the Rowena Crest Viewpoint is a mind-expanding experience—but closer at hand there's another showy display, no less sprawling or special and every bit as breathtakingly beautiful.

Steve also noted that shooting pretty pictures at Rowena Crest (especially on a wind-blown day) can be a challenge. Yet he also admitted that the beauty of the wind-swept plateau and the sprawling two-hundred-acre site is jaw-droppingly gorgeous: "It's like green waves flowing across a meadow up here, and it's splashed with purple and yellow and red and orange. The wind gives an effect of rippling water over the surface of a lake or the ocean."

The endless horizon from atop Rowena Crest offers hard-to-resist scenery across the Nature Conservancy's Tom McCall Preserve.

I hope you're lucky enough to spend time in The Nature Conservancy's Tom McCall Preserve in either April or May—to see the unrestrained kaleidoscope of color from such native wildflowers as grass widows, prairie stars, balsamroot, lupine, and Indian paintbrush. Nearly all of the three hundred species that can be found throughout the Gorge grow on this two-hundred-acre preserve. The preserve is an important link in the chain of Nature Conservancy Preserves across Oregon. The site was named in 1982 for Oregon Governor Tom McCall who committed to conservation. Many people, Steve included, like that connection. Steve also stakes out a spot on the trail where he can go to work with his camera when he wants to capture moments of the special time and place.

Steve freely shared some of his hard-earned photo tips: use a tripod to steady the shot, a wide-angle lens to get up close, and an electronic shutter release to get rid of the shakes. But with a smile—he wryly added, don't forget one more thing: "Patience! If you're out here to enjoy this and the shot that you want includes flowers in the foreground with a stunning Gorge scene in the background—just set up and be patient—really be patient for the right light and weather and overall look."

Steve's patience has paid off in a project that he prizes the most of all his work: the "All Oregon Calendar." It is shot and produced, printed and published entirely in his home state. "Well, I was born and raised in Portland and I just absolutely love Oregon! If I can keep the money and the jobs—even just a little bit because we're not a huge company by any means, but if I can keep that in Oregon then I think I'm helping a little bit."

The preserve contains two trails. The one-mile Plateau Trail begins at the interpretive sign at the center of the preserve. It crosses the plateau to cliff edges at the north and encircles a permanent pond. The three-mile McCall Point Trail is open each spring through fall and begins from the south side of the vehicle turnaround with a thousand-foot gain in elevation. At the top, you are rewarded with spacious views of the Columbia Gorge and the Cascades.

Safety Tip: Watch out here for ticks, rattlesnakes, and poison oak.

You'll want to explore the Tom McCall Preserve more than a little bit—perhaps to wander the mile-long trail toward the Columbia River or the three-mile version that loops uphill. Both are fine adventures for folks with time and patience and a love of the Oregon outdoors. The Tom McCall Preserve is the sort of place that will satisfy your curiosity, let your heart soar, and perhaps restore your soul in the beauty that is found in Oregon.

For More Information

Where: On the Old Columbia River Scenic Highway, 11 miles east of Hood River

Phone: 503-802-8100

Watch the Episode: www.traveloregon.com/rowenacrest

Rockhounds Go Holleywood
Sweet Home's Petrified Wood

I try hard not to leave any stone unturned in my search for great outdoor getaways and I recently went a long, long way back to a time when Oregon was a hotbed of volcanic activity. I joined a group of self-proclaimed rock hounds who love to uncover secrets in the soil.

You could call Brad Newport's backhoe a "time machine" as it crawls across his Holleywood Ranch near Sweet Home, Oregon. "Everyone has his or her hobby," noted the ranch owner. "For some people it's fishing or hunting—crafts—and for me, it's right here—under the ground. I love it so much because I know that everyone who comes out here is going to have a great time. You just can't help it if you're a rock hound." Each chunk of earth that Brad's "time machine" lifts out is a piece of Oregon prehistory. This time, the rock hounds who gathered to sort through the dirt and debris were members of the Tualatin Valley Gem Club.

Each has come to Brad's ranch for a different reason: some say it's for the discovery of something new, others say it's for the value of a newfound treasure—all seem to agree, it's the beauty of what they find— petrified wood. "Each piece is pretty—glassy, they take a polish, they shine—especially petrified wood—it has so much character," noted geologist Taylor Hunt. The Holleywood Ranch doesn't have cows, sheep, or horses—but it does have something more wonderful.

Cedar, maple, alder, oak, plus fifty-four other known wood species—all of it petrified wood dating back millions of years—have been found here. It's the site of an ancient collection of wood that washed up on these Cascade Mountain foothills millions of year ago—a time when Sweet Home, Oregon, was oceanfront. All of it is down deep in the ground—and requires shoveling—scraping—wiping— thirty million years of mud to bring to the light of the twenty-first century. Taylor described what it all might have looked like so long ago: "We would have looked out to open ocean or an inlet or bay—there could have been driftwood here, but looking behind us there wouldn't have been any Cascades—just going in a straight shot into Eastern Oregon."

Once upon a time volcanic activity was common across the Oregon landscape—Taylor said, think of Mount St. Helens times 100. "Roughly thirty million years ago that velocity with huge volcano eruptions like Mount St. Helens ripped the trees up—branches, logs, everything—and brought it this way and then it got deposited as outwash that's followed by ash that buried it and fossilized it."

Most of the petrified wood is small fragments from the past, noted club member Carl Weaver, who had his hands full with scores of rocks that he found: "This is my first trip here and it is looking like it's going to be a good trip with lots of rock for only thirty minutes of digging. I don't think that's too bad because I've been some places where you dig six to eight hours and only had two to three pieces to show for it—so this is pretty good."

Every now and then someone gets lucky—like John VanLoo who found an intact petrified branch from off a larger tree. "That's a trophy right there," noted the excited John. "It's actually the first log I've ever found and I was shaking as I dug it out. I was pretty excited."

All the rock hounds agree that the mystery of their unique adventure keeps them coming back for more. "Ah, it's the camaraderie," noted Carl. "Getting with other people and visiting and everybody gets a chance to share their finds that way. Plus, you always know you're going to be the one to come home with a super big piece. Everyone has fun with it that way too." Brad noted that rock hounding is a "blood sport!" Once it's in your blood, it never, ever leaves: "I do like it when other people find something cool, especially when it's my son or daughter, but I still want to find it—to be the first human that's seen something that old—it's just the rock hound in me."

For More Information

Where: Holleywood Ranch, 26250 Old Holley Road, Sweet Home, OR 97386
Web: www.holleywoodranch.com
Phone: Brad Newport/Holleywood Ranch owner: 541-405-5990
Watch the Episode: www.traveloregon.com/digginghistory

A Sublime Spring View
Mount Hood

On a fine sun-kissed spring day, Portland's hip-pocket mountain—Mount Hood—is a scene fit for framing. It's the size of it that steals the view and your heart. Sprawling across the horizon and rising to nearly twelve thousand feet in elevation, this magnificent mountain and its expansive national forest have long captured imaginations.

Following thousands of grueling miles on the Oregon Trail, emigrants came up against one final obstacle: the massive bulk of Mount Hood. Later, we fell in love with it and built highways to it and around it, and then we embraced it as a playground. The beauty of its isolation and the majesty of its dominance compel many Oregonians to admire and lovingly refer to it as "our mountain."

As winter's grip gives way to riotous spring, Mount Hood and the Hood River Valley countryside invite folks to play outdoors. The drive up the valley is a scenic excursion that may leave you wide-eyed and slack-jawed for the journey.

I love to ramble across the valley at this time of year, when many roadside farms are opening up and shaking off winter's lonesome run, and many local families like Lynn and Dolly Rasmussen are eager to see new faces. Lynn said that their Rasmussen Farms has operated a large flower-produce-gift stand for more than fifty years: "I began after the war—World War II—at a time when everyone raised their own products right at home and so we had chickens and we had pigs and of course, in those days that's just what everyone did."

A friendly place to stop and shop and every season offers something different—and right now? Dolly noted, "Well, plants for the garden, plants for baskets, containers, flower garden items and most are grown right here at the farm. People are anxious to get outside and enjoy themselves in a very scenic, rural, and safe area. You could come here every weekend all summer long and never do the same thing twice."

Picture-postcard country—in the valley and on the drive beyond! It gets even better on the short side trip to Lost Lake, where you may believe you've found heaven. It certainly feels close as you travel one of the prettiest byways you'll ever enjoy on the twenty-mile trip from Hood River to Lost Lake. Roy Hilmick, former owner of Lost Lake Resort, noted, "As you drive up here from the valley, you get to see all the rhodies pop out this time of year in an explosion of color. There are several miles of rhododendrons and bear grass too—it makes for quite a show."

At three thousand feet in elevation, Lost Lake is a small body of freshwater tucked into the northwestern flanks of Mount Hood. Deep and clear with more than two hundred surface acres, Lost Lake supports a variety of fish for the angler's pleasure, including rainbow and brown trout and kokanee (landlocked sockeye salmon).

No motors are allowed on Lost Lake, so this is rowboat country—and yes, you can rent a canoe or paddle boat at the lake's resort. "It's a great little store," added Roy. "It has everything that the campers might need and then there's seven cabins, rustic mountain cabins—woodstove, wood furnished, comfortable beds—people burrow in those cabins and they are just happy as can be."

US Forest Service campsites line the shore and many offer stunning views to the lake—and on a clear day—Mount Hood steals the scene, so bring a camera for plenty of photo ops as you enjoy a delightful three-mile hiking trail that wraps around the lake for closer inspection. "Mother Nature at its best," according to Roy. "Just a real beautiful place to come and relax."

I love this area for the simple peace of mind it brings me and the absolutely stunning view of Mount Hood, sometimes two views, if you consider the glimmering reflection you'll enjoy as you gaze across the lake to the mountain Oregonians cherish.

For More Information

Rasmussen Farms
Where: 3020 Thomsen Road, Hood River, OR 97031
Web: www.rasmussenfarms.com
Phone: 541-386-4622; Fax 541-386-4702

Mount Hood National Forest, Lost Lake Resort
Where: PO Box 90, Hood River, OR 97031
Web: www.lostlakeresort.org
Phone: Mount Hood National Forest: 503-667-0511; Lost Lake Resort: 541-386-6366

Watch the Episode: www.traveloregon.com/mthoodviews

Supper from the Sea
Razor Clams

Oregon's beaches are popular destinations for all sorts of recreation activities and each spring one of the most popular sandy stretches is along eighteen miles of shoreline in Clatsop County; it's where thousands of razor clam diggers have recently discovered one of the best clam seasons in years.

As springtime moves into high gear, the best low tides of the season bring a bounty of seafood close at hand. Local resident Steve Fick likes to say, "When the tide goes out, my dinner table is set—with razor clams." Steve grew up in Astoria and he really digs this recreation: "Oh, Grant, there are clams galore this season—one of the best, most plentiful clam 'sets' in recent history. The biologists say the harvest could exceed one million clams. Wow, huh?"

That much is certain, but if you've never dug this sport—how do you get started? Steve handed me a "clam gun," the tool of choice for beginners learning the ropes of clam digging. It's a hard plastic tube, with a covered top that has a handle built into it, plus there is a small hole on the top so that the tube acts like a siphon.

You press the tube or "gun" down into the soft sand up to three feet deep, and then place your thumb over the hole, lift and pull the tube full of sand—and hopefully, the razor clam—back up to the surface. "Try that clam hole right there, Grant," advised Steve. He pointed to a small, quarter-sized dimple in the sandy surface. "The clam's neck is just under that dimple. It's a giveaway sign that there's a clam down there. Go for it!" And so I did—the tube easily slid down its length, then I covered the hole and lifted the tube full of sand that held a dandy four-inch-long razor clam.

It was slick and it was easy! So easy that anyone can do it. In fact, it's hard to call the activity "work" when the clams are so plentiful. According to Steve the stretch of Clatsop County beaches between Seaside and the Columbia River is "where

95 percent of all the clams in Oregon are dug." Steve is an old hand at the clam game—he can even spot the critters in the surf: "Well, sometimes when they're feeding, they stick their neck up and out right in the shallow surf line—it makes a little V and we call those 'knickers.' Once you get the knack for spotting them, it's easy."

Steve relies on a short-handled shovel with a long steel blade—a clam shovel that's specially designed to quickly dig deep enough to get your hands on the speedy razor clam. Speed is critical because the razor clam moves through soft sand like a hot knife through soft butter. "You go about two inches to the side of the dimple and then you pull the shovel toward the hole," said Steve.

"You pull the sand up and reach your hand in underneath. Feel for the neck and pull the clam up—but not too hard or you pull the neck off." It's a technique that takes practice, so first timers usually stick to the clam gun technique for a successful clam digging adventure. But be cautious—Steve noted that the clam gun technique has drawbacks, as there's greater potential to break the clamshell with the gun rather than shovel.

The Oregon Department of Fish and Wildlife manages the clam resource and there are important rules and regulations to note: A state shellfish license is required for clam diggers fourteen and older. Each clam digger must dig their own limit of fifteen razor clams and you cannot put any back. Remember: even if you break a shell or dig a small clam, the first fifteen that you dig you must keep.

It wasn't long before each of us had dug our limit when Steve smiled and said, "I never met a clam I didn't like—to eat. Let's go!" With that, we were off to his kitchen for a quick lesson on how to prepare our clams. "First, I like to rinse them off—get as much sand off the clams as possible."

Steve is as skilled in the kitchen as he is on the beach and makes quick work of our thirty clams. He offered a tip—he gives the clams a quick dousing of hot water—enough to open the clams but not cook them and he quickly followed the hot water with a cold-water shower. The icy-cold water stopped any cooking of the clam. A few quick flicks of his small sharp knife and he cleaned each clam of its stomach contents. Then he doused each in an egg bath; that was followed by coating each side of the clam in soda cracker meal. The combination provided a nice coating to both sides of the clam. The preheated (medium high) frying pan contained a generous amount of vegetable oil. Steve cooked the clams less than two minutes a side (golden brown on each side) and he cautiously advised that overcooked clams taste "like rubber and are too chewy."

The meal of cooked clams provided a satisfying reward, the sort of activity that builds strong memories of the Oregon outdoors: "It's the whole process—to me," said Steve. "It's a lot of enjoyment to come down here to the beach early in the morning, dig clams, walk around—take the whole family down. You feel like you've really accomplished something at the end of the day . . . I enjoy that."

For More Information

Where: Seaside, South Jetty Access is at Sunset Beach, 10 miles south of Astoria off US Highway 101.

Web: www.garibaldimarina.com

Phone: Oregon Department of Fish and Wildlife: 503-947-6000

Watch the Episode: www.traveloregon.com/razorclamming

How to Dig Horsenecks, Cockles, and Steamers

Shovels and weeding rakes can be a sure sign of spring when gardeners go to work in their yards—but they don't always have to be used for work. Oregon's springtime super low tides are the best because that's a time when the dinner table is set. Mitch Vance, shellfish biologist with the Oregon Department of Fish and Wildlife (ODFW), said that any of the really good low tides during daylight hours provide ample opportunities to harvest Oregon's varied bay clam species. "Some folks like to get out as early as possible and have more digging opportunity; they follow that tide as it goes out, looking for new exposed areas and then work back as the tide turns to flood."

Norm and Bonnie Clow recently traveled to Tillamook Bay from their home in Dayton, Oregon. They were among the first early risers to explore the exposed sand and gravel bars on a sunrise clamming adventure. The Clows have been digging their dinner on the bay for more than sixty years and said that the 4 A.M. wake-up call was "no big deal!" Norm offered his best advice for the novice clam digger: "Keep digging! Usually, the clams are thick enough that if you dig one hole and excavate out, you will have little problem harvesting a limit."

April, May, and June each provide many super low minus tides that occur early in the morning. This is the favored time for digging bay clams with names like horsenecks, qua-hogs, steamers, and cockles. Jeff Folkema, a local guide and the owner of Garibaldi Marina, showed off a half dozen of the prized horseneck clams that he harvested from the bay. He said they are called "gaper" clams because of the "gape" in the shell where the neck pokes through. "This is a nice size," he said while handling a hefty two- to three-pound grapefruit-sized bivalve. "This is pretty average size with a lot of meat. A good sized clam but I have seen much bigger too."

Jeff added that clam diggers fourteen years and older are required to purchase an Oregon shellfish license. "And remember that each person who is harvesting clams must have their own container—a bucket or a clam net on their belt—even a plastic bread bag will do—because you cannot lump other people's clams into your container—you'll get a ticket for that."

Keep your eyes open for the ODFW placard that show pictures of the different clams species along with the harvest limits and other regulations. Mitch offered: "If you're digging it really helps to know what you're after so you can understand the regulations around that species." He added that abundant food and reliable cold, clean water contribute to perfect habitat for bay clams' populations in most of Oregon's coastal estuaries. There is also a tasty reward for the clam digger's efforts—bay clams can be delicious, according to local resident Don Best, who showed off his limit of quahog clams.

One of his all-time favorite recipes is an old-fashioned clam fritter: "All it takes is a little cracker crumb, flour, and egg—perhaps some chopped onion. Chop up the clams, mix them with the batter, and fry them in a skillet with oil. They are awesome that way!" Mitch added that in addition to supper from the sea, digging bay clams can provide hours of family fun for each member of the family: "Oh, it is really good for families because it's so easy and there's not a lot of gear—just a shovel or a rake—so get the kids in some boots and get them out here and have some fun in the sand."

Don Best's Clam Frittters

Makes 15 to 18 fritters; serves about 4.

Vegetable oil	2 eggs
1 cup unsifted flour	½ cup milk
2 teaspoons baking powder	¼ cup reserved clam liquid
½ cup bread crumbs	1 tablespoon vegetable oil
½ teaspoon salt	2 cups chopped clams

In a deep-fat fryer or large, heavy skillet, heat oil to 375°F. Sift together flour, baking powder, bread crumbs, and salt; set aside.

In a medium mixing bowl, beat eggs, milk, ¼ cup reserved clam liquid, and 1 tablespoon oil. Stir in dry ingredients and clams. Drop mixture by heaping tablespoonfuls into hot oil. Fry until golden on all sides. Drain on paper towels. Refrigerate leftovers (if there are any).

What a Fluke!

Cape Lookout State Park Trail

Tillamook County's Cape Lookout State Park Trail lures you along with splendid scenery at every turn with moments of wonder and surprise and sights that are simply breathtaking. Clyde Reid, a Whale Watch volunteer (an Oregon State Parks program), cautioned that the Cape Lookout hike is not for the faint of heart. "It's not an easy walk! It's a bit of a scramble, so you should wear layers of warm and water/wind resistant clothing and sensible shoes—I've seen people out there in flip-flops and cutoff shorts and that's not a good idea."

The trail courses the full length of the cape's southern edge and while it is fairly flat there is a slight gradient drop, which means it's slightly uphill all the way back out to the parking area. It's a five-mile round-trip and you should allow up to four hours of hiking to complete the entire trip. It is also muddy in spots and marked by steep drop-offs.

The spring whale migration begins in mid-March when the sixty-foot mammals leave Alaska's Bering Sea for the warm-water

You can enjoy amazing views of migrating gray whales from atop Cape Lookout.

lagoons of Baja Mexico, where the females give birth. To see them from a land-based site, you have to get as far up or out as possible, such as on a high overlook or a jutting headland. In fact, the higher the elevation and the farther out, the better. That's what makes Cape Lookout one of the choice land-based whale-watching sites along the entire coast.

The 2.5-mile trail traverses through a second-growth forest of fir, spruce, and hemlock. The hike offers expansive southerly views of the Pacific Ocean and Cape Kiwanda. In April the trail is flanked by one of the most prolific stretches of blooming trillium I've ever come across, and other colorful wildflowers are also at hand. This is my favorite place for watching the great mammals of the sea. When they're visible, they're so close that they seem to just lounge in the ocean water two hundred feet below.

Along the way, be sure to keep the binoculars easy to reach and ready for anything. On our adventure, we spied eagles, lounging harbor seals, and thousands of murres, a common seabird, floating on the ocean surface far below. At the end of the line, you will discover why many call Cape Lookout the "best seat in the house" to watch the gray whale parade that goes past Oregon's shores each spring.

There is not another experience along the Oregon coastline quite like this for whale watching; not only are the giants of the deep passing by seemingly just out of reach, but many of the sixty-foot-long mammals detour around the cape's southern flanks where they lounge about, resting and feeding before continuing their ten-thousand-mile journeys. Gray whales left warm Baja lagoons weeks ago and now they are bound for the cold, productive waters of Alaska's Bering Sea. Clyde said that your best chance to spy them is when they rise to the surface to take a breath and mark the moment with their "blow" or exhale. "It's not a waterspout as many think," said Clyde. "It's a big cloud of compressed CO_2. These animals are the size of school buses and they have lungs the size of refrigerators. There's no mistaking it."

Here's a hint that may help you to find the whales faster too: scan the ocean with your naked eye, looking for the telltale blow. Once you see that, focus in with binoculars to get a good close-up look. Clyde added, "You might see their backs, might even see their flukes or tail when they dive to go deep. That's always exciting." Even more exciting (and a bit rare) is a breech when the giants seem to fly out of the water. Local coastal landscape and wildlife photographer Don Best was ready for that dramatic moment with his camera, tripod, and a 500mm telephoto lens.

In his photos he likes to show the true size of the animal—how does he do it? "How do I get that perfect shot?" Don quickly fired back: "Oh, that's easy—patience, patience, and more patience. You have to be looking at just the right spot at just the right moment—so it takes real concentration not to look away. I don't always get that good shot right away and I take many, many pictures for just the right one, but that's the beauty of digital cameras."

Gray whales swim up to one hundred miles a day and most rarely stop to rest. So hurry to the coast and especially Cape Lookout before their show is gone. "Even if you didn't have a camera, this is a great place to come," added Don.

Clyde nodded in agreement as another whale surfaced just offshore and noted: "It's just really fun! When you can get so close to a wild animal it's really great. That's probably why there are more than a thousand Oregon State Parks' Whale Watch volunteers up and down the coast. It's a fun way to spend your time."

Also, when talking with others (and there are usually other intrepid hikers at the end of Cape Lookout) try to find a common language for distance or location so everyone can enjoy the show. There's nothing more frustrating than hearing "I see it!" and you haven't a clue where to look. I use my fingers! That is, when I spy a whale on the sea, I'll raise my hand horizontally to the distant horizon, count the number of finger widths from that line to the whale, and tell others to do the same. It really works!

The spring migration of gray whales continues through mid-June. Most will simply pass by, but it's amazing how often I'll find a half dozen just loafing off the end of the cape. They're quite mottled in appearance from the barnacles that cling to them, and from this unique vantage point you enjoy a perspective on their behavior that is simply unmatched.

For More Information

Where: Cape Lookout State Park is off US Highway 101, 12 miles southwest of Tillamook.

Web: www.oregonstateparks.org

Phone: Cape Lookout State Park: 503-842-4981 or 800-551-6949; Whale Watching Center, Depoe Bay: 541-765-3304

Watch the Episode: www.traveloregon.com/capelookout

Golden Flower of Prosperity
Kam Wah Chung State Heritage Site

There is a timeless feeling at some places in Oregon's high desert—not just across the vast landscape—but with imagination, you can also experience it on the back roads or neighborhood streets where life passes by as it did a century ago. So it is with the Kam Wah Chung State Heritage Site in John Day where imagination and Judy Bracken's description may sweep you back to an earlier time. Chinatown was all around us, noted Judy—an Oregon State Parks ranger. "The laundries were all along one side of the street and over in the corner was a brothel and a bar—and then we have Kam Wah Chung."

The Kam Wah Chung, or "Golden Flower of Prosperity," was a general store and herbal medicine shop that operated for more than half a century—including a time when thousands of Chinese laborers worked in the region. In 1887, two young immigrants, Ing Hay and Lung On, bought the Kam Wah Chung and Company building. They sold large amounts of mining supplies and staple goods to the miners who came out of the hills to stock up. Perhaps the most important function of the building was as the medical office for "Doc" Hay, as he became known. According to Judy, Doc Hay became the most famous herbal medicine doctor between Seattle and San Francisco. "He took your pulse, told you what was wrong with you, gave you Chinese medicines and herbs, and made you better. Doc Hay cured influenza, blood poisoning, even broken bones with a thousand different herbs [still stacked on wooden shelves in a nearby tiny cubicle]. You might have gotten fawn skeleton, antler, or other bones ground up in powder and put in your medicine—and he would cure you."

Judy added that Kam Wah Chung was the social center for more than two thousand Chinese: "They had baking powder, rice, sugar, flour, beans—everything you might need but there was so much more! This is where you would come to find a job—you could have letters written home because a lot of the miners were illiterate. You could come here and gamble, smoke, drink—have a nice relaxing time." In addition to food for the stomach and solace for the soul, you might also find a cure for what ailed you.

Even more remarkable—the shop was locked up for twenty years, and when it reopened in 1969, perfectly preserved artifacts were revealed. From a box of Wheaties—the Breakfast of Champions—to marshmallows sealed in a can—the stone and brick structure protected the building's contents from blistering heat or frigid cold. Christina Sweet, an Oregon Parks and Recreation Department curator, added that we also know much about the men and their place from the records because Doc Hay and Lung On kept everything: more than twenty thousand letters, accounts, and correspondence. "They provide a detailed picture of the Chinese in Oregon," noted Christina. "The letters and the records go everywhere, so we are learning about the Chinese in John Day and what they did here and also what happened in the community and the Chinese in different areas of the state."

Like everything in this wonderful state park time capsule, all of it is perfectly preserved! Just like the story of the unusual men who ran a business that became a legend. "These men changed the community," added Christina. "They made this area what it is today—initially, they were very much the outsiders but then each really became a part of the community. They were well loved by hundreds of locals and this is a part of our Oregon heritage. We want to celebrate it and preserve it through Kam Wah Chung."

For More Information

Where: Located off US Highway 26 at 125 Northwest Canton Street, John Day, OR 97845

Web: www.oregonstateparks.org

Phone: 541-575-2800 or 800-551-6949

Watch the Episode: www.traveloregon.com/kamwahchung

Oasis in the Desert
Malheur National Wildlife Refuge

I am a big fan of Oregon's wide-open spaces, especially east of the Cascade Mountains—where the distances are great and people are few. My love affair with the high desert runs deep and that's easy to understand since it's where my fondest childhood memories are rooted in family times centered on camping or fishing adventures.

At the Malheur National Wildlife Refuge near Burns, Oregon, you can begin to build your own family memories by letting the voice on the radio guide you across new territory that will take your breath away. Tom Hall is that voice, the man who recorded a unique audio tour guide to help you discover a wildlife wonderland in Southeast Oregon. It's a CD that you can check out anytime and enjoy a personalized tour of the Malheur National Wildlife Refuge. "Everything on the Malheur Wildlife Refuge tends to be in movement this time of year," noted Tom, a longtime refuge volunteer. "It is constant motion out here and the trick for the visitor is to catch up with the wildlife to see and learn more. The CD gives the visitor an extra edge to enjoy the place."

Tom and his wife, Sally Hall, have helped visitors explore the refuge each summer for the past five seasons at the US Fish and Wildlife's visitor station at Malheur Refuge. "It's the variety of birds, the landscape, and the people who come to visit," added Tom. "It's all interesting."

Tom's advice: bring binoculars and a bird identification book because the sheer number and variety of nesting birds is staggering. "You will easily see forty or fifty different species on a spring-summer weekend," noted Tom. "A bird book is a really good thing because you're going to see a lot of unusual birds like avocets, stilts, white-faced ibis, and then plentiful waterfowl like redheads, mallards, canvasbacks. We have an island of pelicans where there will be ten, twenty thousand white pelicans rafted up together. It's incredible to see so many birds and so many species too."

Astounding views to countless sloughs, wetlands, and ponds wait for you at Malheur Wildlife Refuge.

Spring's coolness still washes over this remote rimrock country where history hangs around longer than most places. Paiute Indians lived off the land eleven thousand years ago, moving between Malheur and Harney Lakes with the seasons. The native peoples were followed by relative newcomers in the nineteenth century: miners, trappers, and pioneers who settled, scratched out a living, and built towns that rose above the desert.

Signs of those times are still visible too at a place where Western hospitality is served daily at the Frenchglen Hotel. Built in the early years of the twentieth century, Frenchglen Hotel wasn't designed for luxury but as a rest stop for travelers on the long journey across the high desert. So the bedrooms are small but the hospitality is huge and warm in the family-style dining area where three meals a day are prepared and served to visitors who choose to enjoy a more laid-back vacation stay.

Manager John Ross said the hotel is now an Oregon state park and you will not find phones, radios, or television at the Frenchglen Hotel. "We are remote and the country is rugged, but we try to offer a bit of homey comfort that tends to attract a certain visitor who enjoys all of that."

Nearby, the Peter French Round Barn Heritage Site is another state park and a must-stop for visitors who want to explore a one of a kind barn design. Designed and built in 1880 by Peter French, a cattle baron who built a sprawling empire that dominated the region for more than twenty-five years, several giant juniper posts support a stable while an outer circular track lined in stonework provided a wintertime exercise area for horses.

John added, "There were three round barns at one time, but this one is all that's left and it has been well preserved and maintained by the state parks folks. We're lucky to have them." Just down the road, you can stroll even further back in time at Diamond Craters Outstanding Natural Area, a Bureau of Land Management site that is spread across seventeen thousand acres.

Oregon's roadside geology is worth a pause to consider at "Diamond Craters" where you can easily imagine a time, many thousands of years ago, when lava exploded, churned, and oozed out of the ground during a period that lasted for more than fifteen thousand years. It is a geologic wonder that will connect you with an interesting chapter of Oregon's volcanic past. In fact, there's so much to see in this timeless landscape where distances are great and people are few and Tom Hall insisted visitors must bring one thing with them when they come: "Patience! You cannot come here in a day and take all this in—you cannot take it all in in a weekend. Sally and I have been here five years and there's still so much to see with plenty to enjoy outdoors in the wide-open spaces."

For More Information

Malheur National Wildlife Refuge Headquarters
Where: 3691 Sodhouse Lane, Princeton, OR 97721-9502
Web: www.fws.gov
Phone: Malheur Refuge Visitor Center: 541-493-2612

Frenchglen Hotel State Heritage Site
Where: State Highway 205 South and Frenchglen Highway
Web: www.oregonstateparks.org
Phone: For reservations call 541-493-2825; for information call 800-551-6949.

Diamond Craters Outstanding Natural Area
Where: 55 miles southeast of Burns, OR; auto tour begins at State Highway 205 at Diamond Junction.
Phone: 541-573-4400

Watch the Episode: www.traveloregon.com/highdesert

Hiking to New Heights
Saddle Mountain State Natural Area

GETAWAY #35 – OREGON COAST

O n a clear day—even from a distance—Saddle Mountain steals the scene across the Oregon Coast Range: a distinct landmark that's hard to deny! Maybe you've heard about Saddle Mountain State Natural Area, just off the Sunset Highway (US 26 across the Coast Range), which links Portland with the Oregon communities of Seaside and Astoria. The park's entrance is marked near the junction with State Highway 53, just thirteen miles east of Seaside.

The park's unique geology and rugged geography make it a stand-alone feature from a distance. The dark hues of Saddle Mountain rising above all it surveys hint of an ancient story that's out of place in an otherwise emerald green sea of second-growth Douglas fir trees. As you make the seven-mile drive up a narrow lane from the highway to a small parking lot, the view straight up to the gigantic mountain is awesome.

It's a mountain with a history, that's for sure—one that began more than 250 miles away in eastern Washington. The peaks of Saddle Mountain are composed of a single thick layer of Columbia River basalt formed from lava that flowed more than fourteen million years ago. Today the basalt breaks away from the mountain in chunks that are easy to see as cracks, crevices, and bands of geologic time. As you begin your trek up to the Saddle, you'll also discover a bonus: You can hike and camp at one of the ten tent sites in this small Oregon state park. It is hard for hikers to resist on an Oregon state park trail that will steal your heart. Shelley Parker, an Oregon Parks and Recreation Department ranger, said that Saddle Mountain is cherished for its wildflowers, hiking, and spectacular views.

"It is something that must be experienced. It begins with a moderate climb but then it levels off as you experience a coastal rain forest with Sitka spruce and Doug fir trees. You see remarkable geological features with big rocky boulders and out-

While hiking the 2.5-mile trail to the top of Saddle Mountain, take comfort in this fact: the return trip is all downhill.

crops and you will see really amazing mosses and lichens that you won't see anywhere else."

The first mile or so of the 2.5-mile hike up the mountain is pretty gentle, under a shaded canopy of hemlock, fir, alder, and maple. You'll also notice a fairly steady twenty-degree incline. This raises an important issue about proper footwear: Invest in it! A well-fitting boot is critical for an enjoyable hike up Saddle Mountain. Please don't wear tennis shoes, sandals, or other street shoes. Even running shoes won't give you the ankle and arch support you'll need later when you face the toughest, most challenging part of the trail.

Soon, you're above tree line, where the trail suddenly steepens and opens onto grassy meadows covered in a riot of wildflowers. Before long, you're face to face with the namesake—the saddle and then the summit—bare double peaks that loom ahead. The last half mile across loose basalt shale covering a narrow ridge with only a cable as a handhold is really the toughest part, but you're almost to the top and you can see the hike has been worth it.

Although water is rare, cool springs seep and replenish a surprising number of plants with a distinct sound that also soothes the soul. "The trail is a steep climb the last half mile," noted Shelley. "It's definitely not for anyone who's afraid of heights! It's quite rewarding when you get to the top because you made the climb but also you have a spectacular panoramic view of the Pacific Ocean and the Cascade Mountains."

At 3,283 feet, Saddle Mountain is the sixth highest point in the Oregon Coast Range, and as such it offers up drifting clouds so close you'll feel as though you can reach out and touch them. Also, you can easily see the tale of Saddle Mountain's unique geology in the broken basalt rubble and take a moment to consider its origins way over in eastern Washington.

Each day's view is different; in spring the ocean is often obscured by clouds. That means it can be downright cool too! So dress warmly—in layers—and be sure you wear sturdy hiking boots with good ankle support for your climb and the descent back to the parking lot. Allow about five hours for the nearly five-mile round-trip hike and comfort yourself with this: The last 2.5 miles are all downhill. "It's one of the gems of the Oregon coast for sure!" added Shelley. You may choose to make the park a longer stay at one of the ten primitive campsites. Each is perfect for a tent—no trailer space, although trailers are allowed in the parking area. But be aware that there are no hookups for water or electricity.

Let Saddle Mountain State Natural Area be but the start of your back road journey. Next up—the nearby Lower Nehalem River Road is accessed at Elsie, Oregon. A few short miles down the road you'll meet Henry Rierson Spruce Run Park—a fine place to call it a day. Most cross-Coast Range tours are highway blurs, but not the Lower Nehalem River tour. It's the sort of pike my dad would have relished when I was a kid—windy and springy and narrow. You must slow down to drive it. It begins near Elsie, Oregon, at Sunset Highway and stretches nearly forty miles through Coast Range mountains to its junction with State Highway 53 at the marked town site of Mohler.

This roadway winds about in a dizzying fashion, sometimes straightening out to allow views of the river before bisecting campgrounds, such as Spruce Run County Park. I discovered Spruce Run by happenstance—on a trout-fishing adventure during college days—and found a camper's heaven that I've returned to many times. A logging community thrived here in the 1940s and, in fact, Spruce Run is dedicated to the many logging families that settled in the region. They built a village complete with a school, dance hall, post office, and general store at a time when timber salvage of the massive and successive Tillamook Burns of the 1930s and 1940s was pressing. You won't feel a bit pressed for time at this rambling riverside park, especially if you stay overnight under its towering firs.

Assistant District Forester Ron Zilli said that the Oregon Department of Forestry manages the campground: "Most times on the weekends you can still find a spot out here—you may not get a spot adjacent to the river, but there are thirty-one spots here and most times you can find one." Spruce Run campsites (many are streamside) go for $10 a night and each is available on a first come, first serve basis; no reservations are accepted. Four miles up the road you can get lost on purpose—with a rod and reel and a chance to catch fish at Lost Lake. Ron added that "Lost Lake offers fishing for both bank anglers and canoe fishermen. It's stocked by ODFW throughout the year and even though it's a shallow lake, it's an easy place to reach. When you're there, you feel miles away from anywhere."

The Lower Nehalem River Road winds and twists about with views of the Nehalem River. Once back to straight-as-an-arrow State Highway 26, look for landmark "Camp 18," a popular rest spot known for its restaurant and these days—something new. Mark Standley said that the Camp 18 Logger Memorial Museum is a place to remember those who gave their lives to Oregon logging.

A crowning museum centerpiece greets you at the entrance: a life-sized bronze of a hardworking logger with actual logging equipment, even a full-sized tree. It's a remarkably accurate work of art: the logger's pants and sleeves cut short so as not to hang up on limbs or brush—a firm grip on his working chain saw with a falling axe within easy reach. "It is just awesome," noted Mark. "Most people walk in and find it so incredible as a way to keep those logging memories alive. It's just a good thing." That's what you'll be saying about this backcountry byway—where the Nehalem River flows to the sea and the mountains soar to the sky—a stretch of Oregon that will keep you coming back for more.

For More Information

Where: Off US Highway 26, 8 miles northeast of Necanicum Junction at State Highway 53.

Web: www.oregonstateparks.org

Phone: 800-551-6949

Watch the Episode: www.traveloregon.com/dizzyingheights

Hidden in Plain View
Ki-A-Kuts Falls

The Tualatin River meanders through neighborhoods and industry on the western edge of the Portland Metro area. It is a slow moving stream flanked by towering trees that puts on quite a colorful show each fall. Yet, natural drama is only part of the Tualatin River's story on a getaway that takes effort, planning, and persistence according to a small platoon of adventurers from the Tualatin Riverkeepers (TRK), a local conservation group.

The group had gathered at Menefee Park in Yamhill County to compare notes and prepare their gear for a daylong hike into one of the most stunning and surprising sites of the Tualatin River watershed. "It's rugged, it's treacherous, and you need a good topo map, a compass, and a GPS would help you find it," noted longtime Tualatin Riverkeeper Paul Whitney.

Tarri Christopher, a TRK member agreed, "Not everyone can do this. This isn't 'take your entire family and go on a stroll' hike. You have to be prepared—you have to be fit." Fit enough to tackle steep, relentless, and unforgiving terrain along the upper Tualatin River in the Oregon Coast Range Mountains. Lew Scholl joined the expedition too. He had been on a trip like this before but way back in 1993 when he accompanied five friends from TRK who stumbled onto this remote stretch of the river.

It was meant to be a two-hour hike but it turned into an all-day bushwhack. "The six of us got together and we were led by then-TRK President Rob Baur. We were just going to stomp down the river and chase a rumor about a significant waterfall. We really didn't know what we were getting ourselves into as there was no trail and we constantly had to wade across the river, doing whatever it took to get downstream."

After hours of scrambling and rambling up and down the steep-walled river canyon, marked by big trees, huge boulders, and sheer rock cliffs the group heard something loud and constant. Lew said it sounded like thunder, but it was a waterfall that wasn't on any map. "We looked at each other and said, 'Hmm, that sounds like water rushing,' and we got up on some rocks and looked down and holy smokes, it's a forty-five-foot waterfall!"

The thick cord of white-water rushed and then spilled out of a hidden cleft in the ancient basalt rock. It was certainly a well-deserved reward for his efforts, but Lew couldn't really believe that no one had ever heard of it. "It was interesting because obviously the area was logged over. So, someone knew about the falls at one time. In a way, we rediscovered the falls."

Lew added that they submitted a name for the waterfall to the State Geographic Names Board and eventually the waterfall was added to government maps. In 1999, the Confederated Tribes of the Grand Ronde recognized through a tribal ceremony the cascading "Ki-a-Kuts (kia-cuts) Falls," named for the last chief of the Atfalati Indians, a local band of Kalapuya Indians.

"The elder KiaKuts stood up for his people back when Joel Palmer of the US Indian Bureau tried to get the natives to move off their land," said Lew. "The chief said, 'No, we don't want to go to a distant reservation—we want to stay right here. Why can't you make a reservation here for us? The only thing I want is for the settlers to stop harassing my children.'"

"It's a fitting name because the falls were not discovered by the Tualatin River-keepers," added Tarri. "The falls were here long before any of us knew about it. Native people knew the place long ago, so it should be rightfully recognized that way."

Flanked by basalt columns and cliffs, Ki-a-Kuts Falls is a timeless and serene moment that is fitting reward for the effort that it takes to reach the restful site. Brian Wegener, a TRK member, added, "It is hard to believe it's the same Tualatin River that most of us know in the Portland area. It is so different up here from what it looks like down in the valley. If you're adventurous and in good health and you can use a map and compass and find your way, it's a beautiful place to be."

Tarri agreed and added, "If you see where it comes from—to see the beauty of it—I think we're more likely to take care of it. It's a special place and it's worth the effort to get here."

Special Note: The Tualatin Riverkeepers is a good place to start for specific directions to Ki-a-Kuts Falls. In fact, consider attending their annual fund-raising event in April. You can join in the fun and learn more about the rugged hike. It deserves special note that planning and preparation are critical if you want to visit Ki-a-Kuts Falls. That means good hiking boots with proper arch and ankle support, plenty of water, food, rain gear, and a first aid kit.

Remember that it is a remote area with unreliable cell phone service and private logging roads. It is advised that you check with the Forest Grove office of the Oregon

Department of Forestry for information about road closures. You may also want to visit early in spring because when fire season begins, access roads through private timberland close down.

For More Information

Where: Tualatin Riverkeepers, 11675 SW Hazelbrook Road, Tualatin, OR 97062

Web: www.tualatinriverkeepers.org

Phone: 503-218-2580; Fax: 503-218-2583

Watch the Episode: www.traveloregon.com/kiakutfalls

A River Song
Nestucca River Scenic Byway

The Nestucca River sings on its way to the sea and along the narrow winding roadway that follows it you may hear its song. Be prepared to spend some time and savor the road that threads through the heart of these mountains. It's a place where milky white wisps of clouds dance above giant Doug fir trees or tiny wild iris bunches burst to life close to ground. I am on a back road so significant that the Bureau of Land Management designated eleven miles of it a National Scenic Byway.

You certainly won't worry about getting lost on this scenic byway because right at the very start—at Dovre Campground—there's a huge wooden map to show you the way—plus, it identifies several different campgrounds that invite you to make a longer stay. The byway's campgrounds are sheltered under a cool canopy of big-leaf maple and alder.

There are a dozen campsites tucked away at Dovre, plus a larger covered picnic site for a possible family gathering. But don't get too comfy in the campground! Soon, it's time to trade in the truck and the roadway for a different trail. Sometimes the campgrounds are but a starting point that can launch you onto side trips like the short hike up Dovre Creek where you can enjoy the Dovre Creek Waterfall. It's a stunner of a cascade-style waterfall in spring and summer—and offers cool respite when the day heats up. There is so much unmatched rugged beauty on this byway.

As you continue your drive west on the byway, keep in mind that the road parallels an ancient river—marked by forty-million-year-old basalt rock formations that, even on cloudless days, are drenched from seeping groundwater. The water drips and drops across the lush moss and water-loving wildflowers that hang from the rock walls. Soon, you will reach Fan Creek Campground and it is the place to be for more riverside fun—towering trees set this site apart that also offers larger RV

Don't miss Dovre Creek Waterfall! It's but a stone's throw from Dovre Creek Campground along the Nestucca River Backcountry Byway.

sites for the motor home crowd. Stop in at Alder Glen Campground for a whopper of a waterfall.

You may be drawn to the wildflowers that grow right next to even more shoreline campsites—in fact, one in particular rests just across from the namesake falls. It is a dandy campsite for the falls will lull you to sleep at night. You are apt to find me along this river in summer—especially on a day when sunshine abounds and a fairy slipper orchid waves you along the river as it rolls toward the sea with its magical, ageless song. If you like to travel in Oregon, the Nestucca River Scenic Byway is not to be missed!

For More Information

Where: Bureau of Land Management Salem District Office,
1717 Fabry Road SE, Salem, OR 97306
Phone: 503-375-5646
Watch the Episode: www.traveloregon.com/nestuccariver

Colorful Delights

Marys Peak

I recently climbed to new heights—high above the Willamette Valley—to reach a mountain peak that you may have missed. It's noted for dizzying views of the sprawling valley and high Cascade Mountains too, so put on your hiking boots and don't forget the camera as we travel high atop Marys Peak.

It's the size of it all that steals the scene on a back road adventure that rises and winds for a daylong getaway. You're on the trail to the mountain called Marys Peak, the highest point on the Oregon Coast Range and it may just steal your heart along the way. It is something special on a day when soggy skies clear and sunbeams light up a scene that's filled with so much vibrant color: from crimson paintbrush to brilliant blue larkspur or stunning yellow wallflowers. These and other wildflower species are at your side as you explore the lush meadows, dense noble fir forests, and the many hiking trails that link all of it together.

In fact, more than twelve miles of trails crisscross Marys Peak, nearly all of them connected to the spacious parking area where many folks begin their adventures. The most popular trail is the mile-long Summit Trail that leads you up a moderate grade. Soon, you're face to face with an amazing scene: a bird's-eye view of the grand Willamette Valley.

You easily spy the small town of Philomath—then the larger Corvallis just beyond. Even a hazy day cannot diminish the stunning size of the many Cascade Mountain peaks you can see: Rainer, St. Helens, Adams, Hood, Jefferson, and the Three Sisters are easily picked out against the eastern skyline. While to the west, Newport's beaches are often seen with the breaking surf line just twenty-six miles away. It is a glorious view, no doubt about that—but all these high Cascade Mountain peaks may leave you wondering, what about the namesake: Marys Peak. Well, who was Mary?

Some anecdotal stories suggest an Indian legend and linkage—for this place had been called a "house or home of spirits" by ancient peoples. Other tales suggest a pioneer lineage a century old or longer when pioneers first settled the Oregon country. There is a nearby town site of Marysville and a nearby Mary's River, but the fact is no one really knows and so the history behind the naming of Marys Peak remains a mystery. It's no secret that the wildflower show draws a real crowd—not just of people, but swarms of butterflies seem to hover just above bloom top across the open meadows. The fragile insects come in many sizes and colors, but keep an eye out for the larger swallowtail butterfly for it's a favorite and hard to miss.

The summit of Marys Peak isn't hard to miss either; its distinct array of metallic antennas for radio, cell phone, and broadcast television transmissions makes it a landmark mountaintop for miles around. At more than 4,100 feet in elevation, Marys Peak stands tall among Coast Range peaks and so the variety of trees, insects, flowers, and grasses are distinct and rare in Western Oregon too. That alone makes the site worth a visit. Perhaps you'll consider a longer stay. If you packed a tent, sleeping bag and food, nearby Marys Peak Campground's secluded sites offer an affordable overnight stay. At the least, do bring hiking boots and a camera on this getaway— they will provide you a comfortable and enjoyable way to savor Marys Peak: a unique mountain of dizzying heights and colorful delights.

For More Information

Where: Siuslaw National Forest, 3200 SW Jefferson Way, Corvallis, OR 97331
Phone: 541-750-7000; Fax: 541-750-7234
Watch the Episode: www.traveloregon.com/maryspeak

It Will Make You Feel Small
Valley of the Giants

The Valley of the Giants makes you feel small in a secret place that lets your heart soar as tall as the giants that live there. I recently joined a small troop of travelers led by retired Bureau of Land Management (BLM) Forester Walt Kastner. We traveled for hours deep into the Oregon Coast Range to explore a unique fifty-one-acre grove of old-growth Doug fir trees.

Walt pulled the metal tape from its spring-loaded container to measure the circumference of a nearby giant—he stretched his arms and pulled the tape all the way around the huge tree and after a few minutes: "Finally. Twenty-seven feet! Wow!" noted Walt. "By my formula that's a nine-foot diameter—and perhaps 450 years old—at the least—probably older."

The giant tree was but one of scores that you will see along the 1.5-mile-long forest trail that meanders through the Valley of the Giants. Walt advised us to pause often and admire the valley's diversity of trees—not just their size but also their placement in the valley.

"If you stop and look around, you can see you've got some very large trees that are deep and complex. Look at how variable the spacing is between the trees—some are clumped up, others far apart, plus there are standing dead trees and downed trees. There's just so much diversity and complexity in here."

The Valley of the Giants is a small snapshot of what much of Western Oregon's fir forests may have looked like perhaps 150 years ago. It is so special a place the BLM has protected the public parcel since 1976 as an Outstanding Natural Area for study and research.

"Forest scientists can come here to study and learn how these types of stands developed and by knowing that, you can incorporate what they find into the management plan for some of our younger stands where you might want to manage for older forest characteristics . . . it's kind of a living laboratory," said Walt.

The North Fork of the Siletz River bisects the valley in classic "pool and drop fashion," noted BLM staff member Trish Hogervorst. A hiking bridge allows you to access the trail and gain entry into a lush forestland that receives nearly two hundred inches of rain each year. "The music of the water is such a wonderful secret in some ways," added Trish. "Not many people make it out here and you'll often be the only one. It's just beautiful!"

The Valley of the Giants is remote and access is limited because private timberland surrounds this public island of old-growth trees. The BLM offers a free brochure with a map and mileage directions. Still, BLM Recreation Planner Traci Meredith noted that it's a challenging route—even under the best of conditions. "You can make a wrong turn pretty easily if you're looking the other way, so stay alert and follow directions on the map."

There is no camping in the Valley of the Giants—no campfires are allowed and you must stay on the moderately graded trail. There is a picnic table along the route, so you are able to stop for a time and enjoy the experience with friends or family. Still, given its remote location, you should plan on a full day to reach and hike through the valley. Traci added, "I love it out here. It's big, open, quiet. It's not considered a wilderness but people sure feel like they're in a wilderness out here."

Dan Wood and Mari Kasamoto were enjoying the giants for the first time and agreed they'd never seen anything like the grove of ancient trees before. They didn't know that Doug fir trees lived so long. "These big trees are amazing because they reach so far up in the air," noted Dan. "But you can't tell how tall they are until they fall to the ground—and there's a few of those around so you can actually see how big and wide and tall they are at the same time."

"It's very peaceful and relaxing," added Mari. "I would definitely come here again. It's so special a place." Call the BLM (503-375-5646) to receive a copy of the recommended driving directions. The map directions begin at Falls City, five miles southwest of Dallas. The driving route is thirty miles but it will take you ninety minutes to reach the valley. Follow the directions closely and carefully.

Caution: much of the route is in large rock or gravel and the logging roads are notorious for puncturing car tires. I discourage taking the family car or van—if you choose to do so, take along a second spare tire.

For More Information

Where: Bureau of Land Management Salem District Office,
   1717 Fabry Road SE, Salem, OR 97306
Phone: 503-375-5646
Watch the Episode: www.traveloregon.com/ORredwoods

A Cross Cascades Escape
The Upper Willamette River

C ross-Cascade links such as State Highway 58, connecting Oregon's pastoral Willamette Valley with the vast high desert, can be busy blurs unless you slow your pace and get out of the race from here to there. I'm convinced that's especially true along the Upper Willamette River watershed where you'll find so many reasons to ease off the gas pedal and explore the region's recreation. It is a fine destination for riverside camping, mountain bike trails, and family adventures. Traveling the highway we have enjoyed amazing secrets and a surprising amount of elbow room for stretching out and playing at the Black Canyon Campground.

The Black Canyon is a splendid Forest Service campground with eighty campsites for either trailer or tent that parallels the Upper Willamette River. Here, the river has a swift, free-flowing character that is quite different from the broad-beamed, slow-moving waterway most downriver residents know so well. Black Canyon is rarely full—making it a dependable place for a short midweek—or even longer—stop. It's a fine campground with riverside sites and views to the water. For the young-

Trade in the auto gas pedal for bike pedals across five hundred miles of mountain bike trails near Black Canyon Campground.

sters, Black Canyon is a marvelous place to skip some stones, roast marshmallows, make s'mores, and share spooky stories by a crackling campfire. From this convenient base camp you can also explore a region that's somehow been missed or forgotten by many travelers.

That's certainly been the case for mountain bike adventurers Ben Beamer and Randy Dreiling. "We are the mountain bike capital of the Northwest—that's the brand we use," noted Randy, a leading force in the trek toward establishing this area as a mountain bike mecca over the past decade, part of the popular Oregon cycling phenomenon. It's an area that boasts five hundred miles of Cascade Mountain trails near Oakridge, Oregon, and Ben said, "People come and experience it and they go tell all their friends and they'll be back next week."

Randy owns and operates Oregon Adventures, a touring and shuttle company centered in Oakridge. He said the blend of plentiful trails with the Cascade Mountain elevation changes offer something for everyone: "You can really test your skills here; testing yourself to see how long you can ride, trying to improve and testing your skill sets to see if you can get better at rocks and roots." Ben added that the Oakridge area has become famous for cross-country rides that last all day and you never see the same terrain twice: "We're also known for having really 'flowy' trails that tend to be in really good shape all summer long—they don't turn to dust because we have good moisture in our soils. For example, here on Salmon Creek—you can go ride on forty miles of continuous ribbon of trail here and you just cannot do that everywhere."

Near Oakridge, explore another site you can't find "just anywhere." The Oregon Department of Fish and Wildlife's (ODFW) Willamette Salmon Hatchery is in the big business of raising fish—specifically salmon, and by the millions each year. You're free to roam the five-acre hatchery grounds and gaze into the raceways and other "show" ponds to marvel at ten-pound rainbow trout or six-foot-long sturgeon. The real treasure in this neck of the woods is when you head indoors to learn about salmon and other wildlife at a unique museum on the state hatchery grounds. Though small in size, the hatchery's museum is large in scope with its varied information displays and exhibits that show off the hatchery's history and the fish and wildlife of the region. Huge plateglass windows separate you from a diorama featuring nearly every small and large forest animal (mounted for the display) that can be found in the Cascade region.

The centerpiece is a two-thousand-gallon aquarium that contains nearly every fish species you can find in Oregon. Here you can go eyeball to eyeball with rainbow trout, bass, kokanee salmon, and many others. Dan Peck, the hatchery manager, modestly noted that visitors can now see fish from a fish's point of view. "When you're looking down on a fish you can never see how truly beautiful the distinctive markings of a fish can be, since you only see their backs. The crimson bar of a rainbow, the red eye of a smallmouth bass—all of those interesting characteristics are lost on us. We've tried to change that."

Dan told me he wanted visitors to see fish and other "critters" they usually never see in the wild, but funding such a facility from his small budget was nearly impossible. So, his staff donated materials and volunteered to create the entire remarkable museum: "We wanted folks to have a better understanding of Oregon and the role that ODFW plays in Oregon's outdoors. From fish hatcheries to non-hunted species, and wildlife viewing opportunities, we're hoping to educate about all of that."

Back out on the Salmon Creek Trail, Randy and Ben agreed that the region has much to offer—whether afoot or rolling along so many miles of trails. In fact, Oakridge is so special a place, the town has taken center stage for two major summertime bike events called simply Mountain Bike Oregon; each event attracts hundreds of riders from across the entire country for the multiday riding experiences. "You could spend a month here and not hit every trail—there's that much here. When you have sixty-two trails in this area, it's pretty special."

For More Information

Willamette National Forest, Black Canyon Campground
Where: Willamette National Forest, 3106 Pierce Parkway, Suite D, Springfield, OR 97477; US Forest Service Middle Fork Ranger District, 46375 State Highway 58, Westfir, OR 97492
Phone: Black Canyon Campground, 541-225-6300; for reservations, 877-444-6777

Willamette Hatchery
Where: 76389 Fish Hatchery Road Oakridge, OR 97463
Web: www.dfw.state.or.us
Phone: 541-782-2933

Oregon Adventures
Where: 47921 State Highway 58, Oakridge, OR 97463
Web: www.oregon-adventures.com
Phone: 541-968-5397

Watch the Episode: www.traveloregon.com/crosscascade

Strike It Rich for Recreation
Green Peter Reservoir

In the Northwest, the pioneer trails are easy to come by—whether you're aware of them or not—and scenic US 20, a popular and fast-paced corridor from the Willamette Valley to the high desert, is no exception. Once called State Highway 54, and before that the Santiam Wagon Road, this roadway connects Albany with Bend, Oregon. About a hundred and fifty years ago it was a line thousands of families chose to reach the promised land of the lush Willamette Valley, where a new life and new dreams might come true.

Today, it offers a dreamy world of recreation that I try to visit each summer near Sweet Home. Fir and hemlock forests flank the route into

Douglas fir forests rim the lakeshore at Green Peter Reservoir.

the Cascades as it follows the Santiam River toward its headwaters with a wonderful stopover that offers camping, fishing, and a backcountry byway at Green Peter Lake, a 3,700-acre reservoir that's earned my respect and dedication for its multiple recreation options. Camping and skiing and swimming and, especially, fishing can be enjoyed here. Anglers try their trolling luck for kokanee, landlocked sockeye salmon, that are as plentiful in Green Peter as the limit of twenty-five fish a day.

A Golden Memory

Quartzville is an historic gold-mining area. The first legal claim was filed by Jeremiah Driggs on September 5, 1863. Within four years more than five hundred claims had been filed and more than a thousand people lived in Quartzville. The name of the town was taken from the gold-bearing rock that came from the mines. It didn't take long for the bust to occur, though. By 1870 the mining had proved unprofitable and the town was abandoned!

The old town site is on private property and nothing but a second-growth forest remains, although a few abandoned mine shafts can be found. With only two private claims remaining in the area, a large section of the Quartzville corridor is reserved for recreational mining. Digging is allowed in dry gravel beds where there is no vegetation, but please fill in any hole you dig. Mining equipment may include gold pans, rockers, sluices, water pumps, and suction dredges equipped with a four-inch or smaller hose.

Brian Carroll, the director of Linn County's Parks, said: "Folks look at the beautiful Willamette Valley, farm country and all, and think that's all there is to us—but the truth is more than half the county is forested. People are usually surprised to learn that the Willamette National Forest is a large part of the county." It is a county that cries out for closer inspection and soon you will discover a bit of unhurried heaven on earth at Green Peter Lake where boating and camping adventures are easy to find. "It's remote and yet it's close," noted Brian. "We have one of the biggest bodies of water in the state of Oregon and it's kind of hidden."

Anglers like Salem resident Kent Cannon go to Green Peter for trout or especially kokanee. Kent used an electronic fish finder graph—plus electric downriggers to reach the feisty fish that can swim to one hundred feet deep. His bait of choice is something right out of the kitchen cupboard called shoepeg corn. "It's the sweetness of the corn they like," noted Brian. "Plus, the shoepeg style has long kernels so they are easier and firmer to put on a hook."

According to state fish biologist Steve Mamoyac, the Oregon Department of Fish and Wildlife manages Green Peter Lake for kokanee and trout. "We stock about 50,000 catchable rainbow trout each year," noted Steve. "We've been stocking about 50,000 fingerling kokanee to augment natural production in the basin too."

The nearby Whitcomb Creek County Park is perfectly suited to anglers seeking a multiday stay. It sports two boat ramps near a campground that offers thirty-nine roomy sites for tent or trailer. While the sites do not offer water or electrical hookups, they do provide plenty of elbow room to stretch out in a pleasant wooded setting. "You can come up here to find that special outdoor experience that's not as crowded as other places," said Brian. The roadway calls you back on western approach into the Cascades where Doug fir and western hemlock trees flank a route called the Quartzville Backcountry Byway. This byway meanders past Green Peter Lake along the clear, cool waters of the Quartzville Creek, designated a National Wild and Scenic River.

It's an amazing corridor of old-growth forest, accented by rocky outcroppings and wildflowers. Some of the giant trees are 450 years old and tower more than two hundred feet tall. All together, the scenery, the fishing, and the locale—so close to the Willamette Valley—provide a fabulous getaway that's close to home. Once visited, you'll return real soon.

For More Information

Where: Linn County Parks Department, 3010 Ferry Street SW, Albany, OR 97322

Web: www.linnparks.com

Phone: Linn County Parks: 541-967-3917

Watch the Episode: www.traveloregon.com/greenpeterlake

Marsh Music
Klamath Lake Canoe Trail

While Klamath Lake feels huge at first glance, you'll feel comfortable and right at home inside the cozy confines of a canoe or kayak as we paddle across the Upper Klamath Wildlife Refuge's designated Canoe Trail where hundreds of bird species make their seasonal home. In the vast Klamath Basin, summer mornings arrive on brilliant sunshine and a soft, cool high desert breeze. It's a place where wide timeless vistas allow your mind and imagination to wander among mountains, grassy meadows, broad lakes, and ponds into rich mysterious marshlands.

You don't need to be an experienced birder to enjoy Klamath Marsh music when you join Darren Roe of ROE Outfitters. We recently joined Darren, his wife, Jen, and their friend Melody Warner on the Upper Klamath Wildlife Refuge. As we loaded our gear into dry bags and prepped for a morning of paddling, Darren noted: "It is amazing to folks that come here for the first time and they always want to know—why aren't there more people here?"

It was an intriguing question as we left the pavement far behind to discover an enchanting world that was all ours to explore. The Upper Klamath Wildlife Refuge Canoe Trail begins near the Rocky Point Resort and extends more than nine miles until you reach a freshwater marsh on the north end of Klamath Lake. "It is splendid and scenic with just a ton of wildlife species," said Darren. "This waterway is mostly fed by freshwater springs in the marshes that help to create these waterways—they actually well up out of the ground."

"And it's a friendly place to paddle too," added Jen. "There aren't a ton of tough turns; you don't need to be an expert paddler. It's really friendly to someone that's just beginning to paddle a canoe."

The braid work of channels that make up the Canoe Trail are defined by bulrushes and cattails and plants called wocus that are always at your side. The marsh is home to hundreds of wildlife species—especially bird life—from small red wing blackbirds that flit from branch to branch in an endless parade of feeding activity to the large and dramatic white pelicans. The big birds arrive at Klamath Lake on nine-foot wingspans from as far away as Baja and will summer in the Klamath Basin's nesting and brooding wetlands.

"Typically we see them flying across the lake and occasionally you'll see a group actually fishing for the perch," noted Darren. Unlike the more common California brown pelicans that spend summer months in the Pacific Northwest, white pelicans actually tip to feed and do not dive to capture their prey. They also work as a unit; a group will circle the fish and then tip over to feed.

Over four-thousand square miles of south-central Oregon and northern California's water natural drainage is stored across the Klamath Wildlife Refuge. While only a fraction of historic wetlands remain today, Darren noted that the Canoe Trail allows the visitor a close-up view into a wonderfully rich and diverse world. "There are so many different mini-ecosystems in the basin," he said. "You will go from crystal clear spring creeks out in the lake where the water bubbles up out of the ground. It is very unique—hard to find all of those things wrapped up in one place."

The abundance of varied bird life includes Oregon's largest concentration of nesting bald eagles, plus diverse habitats that are home to varied wildlife within a national refuge where 80 percent of all Pacific waterfowl are found each fall and winter. Jen added that the Upper Klamath Lake's protected Canoe Trail allows a closer visit that's filled with surprises! "Make sure you take enough time off so that you can really enjoy it. Once you get here and experience the canoeing, kayaking, and fishing, the disappointment is going to be that they couldn't get it all done in one trip."

For More Information

Where: Rocky Point Resort, 28121 Rocky Point Road, Klamath Falls, OR 97601
Web: www.rockypointoregon.com
Phone: 541-356-2287; Fax: 541-356-2222
Watch the Episode: www.traveloregon.com/klamathcanoe

Somewhere Over the Rainbows

Klamath River Rainbow Trout Fishing

Fly fishing is king on the Klamath River, home to the region's famous redband rainbow trout. Who does not love to cast into rivers or streams for big, hungry trout? Mark me down as one who cannot resist the allure of magical places that hold big-finned secrets in the riffles and runs. So it was that I traveled to a designated wild and scenic section of the broad-shouldered Klamath River in Southern Oregon and joined a couple of pros who know just the right flies to cast into the river and provide us a chance to catch the Klamath's redband rainbow trout. The adventure begins south of Klamath Falls on a roadway that demands your attention!

A rough roadway with bumps and jumps and a jarring ride down a single-track dirt road that leaves you wondering: where is this adventure headed? And then you arrive—riverside! Where scenery softens and the world is reborn along Oregon's remote wild and scenic Klamath River. Our hosts, Darren and Jen Roe of ROE Outfitters, told me that the Klamath Canyon is known mostly for its rafting, but wanted to impress me with why it needs to be known for its fishing too.

That began with preparation—so a rod, reel, and waders are required. Plus, a collection of imitations of nature's creations that

This gorgeous Klamath River rainbow trout called redband is a handful.

promise to catch fish. Darren noted his preferences: "Stone flies and redheaded prince nymphs and a salmon fly and a golden stone. You want to unhook your fly, not walk up too close, and just plop it in closely—then pick it up and go a few feet further."

High buttes crown the canyon rims as the Klamath River carves its way through Oregon's volcanic cascade mountain range for eleven miles to the border with California. You can easily watch the canyon come to life: vegetation cools the riverbanks and shade covers the boulders and provides a home for insects: "The biggest passion here is the fly fishing," noted Jen. "It's a great, large population of redband rainbow trout and the food source is really incredible as well as the aquatic life."

The Klamath River is managed as summertime catch and release fishery and that means flies or lures only—no bait allowed. Once I got the hang of the technique—casting and then stripping line—I was into fat rainbow trout too. The fish are wild redband rainbow trout and the river provides a prolific fishery with fat trout ranging from ten to sixteen inches, with some trout reaching eighteen inches.

The river has been protected as wild and scenic since 1994 and it is a special place that's a distant world away from city hubbub and noise and aren't we lucky it's that way! Jen offered that, "It's really just about getting off the main highway and getting out and exploring all of these great things like the Klamath Lake Wetlands and the river and lake fishing—too many people pass it by. They don't think it has anything to offer and that's really wrong."

"It's so peaceful, it's so quiet," added Darren. "It so beautiful too—I think it's just a well-kept secret—I think people just honestly don't know it exists."

For More Information

Where: ROE Outfitters FlyWay Shop, 9349 US Highway 97 South, Klamath Falls, OR 97603

Web: www.roeoutfitters.com

Phone: 541-884-3825

Watch the Episode: www.traveloregon.com/klamathred

June

Up, Up, and Away
Hot Air Balloons

In early morning, when the light is soft and the air is still, there's a sense of peace in the world. But as dawn approaches at the Sportsman Airpark near Newberg, Oregon, that serene silence is all too quickly broken. For this is where Roger Anderson gathers folks who travel from all over the world to let their hearts soar on one of his unique adventures.

Roger's Vista Balloon Adventures has been based in Newberg the past ten years. Anderson and his wife, Catherine, specialize in giving people a bird's-eye view to a corner of the greater Willamette Valley that stretches across Yamhill County. As Catherine noted, "People come with high—pardon the pun—expectations and preconceived notions of a flight in a hot air balloon, but the fact is that first timers cannot really compare it to anything they've ever done because it's so unique."

The balloons are huge—big as houses. Each balloon requires five or six "crew" (volunteers who lend a hand) to assist with each morning's launch. First, powerful fans blow cold air (the process is actually called a cold-air inflate) into the nearly 200,000-cubic feet of nylon fabric. How big is that? "Visualize 180,000 basketballs," offered Roger with a wink and a nod.

Once the balloon has been filled to its limit, ignition occurs as powerful propane gas burners light up and heat up the air inside the balloon. It's what gives the craft its lift. It's really a rather simple premise based upon the fact that hot air rises, but it gives passengers who ride aboard a different point of view to the landscape.

Catherine offered, "When you get up there, the overwhelming sensation is total quiet. It's really pretty cool!" Our balloon was guided by Roger, a veteran pilot with more than two decades experience in lighter-than-air flight.

Roger noted, "The conditions for flying are perfect this morning. A light breeze

Be on time or you'll miss the dawn flights with Vista Hot Air Balloons.

and clear skies—so we'll be traveling across the Willamette River first and then head south towards Dayton and the wine country." Within moments of our easy liftoff, we are two, four, then six hundred feet up in the air and the other "giants" soon appear as tiny, thimble-sized floats on the ground below.

Roger said that he learned about the wind and the weather (critical for balloon pilots) as a sailor. He logged more than fifty thousand miles across the Pacific Ocean as a boat-sailing skipper. "One of the reasons I like to fly balloons is that they can get you into places you can't get any other way. Plus, you don't get in a balloon to go to a particular place, but instead you get in a balloon to be in a balloon. There's no 'have to get there quick' feeling, you just get to look at the world."

One of my fellow passengers, Brian Clapshaw, nodded in agreement and said, "It's quite amazing! I've never, ever had any experience like this ever before. I feel like I'm floating above the sky—I feel like I'm in a glass bubble."

As we soared across the valley, sometimes mere feet above the ground, Roger pointed out something that I might never have noticed if my feet were firmly planted on the soil below. "This part of the Willamette Valley was once a lake—Allison Lake—an ancient body of water that dates to ten thousand years ago and the time of the Missoula Floods era."

Allison Lake was up to four hundred feet deep—and then the lake became a river—and from the balloon basket I could see how the ground rose and fell, just like a river bottom. That wasn't all—it was easy to see how the valley near Newberg was ringed with hills—hills that grow grapes—in fact, wine grapes! "There's the Dundee Hills, Chehalem Ridge, Eola Hill; you can see it all and all of it produces some of the best wine in the world," said Roger. He added that there are hundreds of unique wines produced by scores of wineries and each is easily reached within fifteen minutes of Newberg. With a wry smile he added, "It can be even quicker by air."

But not on this fine summer morning for the wind was building and the ground was heating up. If we waited too long, a soft landing could be—well, challenging! And so, after an hour of delightful touring, the time had come for us to come back to the ground. Catherine and her "chase crew" with their trailers in tow were a short radio conversation away to determine and coordinate on the best landing area. Roger told me, "In twenty years of flying I haven't had two flights that have been the same. Once in a while people will ask do I like to fly by myself? I tell them not at all, because I have a skill set that's great to share."

We touched down on a recently cut "seed-grass" field ever so softly, without even a bounce to the remarkable landing. "Welcome back to Mother Earth," cheered the proud Roger. Hot air ballooning is a lovely and magical way to see a beautiful corner of Oregon and build lasting memories through a unique outdoor adventure.

For More Information

Where: Vista Balloon Adventure's launch site is at Sportsman Airpark, 1055 Commerce Parkway, Newberg, OR 97132; their office is at 23324 SW Sherk Place, Sherwood, OR 97140.

Web: www.vistaballoon.com

Phone: 800-622-2309 or 503-625-7385; Fax: 503-625-3845

Watch the Episode: www.traveloregon.com/upandaway

Lend a Hand and Learn More

Firsthand Oregon

You may get your hands a little dirty and your feet a little wet, but you will gain appreciation for what it takes to protect and preserve Oregon's fish and wildlife resources when you learn how the experts do it "Firsthand." Each spring, as the days grow longer and the promise of summer grows closer, you feel better spending more time outdoors. So, isn't it nice to learn a little more about Oregon while you're out there?

Don't forget binoculars! They make a big difference enjoying the views of wildlife on a Firsthand adventure.

Susan Barnes does what many of us only dream about: she gets to know Oregon's wild places better than we know our own backyards. In fact, she gets paid to learn about the wildlife that live in and around the St. Louis Ponds near Woodurn. Best of all, she'll help you to learn more about the place too—Firsthand!

"It's a wet native prairie and there aren't many places like this in the Willamette Valley," noted the state conservation biologist as she led a small group of curious folks through the 260-acre site.

"Be sure to wear boots because you will get wet," advised Susan.

Each person had signed up to spend half a day with Susan to see and learn more about an increasingly rare habitat type in Western Oregon. Susan specializes in Oregon's nongame species, the animals that are not hunted: "I think it's important to learn what we have in our own backyard because that's what we have the greatest influence over," noted the longtime biologist.

Susan shared her knowledge with folks who had signed up for a tour of St. Louis Ponds in a program called Firsthand Oregon. The program is the result of a new and unique partnership with the nonprofit Oregon Wildlife Heritage Foundation (OWHF). "If we care about places like this, it's best to experience it firsthand," noted OWHF conservation expert Claire Puchy. "Only by getting out here can people truly learn not only about fish and wildlife species but also the conservation issues associated with them. Firsthand gives folks the chance to do that."

The Oregon Wildlife Heritage Foundation has "walked the talk" of protecting, preserving, and enhancing Oregon's natural resources for more than thirty years through programs, outright land purchases, and public projects across the Oregon outdoors. Back in the early '80s they spearheaded the purchase of the lower twelve miles of the Deschutes River and secured public access for hiking, biking, and fishing. They designed and built the popular sturgeon exhibit at the Bonneville Fish Hatchery in the Columbia River Gorge where visitors can see Herman the Sturgeon and his buddies anytime.

Most recently, they developed a new Willamette River fishing dock at West Linn so anglers have a riverside location to cast for salmon and sturgeon. "We do a lot of habitat work," noted former OWHF Director Rod Brobeck. "But we also try to provide access; something we can look at and even stand on—like this fishing dock. It's great for everyone."

The Firsthand Oregon educational tours partner with the Oregon Department of Fish and Wildlife's land managers, field biologists, and others who will spend a day with you, talk about their work, and show you the lands that they are responsible for in Oregon. For example, on a recent tour of the Sauvie Island Wildlife Area, Assistant Manager Dan Marvin explained how successive years of flooding from the adjacent Columbia River have deposited increasing amounts of sediment in Sturgeon Lake. The lake is a critical water body in the wildlife area and it's beginning to fill in. That could lead to long lasting effects for hundreds of thousands of waterfowl that migrate to the island each fall season. "Basically the lake is shrinking," noted Dan. "The overall value of this wetland area will be lost as more sediment is deposited through the years."

The range of Firsthand classes is remarkable too—including hatchery visits for the chance to learn how salmon spawning is done—to turtle trapping techniques to see and learn more about Oregon's native amphibian populations—plus many more classes emphasizing outdoor education—it's perfect for the curious. "It's a great opportunity for informing the nonhunting public, which is the majority of folks we see on these tours," said Dan. "They can see what our programs entail and what goes into it to make it such a successful program."

Back at St. Louis Ponds, Susan said she enjoyed the chance to teach others with Firsthand wildlife observation techniques. Bryce Peterson said he enjoyed learning how Susan does her job: "It's an opportunity for me to learn more for sure, about native birds, their habitats, and how I can help—even if it's just in my backyard by protecting and enhancing native plants." It's real science that's fun, takes you to a new place, and can help determine conservation strategies that will make a difference for the future of Oregon wildlife. "Getting people outdoors to see firsthand what's in their backyards can make all the difference in the world—for information, awareness, and appreciation," noted Susan.

For More Information

Where: Oregon Wildlife Heritage Foundation, 1122 NE 122nd, Suite 114B
Portland, OR 97230
Web: www.owhf.org/firsthandoregon
Phone: 503-255-6059; Fax: 503-255-6467
Watch the Episode: www.traveloregon.com/firsthandOR

Flying Fish
High Cascade Trout Stocking

O n an early morning in summer—when the air is cool and the scenery quiet, snow-capped Mount Hood is a marvel! But for one week every other June, Oregon's Cascade Mountain silence is broken when a Bell U1H1 helicopter, owned and operated by Columbia Basin Helicopters of Baker City, takes flight with a load of "flying trout."

"We start our trout stocking at the Oregon-Washington border and end at the California-Oregon border and we do the entire Pacific Crest Trail from one end of the state to the other," noted Oregon Department of Fish and Wildlife's (ODFW) Kurt Cundiff. "It's a pretty awesome view—you get to see a lot of different lakes and areas that most folks just don't visit."

Oregon's high Cascade Mountain areas are remote and difficult to reach—usually by horse or on foot, so Oregon Department of Fish and Wildlife's aerial stocking program delivers tens of thousands of the so-called flying trout on time and on target into nearly four hundred high lakes—in one week. Chief pilot Dave McCarty logs more than twenty-two thousand hours in the chopper and said that he wouldn't trade the adventure for any other job. "I love this job! I see the entire Cascades in one week and it is just amazing! I approach each lake by looking it over first, seeing which way the riffles are blowing on the water. [This helps determine which way the wind is blowing.] If you get turbulence or downdraft you can feel it dragging you a bit, but for the most part it flies real nice."

Dave pilots up to four flights a day during the weeklong project that had ground support crews scurrying into action on his return to the base. The base this time for the Northern Cascade flights was the Mount Hood Meadows Ski Area's Sunrise Lodge parking lot. On the ground, tens of thousands of baby rainbow, cutthroat, and brook trout are loaded aboard a special unit called the Aerial Stocking Device, or ASD.

ODFW engineers built the fish-hauling unit back in '97. Ground crews load up to four hundred of the three-inch-long trout into each of thirty aerated tanks on the remote-controlled device. The device sports a rear tailfin and an aerodynamic nose that lend a familiar look—like a miniature space shuttle. The history of Oregon alpine lakes' trout stocking is rich and colorful. In the early days of the twentieth century, horse pack trains made long arduous treks into the Cascades to deliver the baby fish—it was a summerlong effort to reach all of the lakes, which were often frozen over or closed due to slides.

In the 1960s, fixed wing aircraft took over and then helicopters cut down on time and expense. Today, the helicopter with its remote-controlled unit hanging sixty feet under the ship's belly will fly into nearly four hundred lakes in just one week.

"The navigator has a list of the lakes that identify which fish species go into which water body," noted project manager Kurt Cundiff. "The navigator gives that information to the bombardier who sits behind him. When McCarty says 'go ahead and release fish,' the bombardier presses a button on the remote controller. That will release the appropriate compartment on the device that holds the fish. It runs real smooth." ODFW Biologist Erik Moberly said that the fish do well in Oregon's high lakes but in some years not all lakes will be stocked. "That's because a lingering winter finds most lakes above six thousand feet still frozen over so they'll have to wait until next time—that's two years from now."

The baby trout thrive and grow fast in the nutrient rich lakes—they will grow to catchable size in just one year. A recent angling survey noted that one out of four of the state's 600,000 licensed anglers participate in High Cascade lakes fishing opportunities and they are a dedicated group who say they return year after year. The project is funded through the sale of Oregon angling licenses and tags and the net benefit of the project is significant. Managers said that for every dollar spent on the weeklong aerial trout stocking of Oregon's high lakes an additional sixteen dollars is generated in the Oregon economy by the anglers and campers who journey to the remote areas.

Erik, an avid angler and backpacker himself, added that the project provides unique Oregon angling opportunities to those willing to go the extra mile and find adventure. "It's rewarding to go into the wilderness with a rod and reel on your backpack so you can catch your dinner. If you've never been out to the wilderness to see some of these gorgeous lakes, you really owe it to yourself to get out there. Oregon is such a beautiful place."

For More Information

Oregon High Lakes Trout Stocking
Where: 3406 Cherry Avenue NE, Salem, OR 97303
Phone: 503-947-6000 or 800-720-6339
Watch the Episode: www.traveloregon.com/flyingtrout

Soft Sides of an Iron Giant
Iron Mountain Trail

Some Cascade Mountains are cloaked in a mysterious presence, yet when the moist fog blankets move on and the view clears, the beauty of spring's first seasonal blush is astounding. This is no more apparent than on the drive to the Iron Mountain Trail, a route made for savoring the quiet side of spring. Make your first stop Cascadia State Park, a place meant for the quiet times, and learn about an intriguing chapter of Oregon history. The serene camp setting was once a center for those seeking health remedies from the nearby mineral water that still bubbles out of the ground.

Lore tells of a former slave who discovered the springs in the 1880s and how people then flocked here to taste the water. Visitors spread the word about its medicinal benefits, and soon people pitched their tents to stay longer. One enterprising gent, George M. Geisendorfer, purchased 300 acres in 1895, including the mineral springs. He developed a resort complex with a health spa that grew to include a post office, hotel, and camping area that became a vacation destination for thousands. The spa operated for a half century until Oregon State Parks purchased the 254-acre property in 1941.

You'll find picnic tables and group picnic shelters spread across a huge area of large meadows flanked by large old-growth Douglas firs. There are twenty-six primitive campsites with barrier-free restrooms at Cascadia too. I enjoy stopping at Cascadia for the three-quarter-mile hike to Lower Soda Falls. From the group camping area, look for a sign marked "Soda Falls." Walk upstream along the creek until you see the falls spilling over the edge of a tall cliff and following a course through a vertical crack in the cliff face and falling 180 feet in two tiers among moss-covered rocks.

Just a few miles up the road past Cascadia, take a short hike on the wild side to meet resident Roosevelt elk. You'll need a spotting scope or binoculars to enjoy this show, but the novelty of the experience is worth your time at the Walton Ranch

Interpretive Trail. A pasture on the south side of the Santiam River is surrounded by steep ridges that are blanketed with fir and alder. The best viewpoint is from a platform at the end of an interpretive trail, where information kiosks tell the story of the herd, which was transplanted here by the Oregon Department of Fish and Wildlife. The elk have adapted to their new habitat and are doing very well! While elk viewing is best in winter, the herd of thirty-five to forty can still be seen here in spring. Early mornings and late evenings are best.

If time is on your side for a daylong excursion, discover the spectacular bursts and hues of an amazing array of red, blue, and yellow alpine wildflowers that steal the scene at the little-known geologic wonder named Iron Mountain. This destination will challenge you with its 1.7-mile hike and 1,500 feet of elevation gain. The Iron Mountain Trail leads through stands of trees and up the side of the mountain at a moderate grade. It branches about halfway up—stay to the right and you'll soon be zigging and zagging along a series of switchbacks up an even steeper grade. There's quite an impressive show as you ramble through meadow after meadow exploding with varied blooms.

Botanists tell us soil, moisture, sunlight, and temperature all dictate a plant's survivability, and life here must certainly be sensitive to all of that for practically every wildflower that grows in the western Cascade Mountains—over three hundred species—can be found along this trail. While the hike is steep, narrow in places, and full of switchbacks, you can pause often and slowly savor the likes of the rosy foxglove, sapphire lupine, or crimson paintbrush that are always at your side. Then there's the geology of the place: Oxidation has cast many of the ancient and exposed cliffs, outcroppings, and spires in varied hues of burnished red. Once atop the bare, volcanic summit, you'll find a Forest Service lookout (occupied in summer) and plenty of flat open space to spread out a lunch and enjoy the surrounding views.

For More Information

Cascadia State Park
Where: On US Highway 20, 14 miles east of Sweet Home, OR
Web: www.oregonstateparks.org
Phone: 541-367-6021 or 800-551-6949

Willamette National Forest
Where: Willamette National Forest Supervisor's Office, 3106 Pierce
 Parkway, Springfield, OR 97477
Phone: 541-225-6300

Watch the Episode: www.traveloregon.com/irongiant

Monumental Recreation
Newberry National Volcanic Monument

Not too many years ago, I frequently asked my young sons, "Are you ready to go camping?" Usually, that question arrived just as their summer vacations set them free from school. I felt it was time for us to find some freedom on the road—in some of the same places I had explored as a child. "Oh yesssss, Dad," came the choral reply from a troop of eager small fries, "Let's go camping!"

That's the way it worked around my household and it remains true today: when the mood to move strikes us there's no better way to celebrate summer than packing up and moving out toward our annual camping adventure at Paulina Lake. We like to leave busy US 97 near Bend behind and follow the lonesome trail high into the alpine reaches of the national monument at Newberry Crater.

Newberry National Volcanic Monument, created in 1990, includes over fifty thousand acres of lakes, lava flows, and spectacular geologic features. The monument's summit is 7,985-foot Paulina Peak, which offers showcase views of the Oregon Cascades and the high desert. It's hard to believe as you drive through this mountainous area that you are within the caldera of a five-hundred-square-mile volcano that remains very active seismically and geothermally to this day. Geologists believe the park sits over a shallow magma body only two to five kilometers deep.

Named for Dr. John S. Newberry, a scientist and early explorer with the Pacific Railroad Survey, the caldera (the center of the volcano) holds two lakes, Paulina Lake and East Lake. The caldera also includes the Big Obsidian Flow, deposited 1,300 years ago by an eruption. This pyroclastic wonder is over a mile in length and two hundred feet deep, with huge chunks of obsidian scattered about like so many forgotten children's toys.

The mile-long stroll puts you in the heart of gray pumice, brick-red lava, and ebony obsidian, and the contrasting shapes and colors rest side by side. Historians say that Native Americans discovered the glasslike qualities of the obsidian and hand-tooled it into razor-sharp tools for hunting and cleaning game.

Today the fractured, jagged ramparts of the volcano are topped by the pinnacle called Paulina Peak, but a glance down to Paulina Lake's forested shore reminds me of my true interest in this site, and it won't take long for you to discover that camping has long been a tradition here.

Paulina Lake Lodge was built in 1929, and many of the nearby lakeshore cabins were built in the 1930s, according to former resort owner John Hofferd. He told me, "Families have been coming here since the very beginning when it took much longer to get here, but then they stayed much longer too."

Paulina Lake, named for the Paiute Indian Chief Paulina, covers 1,531 acres and is 250 feet deep. It holds rainbow trout, brown trout, and kokanee salmon. Early in the morning, when light is faint and not a hint of wind ripples the smooth water, the lake looks like a welcome mat for anglers. In the icy depths of Paulina, the fish thrive, so anglers come by the boatload to troll, cast, and catch. Like many who visit Paulina, John first visited as a youngster. The lodge sports a photo of a beaming ten-year-old boy, hands tight on the tiller of an outboard: That's John at Paulina Lake! As a kid he fell in love with the scenery, the fishing, and the people who come to enjoy it.

"Grant, people have a super outdoor experience in an atmosphere so clean and clear at 6,400 feet in elevation that the clouds seem but an arm's length away. Laid-back is a great way to describe our place. It's for people who really want to get away from the hustle and bustle of their city lives. They come up here and, within a day or two, all that they thought was so important seems to disappear." That's certainly true! The stress melts away. There is no water-skiing or jet skiing on either Paulina or East Lakes, so life moves here at a slower pace.

Perhaps you'll rest fireside and simply take stock of the abundant beauty at one of the seven campgrounds within Newberry Crater. All developed sites include drinking water, a picnic table, fireplace, toilet, and access to boat ramps. Both Paulina Lake Lodge and the East Lake Resort offer rental cabins. And hiking trails abound, including one around Paulina Lake (seven miles) and around the entire crater rim (twenty-one miles).

For More Information

Where: Deschutes National Forest, 63095 Deschutes Market Road, Bend, OR 97701

Phone: 541-383-5300

Watch the Episode: www.traveloregon.com/lavalands

Birth of a River
Metolius River

In early morning light, when the summer air is clear and cool, peaks in the Oregon Cascades like the Three Sisters and Mount Jefferson are marvels. That is especially true from the Central Oregon point of view at a place where the Metolius River is born near the north base of Black Butte, a once-active volcano that rises more than 3,400 feet above the river.

At the head of the Metolius (just off US 20 near Camp Sherman), you can watch as a river comes to life. It bubbles up through an ancient lava flow and forms a shallow creek, then weaves through grassy meadows. The clarity and color and coldness of the water are amazing, ranging from deep blue and turquoise to frothy white water as the flow gains volume from snow-fed tributaries. Bordered by ponderosa pines whose cinnamon-colored bark seems to glow under dazzling sunshine, the river splashes and speeds up as the Metolius reaches its full size on a sixteen-mile journey toward Lake Billy Chinook.

Little wonder the Metolius, and its 8,560-acre river corridor, were designated one of America's Wild and Scenic Rivers in 1988. Clear water, green meadows, and majestic pines draw thousands of visitors and anglers to the Metolius each year.

In nearby Sisters, Oregon, the folks who live and work in Central Oregon like it that way. That includes Jeff Perin, local fishing guide and owner of The Fly Fisher's Place. Jeff is often found creating hand-tied imitations of nature's creations and said "artistry and utility go hand in hand" for one of the hottest recreation activities around: "What I think is really cool about fly fishing is that regardless of where you are in the sport, how much gear you have or don't have—it's still the same sport and everybody can do it. Plus, it's so beautiful here and we have so much great water—at any given time in Central Oregon, there's always some place to go fishing."

Jeff often goes to the Metolius River near Wizard Falls, a rough and tumble stretch broken by moments of calm water. Jeff has cast into the Metolius for more than twenty-six seasons and he loves to cast flies to tempt wild trout to bite. But the trout are not "easy pickings"; in fact, Jeff said it's one of the best "cat and mouse games" in Oregon; a fine complement to the river's character: "You don't have spring creeks like this in too many places where the water just bubbles out of the ground at 50°F and here we are on a 90°F day and we're fishing in cold, clean water. It is such a special place."

It is so special a place that the Oregon Department of Fish and Wildlife has operated the nearby Wizard Falls Hatchery since 1947. Manager Steve Hamburger said that 45°F water was the reason; the perfect water temperature for raising trout. In fact, more than four million baby trout are raised at Wizard Falls Hatchery for release into scores of lakes and ponds across Oregon. Visitors come from all over the state too and stroll the thirty-five-acre hatchery grounds that Steve said is more akin to a parkland than a fish hatchery. "These old ponderosas and Douglas firs are hundreds of feet tall and hundreds of years old. Plus the cool, inviting grass lawns—hey, you'd feel comfortable pitching a tent and laying out a sleeping bag right here." He chuckled and with no small amount of pride continued, "We've been told many, many times by visitors that this is one of the prettiest—maybe the prettiest—fish-rearing facilities in Oregon."

The smooth and steady Metolius River challenges the best fly casters like Jeff Perin from nearby Sisters.

Nearby campgrounds make the living easy too. There are ten US Forest Service Campgrounds along the Metolius River that offer a place to stay and relax. There are no hookups, phones, or TV at these camp sites; it's self-contained camping without fancy conveniences. Steve said that seems to be okay with the campers who return to the Metolius River area season after season. "They came here when they were kids and now they have kids, so bringing their youngsters out carries on from generation to generation. They really do enjoy that and the kids love it."

The Camp Sherman community comprises many homes, a post office, a restaurant, and a general store with a fly shop. It is an extremely popular area, so expect crowds during the peak summer season. If you hope to camp during late summer, your best hope is midweek because the campgrounds often fill up on weekends.

"Just a super destination!" Jeff told me later at our camp as we reveled in the evening quiet. "The Metolius is a difficult river to fish for the beginner. In fact, each year thousands of anglers come and get skunked, yet they still manage to enjoy themselves soaking in the peace and scenery. The campgrounds are clean and the scenery is unbeatable and the weather—well, with more than two hundred rain-free days a year, you can depend upon the Metolius for comfortable conditions." Jeff added, "This belongs to everybody in Oregon and they should all come see it, enjoy it, and be proud of it—it's that special a place." The Metolius River may run through the heart of Central Oregon, but it also builds lasting outdoor memories in the hearts of the people who visit each year.

For More Information

Where: Deschutes National Forest/Sisters Ranger District Office, Pine Street and US Highway 20, Sisters, OR 97759

Phone: 541-549-7700

Watch the Episode: www.traveloregon.com/metoliusriver

Looking Back in Time
Lava Lands

I am always on the lookout for Oregon's "touchable history," interesting, unique lessons that show us more about the place we call home. Recently, we got in touch with a real historic hotbed of geologic history across a landscape that was a true hot zone of volcanic eruptions, magma flows, and a birthplace of mountains—evidence that's obvious not only above ground, but below the surface too at Central Oregon's Lava Lands inside the famous Newberry National Volcanic Monument.

I pointed my travel compass into the Oregon Cascades and a campground I'd heard of for many years but had never veered into during cross-mountain treks. LaPine State Park is just off the famous Century Drive near Bend, Oregon, which winds over a hundred miles past watery gems with alpine mountain views. Lakes with names like Sparks, Hosmer, Davis, Elk, and Todd offer scores of campgrounds the family will enjoy, but LaPine is quiet and out of the way and no one seems to know why. Certainly it can't be for lack of recreation, for aside from the standard state park fare of hiking and biking trails, the 2,400-acre park and its 150 camping sites rest alongside more than five miles of the free-flowing and refreshing Deschutes River.

Lava Lands Visitor Center

First, travel to the Lava Lands Visitor Center, headquarters for all of the Newberry National Volcanic Monument and a super place to get well grounded, so to speak, on the geologic history that created the five-hundred-square-mile region. The visitor center offers displays and exhibits and rangers who can school you well before you head out to see the terrain. Larry Berrin, a former US Forest Service spokesperson, said that there are four hundred buttes or cinder cones that date to the time when volcanoes ruled the landscape near Bend.

"The Trail of the Molten Lands gives you a perspective but then coming up to the butte and seeing it—wow! It keeps going, it's not just right around here—it's not just this cinder cone. It actually flows and continues on." Larry added that lava either exploded into the air or oozed out of the ground for miles around—the trail allows you a close-up view of the power of nature. "It knocked down every tree in sight and wherever it went, nothing lived. So, anything you see now came after the flow—seven thousand years of growth on the flow itself . . . there's not much growing on this lava field, it's pretty barren."

Lava Butte

You can hike or drive to the top of Lava Butte. The way up the narrow, winding lane prepares you for the stunning display you'll find at the top. Lava Butte erupted several successive times beginning about seven thousand years ago with enough basaltic rock to build a roadway six times around the planet. The lava from these cones flowed for miles—not only above ground but below too.

Lava River Cave

A mile south of the visitor center is Lava River Cave, a mile-long lava tube, Oregon's longest. Larry said the chance to go underground and view the lava's unique legacy is "an opportunity to plunge yourself into a primitive environment." Lava River Cave's entrance is nicknamed "the collapsed corridor" because the cave's air mixes with the outside air to expand and contract the cave's walls and ceiling. But rest easy for there's no record of rock fall over the past century.

Your cave adventure is perfectly safe as you reach the smooth sandy floor. Be sure to stop along the way and examine what at first glance looks like a sort of glazed donut effect on the cave walls. "What you see here is almost like candle wax I guess," noted Larry. "It isn't, but it looks like it is. People think that the water is mixing with minerals and dripping—but that's not what's happening—this is solid basalt and hasn't changed in seventy-five thousand years. When the gases got trapped, they remelted the walls and all the walls started dripping again after they hardened." You can proceed for over a mile down an eerie passage through a tube where lava flowed, twisted, turned, and drained away. You lose your sense of space and time and direction the minute you go into the cave and turn the lights out. What remains is a lava tube that's dark, cold, and massive. You must carry a flashlight or a lantern, of course, and when you put the light down low, and it's really quiet, it's also very spooky. Larry added, "The people who are very perceptive will put their lanterns down and out or set them aside and walk and sit and enjoy the silence of the cave."

There is a nominal entrance fee, and lanterns can be rented to view this cavern. Be careful of ice and always carry two light sources if you descend into the cave. It is an eerie experience—best enjoyed on a tour—which take place each afternoon—and like all of the lava lands experience—teaches you much about a unique chapter in Oregon. Lava River Cave is open May 1 to October 15. Wear boots to protect your feet and allow an hour for your trip. Remember, it's akin to being in your refrigerator, so dress for the cold. Lighting is also critical and while lanterns can be rented, I always take a backup flashlight too.

For More Information

Lava Lands Visitor Center
Where: 58201 US Highway 97 South, Bend, OR 97707
Phone: 541-593-2421

LaPine State Park
Where: Off US 97, 27 miles southwest of Bend, OR
Web: www.oregonstateparks.org
Phone: 541-536-2071 or 800-551-6949

Watch the Episode: www.traveloregon.com/lavalands

A Jewel Anytime!
Diamond Lake

If you're on the hunt for one more Oregon summer vacation destination, consider a place that feels a million miles away from city hubbub, noise, and everyday routine. Escape into the watery world of Southern Oregon and the gem of Oregon's Cascade Mountain lakes where hungry rainbow trout are often on the bite at Diamond Lake.

The Umpqua River Scenic Byway provides glimpses into a water lover's playground. Across nearly two hundred miles, the riverway draws those who cast flies to big fish or those who grab paddles to tackle big white-water waves. Many folks are drawn to the quiet times down hiking trails that seem all yours to explore at places like Watson Creek Falls. From the parking area, it's little over a half mile up a long steady incline to reach the falls. A wooden bridge crosses Watson Creek and offers an excellent view of the stunning falls. Watson Falls is the highest waterfall in southwest Oregon and the nearly three-hundred-foot-tall plunge-pool affair roars over a basalt lava cliff and flows into a shallow bowl below. It is worth a pause or a picnic lunch.

Leave the falls behind and continue a short sixteen-mile drive east to reach the gem of Oregon's Cascades called Diamond Lake. It's where anglers have "caught on" to a really good thing: plump and plentiful rainbow trout. Laura Jackson, a fishery biologist with the Oregon Department of Fish and Wildlife, said that back in 2006 it was a different story. Most aquatic life in Diamond Lake had nearly died from a takeover by a nonnative fish species that had grown to number in the millions.

Someone had let loose a fish called Tui chub in Diamond Lake and over the years the fish reproduced so fast, the prized rainbow trout didn't stand a chance. "Back at that time," noted Laura, "Diamond Lake had an estimated 98 million Tui chub. About 90 million of them were juveniles that couldn't reproduce, but 8 million were reproductive so it really threw the lake's ecosystem out of balance."

Diamond Lake was poisoned on purpose in 2006 with a common chemical pesticide called rotenone. Eleven boats spread hundreds of pounds of the chemical across each nook and cranny of the lake. Officials closed all access to the water for a time and the wait was worth it, added Laura. "The treatment in 2006 was followed by stocking in 2007 and a little fingerling that we release in June or July will be eight inches and catchable by August or September. Now, it's a tremendous lake with a great fishery."

Rick Rockholt has helped to manage the Diamond Lake Lodge and Resort over the past three decades and said that the trout turnaround has been remarkable. "It has brought back many, many people who agree that the fishing is even better now than the good old days." Diamond Lake Resort owns a pontoon boat that was purchased from the leftover pontoon-style boats the state had employed in the chemical treatment project. Now, it's a guide boat and the folks who operate it furnish everything you need including rod, reel, worms, and a bobber. It doesn't take long to catch large trout. The full-service resort also offers rental cabins for folks who enjoy an overnight stay and smaller rental boats so you can head for the water.

If you are looking for shoreside camping there are plenty of options to consider: "The US Forest Service has 450 campsites in three different campgrounds around the lake," said Rick. "Half of those can be reserved and the rest are first come, first serve, so you can usually find a place to camp here." Diamond Lake is an Oregon destination where unmatched Cascade Mountains scenery rules and warm hospitality is king. It's a timeless place perfect for building lasting family memories of camping time together in the great outdoors.

For More Information

Where: 350 Resort Drive, Diamond Lake, OR 97731
Web: www.diamondlake.net
Phone: 541-793-3333; Fax: 541-793-3309
Watch the Episode: www.traveloregon.com/diamondlake

Three for the Price of One

Sunset Bay, Shore Acres, and Cape Arago State Parks

This is the time of year when I refuse to let the grass grow under my feet because there is simply so much to see and do across Oregon. That's especially true along a unique section of the Oregon coastline where you'll find three glorious Oregon state parks called Sunset Bay, Shore Acres, and Cape Arago. I am thrilled with each visit to this region. You actually get three state parks for the price of one vacation and each is within two miles of the other and all are connected by road, bike trail, and hiking path. Each park is distinct, easy to reach, and offers unique perspectives on coastal Oregon's recreation experience.

Sunset Bay is a small overnight campground, with seventy-two tent sites and sixty-three trailer sites. The park also features a hiker/biker camp, plus ten group tent camps. Hot showers and flush toilets are available to all campers and provide a welcome comfort zone. There's plenty of elbow room and trails to explore across the park's twenty acres, according to park manager Preson Phillips. That's especially true along Big Creek, which flows for a half mile through the heart of the forested campground into the namesake bay: "Suddenly out of a regular coastal highway, you come into a lusher, greener area where the trees are mature and then you drop down and off to your right is the bay. It's not an area that gets crowded so it's very easy—even on a busy day—to come in and find a place to visit."

He added that you can also "camp light" inside one of the park's eight yurts: "All you need to bring is bedding and another method to cook some food on the outside and you're ready to go. There are bunk beds, futon couch, a table, chairs, and lights—and heat and opening skylight as well."

Thomas Hirst, an early settler in Coos Bay, named Sunset Bay back when fishing boats and other shallow vessels used it as a protective harbor during violent

Wind-shorn and wave-battered cliffs mark the coastline at Shore Acres State Park.

storms. But I feel the wind-shorn, wave-battered cliffs hint of some far-off shore—say, Polynesia? Or Alaska? Legend has it Sunset Bay was also used by pirates, and a glance toward the ocean suggests the reason: The small bay is set inside steep sandstone bluffs and has a narrow passage to the sea that's difficult to discern from the ocean.

A mile away, a much different environment waits for you at Shore Acres State Park. Here, the wildness is tamed at a parkland that puts a smile on your face. You see, Shore Acres is the state park system's only botanical garden.

My first visit to Shore Acres State Park, a mile south of Sunset Bay, is shrouded in a foggy mist that time often lends to an adult's childhood memories. I couldn't have been more than six or seven, but I remember wandering and then wondering who in the world pulled the weeds and mowed the acres of endless green grass. (You see, this was my duty at home, so I always turned an envious eye to manicured yards in well-groomed neighborhoods.)

Shore Acres, built in 1906, was once a private estate famed for gardens of flowering trees, plants, and shrubs brought from around the world aboard the sailing ships of pioneer lumberman and shipbuilder Louis B. Simpson, as well as a one-acre pond and shimmering waterfall. Simpson developed the summer home into a showplace capped by the towering presence of a three-story mansion. The grounds originally contained five acres of formal gardens, but fire destroyed the mansion in 1921.

Simpson began to build an even larger replacement; however, financial losses caused both house and grounds to fall into disrepair in the 1930s. The State of Oregon purchased Shore Acres as a park in 1942. The park offers hundreds of different plant species for you to enjoy as you stroll across seven acres of garden. Preson noted that the park continues to amaze and impress even lifelong Oregon residents: "Folks come in the gate and they say, 'What's that?' And they step in and they're here for hours taking pictures, just oo-ing and ah-ing—and for many it's 'we didn't even know this place was here.'"

A short but easy one-mile hike south takes you to Cape Arago, famous as a resort for Steller sea lions. Well, perhaps "resort" is a bit of a stretch, but the fact is that Shell Island (adjacent to the cape) is the largest Steller haul-out and calving site along the entire West Coast. "It is critical habitat for these federally protected, endangered marine mammals that can weigh more than a ton," noted local eco-tourism guide, Marty Giles, owner/operator of Wavecrest Discoveries. She said that more than three thousand sea lions will haul out on Simpson Reef and Shell Island and that they put on quite a show. "Imagine a group of anxious kids in the back seat of a car on a long trip—you're in my way, you're over my line, move, you touched me—and you can see that kind of behavior going on—they walk over one another and grump at each other and move around."

Any time is a fine time to visit the many viewpoints along Cape Arago's main hiking path overlooking Shell Island, but keep in mind that the offshore rocks, islands, and reefs are part of the Oregon Islands National Wildlife Refuge system, which is closed to public access. So here's a tip: Bring binoculars or a spotting scope so you'll have a front row seat into the refuge proper and a chance to view fascinating wildlife behaviors. Marty added that the three Oregon destinations—linked by hiking trail, they are so close together—offer visitors something new to see each day: "A rocky shoreline and a sandy beach, we have dunes, we have nearby wilderness areas, we have forest—a huge variety of publicly accessible recreational opportunities in a very small area."

Preson agreed and added, "It is so easy to get yourself lost in nature a little bit. Please come visit us and you'll see why." I try to make this collection of wonderful parks a three- or four-day stay—I like to linger and just loaf around the trails, viewpoints, and colorful gardens that this unique Oregon destination offers.

For More Information

Where: Shore Acres State Park is located off US Highway 101, 13 miles southwest of Coos Bay.

Web: www.oregonstateparks.org

Phone: 541-888-4902 or 800-551-6949

Watch the Episode: www.traveloregon.com/threeforone

Shore Acres Holiday Lights

The Oregon coast is a many splendored place boasting unique sights and sounds that will amaze you any time of the year, including a unique holiday light extravaganza at Shore Acres State Park. The park's Holiday Lights offers the very best in community service and a wonderful holiday gift for you to enjoy.

It's safe to say that most holiday lights don't hold a candle to the ones the Friends of Shore Acres State Park put up each year. The folks who show up each weekend beginning before Halloween go the extra mile to light Oregon's only botanical garden state park. If you're quick enough to keep up with the woman who started it all, Shirley Bridgham can tell you how it began—more than two decades ago: "We started with 6,000 lights—just 6,000 lights and one Christmas tree. And then we doubled that each year until we got up to 150,000 lights." With a chuckle, she added, "Then we started going up by 50,000 lights at a time."

Back in those days, Shirley and her husband, David Bridgham, enlisted a dozen or so of their friends to help out. But now, with more than five miles of electric cord and 275,000 lights, the job requires organization and direction. Shirley's figured that out too—with a three-ring notebook that is crammed with pages and maps and photos of the park. "Well, this book shows me what we start with: that is, all the kinds and styles of lights to use and then every single shrub gets a tag. The text that I've developed tells me how many lights, what color to use on the bush, and so forth."

She's not kidding—every shrub, bush, and many of the trees get a tag and eventually one or more strings of lights. Shirley boasts that one time she logged more than eight miles of walking across Shore Acres sprawling seven-acre garden—directing, advising, and motivating her volunteer troops.

Like holiday elves, 1,500 volunteers now follow Shirley and David's lead—while a small, dedicated group of twenty-five or so will spend all of their free time on weekends, putting up the park lights and displays in time for opening night on Thanksgiving Day. They will stretch 3,400 strings of lights and it is hard, painstaking work to get them to look and to work just right. Many say it is also the sort of work that makes them feel good and puts a smile on their face.

David Barnhart (he travels all the way from Seaside on the northern Oregon coast each weekend) said: "I just enjoy the people and the camaraderie. There's quite a group of people out here; usually the same ones every year and it's a lot of work so we couldn't get the job done without them."

Del Willis said that he lives in an apartment in Coos Bay and so putting up the holiday lights in the park is something that he looks forward to each year: "This is for the community, a great thing for Oregon and for the world. Let's face it—it just makes you feel good to do this for others to enjoy."

Preson Phillips, the state park manager in charge of Shore Acres, agreed that people feel good lending a hand to get the

Children of all ages enjoy the Shore Acres State Park's Holiday Lights with wide-eyed enthusiasm.

park ready. In fact, he said that all the work, all of the expenses—even the electric bill—are all paid by the Friends of Shore Acres: "I don't know if I can explain it," noted Preson. "I believe there is something about this site, this garden, this community where pure volunteerism from the community comes out each weekend to make this happen—maybe it's just pride in the park."

Pride resonates across the seven-acre park, despite tough economic times in a county with one of the state's highest unemployment rates, noted David. He said that the worst of times seems to bring out the best in people who want to brighten their park, support their community, and show visitors that they care about the place they call home. David believes that by giving so much of their time and energy to make the Holiday Lights come to life each year, local folks get even more back in return. "This event is a touchstone! This place is where the community comes together and it's a tradition. People know it's going to be here every year and they can be a part of it."

Shirley agreed and added, "It's magic—for thirty-six nights each year—it is magic come true. Especially if you are here when the sun drops out of sight across the ocean out there—the magic that begins at dusk is amazing." David added, "What thrills me is that there are so many adults who don't know the Christmas or the holidays without coming out here to see the Holiday Lights and that's s touching, even rewarding. It puts me in the Christmas spirit."

The Holiday Lights—a magical gift for you from the good friends of Coos County who keep the lights burning in a special place by the sea called Shore Acres. The Holiday Lights are open from Thanksgiving through New Year's Eve; the park is open daily and closes each night at 10 P.M. There is no entry fee, but there is a five-dollar state park parking permit required.

Outdoor Class in Session
Youth Outdoor Day

As summer kicks into high gear, plan on some valuable lessons that will boost your kid's confidence for camping, fishing, exploring, and dozens of other activities at an Oregon Department of Fish and Wildlife event that's a "one-stop outdoor shopping affair" for youngsters and their parents.

Nearly eight hundred youngsters discovered that learning about the outdoors is fun when the lessons are filled with hands-on opportunities at a unique Youth Outdoor Day sponsored by the Oregon Department of Fish and Wildlife (ODFW) at the E. E. Wilson Wildlife Area near Corvallis. "It is the largest outdoor fair of its kind," said Youth Outdoor Day Cochair Steve Sessa. He added, "No one is by a TV, in front of a computer, and there's no one texting right now. Everyone is just engaged in the outdoors and that's just great."

The daylong event offers thirty-five different outdoor recreation activities for youngsters who are able to learn by doing from instructors who donate their time. The instructors bring their skills while twenty-five organizations provide the equipment and assorted gear so that young people can see and feel what it's like to shoot a shotgun, handle a bow and arrow, create a piece of wildlife art, or send out a champion on a long distance retrieve.

Most kids like Morgan Frederick and her sister Sydney have never done anything like it before: "I got over the fear of shooting a shotgun," said a beaming Morgan. "It doesn't hurt my shoulder because I learned how to hold it the right way. Everyone's helpful and offers advice if you need it." Sister Sydney added, "It really is fun. If a kid is outdoorsy at all, they might want to come here and learn a lot more things about the outdoors."

The Oregon Department of Fish and Wildlife staff spent days preparing the

Youngsters take aim at many hands-on experiences when they attend the Oregon Department of Fish and Wildlife's Youth Outdoor Day each July.

E. E. Wilson Wildlife Area to handle the crowds and provide plenty of parking for folks who traveled from throughout Oregon to attend. Scores of staff also volunteered for the flagship event of the agency's calendar year. In fact, more than 250 volunteers offered their time and expertise for the event.

"People are just clamoring to get outdoors with their families," said ODFW spokesperson Chris Willard. "Even though it's billed as a youth event, what you see out here are families engaged in the outdoors and discovering what varied activities mean to them. We hope to show families how easy it is to bond through outdoor activities."

Valerie Duncan said the event was spot-on as a way to engage her three youngsters: "A great place for kids to learn about conservation. We've seen reptile displays, dog training, archery—a lot of activities that we'd never find anywhere else. We're excited to be here and excited to learn more and the atmosphere's wonderful."

The Oregon State Marine Board, Oregon Hunter's Association, Northwest Steelheaders, the NRA, Ducks Unlimited, and the Oregon Wildlife Heritage Foundation are just some of the groups that help the state fish and wildlife agency put on the affair. It is a remarkable event—even more so because the organizers do little to advertise Youth Outdoor Day. It is mostly done through word of mouth . . . because they'd rather provide more activities for the kids. The summer event is really just the start too. There are many other ODFW workshops for kids and their families that continue year-round.

A chill is in the air and for many people that signals the start of Oregon's fall hunting seasons and women who have always wanted to try their hands at hunting have a new way to learn about one of Oregon's premier recreational pursuits and fellas, this one is for women only!

When you go hunting for pheasant, be ready to put in your time and lots of energy—often you are pushing through thick, waist-high grass. At the E. E. Wilson Wildlife Area, newcomer Kelly Ruboin was on her toes because the pheasants can launch themselves skyward in a heartbeat. Kelly joined accomplished hunter Mark Steele, and his hunting dog, Neela, for an afternoon in the field.

Mark is a volunteer guide who gave his hunting services over for a special day designed for women only. In fact, two dozen women gathered on the wildlife area to learn what upland bird hunting's all about. "Okay, Kelly," coached Mark. "Walk right down into this field—a bird could be sitting out there fifty yards or so—if I was a pheasant this is where I'd be hidin' out."

Kelly, like many of the other women, has never done anything like this before. But that's okay because she's taking a class to learn how it's done. The E. E. Wilson Wildlife Area pheasant hunt is part of a unique Outdoor Skills program sponsored by the Oregon Department of Fish and Wildlife called Becoming An Outdoors Woman.

The class was too good a deal for Kelly to pass up. For twenty-five dollars, each woman learned hands-on gun safety, hunting techniques, proper clothing, plus how to shoot and hit what they aim at. Kelly said that her interest in the class was simple: "I'd never done it before and it's just fascinating. I'd love to learn more about it because I've family members who hunt. If I could learn, maybe I could go with them."

Michelle Dennehy, a public affairs spokesperson for the state wildlife agency, agreed and said she was attending the class—not as staff, but had taken the day off from work to participate as a student: "These classes are designed for people like us—people that are new to the sport, a little bit nervous about handling a shotgun, and don't want to be rushed or pushed or anything like that."

Experienced instructors from ODFW offered lectures on firearms and led the students through a number of exercises in proper gun handling and safety. They helped to build confidence in the newcomers with an atmosphere of trust that paid off with relaxation and fun. Betty Rose Richardson agreed with the theme and said, "I love it! There's so much opportunity for hunting and fishing in Oregon's outdoors and this class is wonderful."

That is a message that ODFW would like more women to hear! You see, the agency sells approximately 300,000 hunting licenses and tags each year and women make up just 16 percent of the total.

Rick Hargrave, ODFW spokesperson, said they hope to change that percentage with specific classes that encourage women to participate: "What our outdoor skills program does is plant that seed of interest—if it leads to hunting or fishing, that's great—but if it leads to getting their families outdoors more often that's even better too."

E. E. Wilson offers nearly 1,800 acres for hunters, fishers, hikers, and cyclists to explore throughout the year. Mike Moore, the wildlife area manager, said that the site was a military training facility during World War II and today that means side benefits for the visitor. "Well, we're so accessible," he said. "The road system that was left behind created easy access for people who want to ride bikes, ride horses, and it's also really A.D.A.-friendly. People who require a wheelchair find it a lot easier to get around here than some of the other public wildlife areas."

Today, the area offers wetlands for wildlife, a stocked fishing pond to cast lures, and a wildlife exhibit area where you can see many of Oregon's upland birds on display. Back out in the hunting area, Kelly was on high alert and ready for her shot at a pheasant. She walked the field with Neela out front and on point. Suddenly, two birds erupted from the grass, Kelly tracked one of the birds as it flew to her left and away—she fired, but it was a clean miss! Yet, she turned and smiled—full of enthusiasm: "That was great!" she shouted. "This has been so educational even though I didn't get a pheasant. At least I got a shot off. It's so much fun! I'll be back too."

For More Information

ODFW Headquarters
Where: 3406 Cherry Avenue NE, Salem, OR 97303
Phone: 503-947-6000 or 800-720-6339

E. E. Wilson Wildlife Area
Where: 29555 Camp Adair Road, Monmouth, OR 97361
Phone: 541-745-5334

Watch the Episode: www.traveloregon.com/youthoutdoors

Free Riding
Black Rock Mountain

Mountain bike riding is king of the outdoor recreation scene in one corner of Polk County at a paradise for riders who seek the challenge of steep forested trails and the thrill of thirty-foot jumps. Some say it's the speed, others say it's the jumps, and all agree that Black Mountain offers risk and rewards, danger but excitement plus a true adrenalin rush pursuing their sport. And why wouldn't it?

Speeding down a narrow forested trail, weaving left and right to stay on the right track, jarring bumps and jumps that shake, rattle, and roll you along. Suddenly, a five-foot-tall dirt berm appears out of nowhere and tests your agility as you fly airborne high above the ground. It's the rush of speed and the test of stamina that mountain bike riders find when they travel to one of the hottest locales in Oregon.

It's called "free riding" and it's on a little piece of cycling heaven where the riders catch "big air" across five hundred acres of Oregon state forest at Black Rock Mountain in Polk County. The volunteer organization that makes it all work is called the Black Rock Mountain Bike Association, or BRMBA for short.

Rich Bontrager, the association president, told me that the group is now seven years old and 1,500 members strong. He noted that it all started with a simple dream: "I think we all need to help get people off the couch and out in the forest . . . to see that there's other stuff out here than the city pavement or a computer game—it's that sort of thing that draws folks—something new and different and exciting."

It all begins with designing the features that riders seek at Black Rock; features that include ramps, jumps, and berms—that are approved by the Oregon Department of Forestry and then built by the club members under the Adopt-A-Trail program. The trail designers can also name the varied projects and include imaginative monikers like Sunday Stroll, Grannie's Kitchen, and Bonzai Downhill.

BRMBA members are at Black Rock each day to care for the site and make certain that it's not abused. Rich noted that the concept of a mountain bike destination play area is a first for the Oregon state forest: "Forest managers take a look at our proposals and make sure the ideas won't create an environmental hazard or be too close to a watershed."

Todd Glascow, a BRMBA member and longtime rider, said that feature ideas are really born of the experiences that riders have as they take on trails across the United States. "Oh yes—we ride other areas, see other things, and incorporate them into our own ideas and then take a spin on it. While some material is bought and some donated, a good majority of the wood that we use is fallen timber found in the forest."

Rich agreed and added, "If we do move some dirt we try to cover it back up a little bit so that it can re-naturalize or re-forest itself and look natural again. Once we're done with these structures, we'll actually lay them back out so they decompose in the forest." Some of the runs are so steep that riders can reach speeds of forty miles per hour, so each rider covers up from head to toe with plastic and neoprene rubber protection that they call "armor."

The bikes that they ride are specially designed to take punishing workouts across the forest—aluminum framed bikes with heavy-duty front and rear air shocks and disc brakes are common and the bikes can cost five thousand dollars or more. Wade Youngblood said that beginners can get started for far less: "The used market is a good way to break into the sport—a good used bike goes for about a thousand dollars. If you buy new, you're looking at four to six thousand for a top of the line bike."

Wade's father, Owen Youngblood, said that the affordability of the sport drew him to share the outdoor experience with his son—plus, there's been a bonus: he's lost twenty pounds since he started riding at Black Rock two years ago. "It's always fun to ride with someone who's better than you are because that will push you to the next step . . . and that's why I enjoy riding with my son—he's typically in the lead and I do my best to catch him."

Whether catching big air or enjoying the freedom that comes from speeding down a forest trail on two wheels, the riders agree that there's something for every level of experience at Black Rock Mountain. "You're out here in the trees and you're away from everything else," noted Todd. "You're far away from the daily grind. You can have a stressful day or stressful week and you come out here and ride a bike—it's all gone!"

For More Information

Where: Near Falls City, OR
Web: www.brmba.org
Phone: BRMBA, Dan Shell: 503-679-4948
Watch the Episode: www.traveloregon.com/blackrock

Afoot and Afloat

Clay Myers State Natural Area at Whalen Island

Take a deep breath and savor a place meant for the quiet times at the only Oregon state park that's a coastal island getaway where wildness rules: Whalen Island! A state park property that is prized because there are few folks around and most agree they like it that way. "We don't get huge amounts of use here," noted Oregon State Parks and Recreation Manager Pete Marvin. "You often have the place pretty much to yourself and that makes it nice."

Clay Myers Natural Area includes nearly two hundred acres of forest, sand, and estuary and it's a place meant for tranquillity. The waterway surrounding Clay Myers and Whalen Island is called Sand Lake and it is shallow throughout; it averages just two feet deep at flood tide. The estuary wraps around the island on the high tide and that is the time you will find paddlers like Marc Hinz launching kayak excursions to explore the parkland. "I like to bring folks here to enjoy the quiet, serene, and secluded nature of the waterway," said Marc.

Marc is a co-owner of Kayak Tillamook and he leads tours for a company that specializes in coastal estuary trips: "You don't see many people here because it's too shallow

When the tide goes out at Sand Lake, you'll discover a sprawling tide flat that's perfect for an easy stroll.

for motorized boats." Marc adds that Sand Lake's isolation means paddlers should be prepared to handle any issue that might arise on the water. "Even though it is a shallow waterway, there are deeper parts and the tide does recede out into the ocean. So it's important to wear your PFD [personal flotation device], bring an extra paddle, basic first aid, and a communication device in case you get into trouble."

Whalen Island is tucked between two landmark coastal features. Cape Lookout is to the north, a massive forested headland that juts more than two miles out to sea. Cape Kiwanda is to the south and brings you face to face with an offshore island called Haystack Rock. There is also a giant sandy hillside that is the perfect playground for the young at heart. Don't miss the popular destination that satisfies both thirst and appetite called the Pelican Pub and Brewery. Tillamook County manages Whalen Island Campground's eight acres that offer thirty sites for tents or trailer. There are no water or electricity hookups, so your rig must be self-contained.

Back in 2000, when Oregon State Parks acquired Whalen Island, they built a trail to provide visitors access across the property. The looped trail is two and a half miles long and winds through a forest setting that—every now and then—opens to reveal stunning views to a sprawling sandy beach with breakers just beyond. "The park is unusual for sure," added Pete. "It's an island in the middle of one of the most pristine estuaries along the entire Oregon coast. It is special, unique, and should be prized by those who come to visit. It's Oregon!"

For More Information

Where: Clay Myers State Natural Area at Whalen Island, Tillamook County
Web: www.oregonstateparks.org
Phone: 503-842-4981
Watch the Episode: www.traveloregon.com/whalenisland

The View from the Saddle
Santiam State Forest

On a dreamy summer day, could there be a better find on a simmering afternoon than filtered sunbeams shooting through the overhanging maple leaves and a cool, refreshing creek by your side? Oh, I doubt it! I just knew it was the right place to start an adventure when I arrived at the Monument Trailhead near Gates, Oregon, to meet a small, dedicated group of horseback riders who were to guide me into the wilds of the Santiam State Forest.

Sheila Hoover, co-owner of Into the Wild Equine Adventures, told me that, "There are a lot of people who are interested in horseback riding who just haven't had the opportunity. And this is such a gorgeous place we thought, let's try that." Her husband, Jahn Hoover, quickly added, "For most people it's about 'I've always wanted to ride a horse before . . . always wanted to go horseback riding and try something new.' Well, that's our goal—to make their dreams come true."

Into the Wild Equine Adventures began in 2009 when Jahn and Sheila Hoover decided to teach city folks to ride tall in the saddle aboard their fine stable of Arabian, Percheron, and Tennessee Walker horses to see the outdoors from a different point of view. First, comes the training—not for the horses—(that's happened daily through many years)—but for the people—folks like me who haven't done anything like horseback riding in years. Jahn noted that the reason people need to know how to ride is to feel empowered to work the horse. "If you choose not to be in charge," he said, "the horse will happily be in charge! That means you've put an animal that weighs 1,200 pounds and with the mind of a three-year-old in charge of your destiny. That is not a good plan!"

So, I got to know Venus, a twelve-year-old Arabian mare through a forty-five-minute refresher training course that taught me the basics of correctly sitting in the

You'll be sitting tall in the saddle on this unique adventure in the Santiam State Forest.

saddle, holding on to the reins, and then guiding the horse forward, backward, and turning left and right. "Now, Grant," chided Jahn, "don't let her rub on you! Push her away! That's an aggression."

"Oh," I meekly replied, "She's playing boss?"

"She's testing you," he replied. "That's her first challenge to the relationship." I followed Jahn Hoover's every word of guidance and soon found it easier and easier to handle Venus.

I was soon in control and in the comfort zone, sitting tall in the saddle and ready to ride across new country—in fact, this was country I had never been in before. "It's a gem!" confided Sheila. "The reason we picked this area is that there's about ten miles of trails with a variety of loops and different terrain in a forest that not many people know about. Plus, there are more trails being planned all the time." We were on the Magic Trail and it is one of several that are set aside in the Santiam State Forest for nonmotorized use.

On a warm autumn day, with the temperature flirting with the eighties, it was much cooler under the sprawling canopy of fir, alder, and big-leaf maple. "It is a beautiful section of a temperate rain forest with lots of colorful vine maple and other beautiful trees," noted Sheila. "The trail is well maintained by state forestry crews who do a fabulous job of keeping it in top condition." The trail was gentle with a bit of rise and fall that shifted the scenery and made the ride interesting. It was the sort of riding experience that put my mind at ease and allowed me to really soak up the countryside.

After a couple of hours, we arrived at the Santiam Horse Camp—complete with corrals and fresh water for folks who may wish to make their trip a longer stay. The horse riding community helped the state develop the trails and the campground. Arden Corey, a member of Backcountry Horsemen of Oregon, told me that his group and another called Oregon Equestrian Trails are dedicated to their recreation for many reasons: "I have seen a lot more country on horseback than I would have if I just relied on walking," he noted with a smile. "On horseback, I can see over the sword fern and the salmonberry and it's just a real pleasant experience."

Cristina Stinson, another longtime rider who had joined our trail ride, quickly added, "I have done a lot of off-road riding with motorized vehicles, which I enjoy—but this is just a slower paced activity that lets you look around and take it in a bit more. I don't think you could ask for a more beautiful place to ride." That much is certain! The Santiam State Forest is a fine forest to explore and horseback is a wonderful way to get there. "It's a two-way street," noted Jahn. "We started Into the Wild because we wanted to train and exercise our horses, but also to let people have real riding adventures. They get to learn to control a horse, gain confidence, and to feel good about accomplishing something new."

For More Information

Where: Into the Wild Equine Adventures, PO Box 1188, Mill City, OR 97360
Web: www.itwtrailrides.com
Phone: 503-586-8072
Watch the Episode: www.traveloregon.com/santiamforest

Beauty for All to Enjoy
Opal Creek Wilderness

I f you wish to beat the heat during a late summer hot spell, consider an easy to reach getaway that offers an escape into a cool and refreshing Cascade Mountains wilderness. On a blistering summer day, all it takes is a simple leap of faith to find a cool moment in the gorgeous and refreshing pools of Opal Creek. The thirty-foot drop from the high rocky bluff into the cold Opal Creek pool below is a draw for thrill seekers but it's also place shrouded and shaded by towering, ancient Doug fir trees.

When you walk among the giant trees you'd swear someone left a freezer door open—it's that cool—for the visitors who journey the less traveled trails into Oregon's Opal Creek. Refreshing to be sure—even bone chilling at a reliable 42°F but the creek is one of many small treasures you'll discover across the huge thirty-five-thousand-acre Opal Creek Wilderness and National Scenic Recreation Area.

Opal Creek, in the Willamette National Forest, is more than one hundred miles from Portland. It is a watershed that was once center stage for one of our country's most publicized old-growth timber battles of the past century. Oregon Senator Mark Hatfield capped his career by getting Congress to protect Opal Creek as a scenic recreation area and wilderness in 1996. That action ended the debate over the watershed's ancient trees that date to the Middle Ages.

"Everywhere you look you have 450-year-old trees, but many are a thousand years old, plus the many pristine streams," noted George Atiyeh, a longtime forest activist. Back in the 1970s and '80s, George was a miner who worked a decades-old mining claim "not for gold, but lead, zinc, and copper."

He grew up near Opal Creek, so watershed became his backyard and he grew to love and admire the place. George became a supporter and central figure in promoting and publicizing the features and benefits of protecting and preserving Oregon's fast-disappearing ancient trees. So it is no surprise that today he works with the Opal Creek Ancient Forest Center at a small wooden village called Jawbone Flats in the Opal Creek Scenic Recreation Area.

The collection of cabins and classrooms is where education and tourism collaborate in a unique partnership that draws the curious and the dedicated alike who wish to learn more about the values of an ancient forest setting. "This forest was what the whole west side of Oregon looked like all the way down to California," noted Katie Ryan, the Center's executive director. "There's very little of it left but here you get a chance to immerse yourself in it."

Many old- growth trees in the Opal Creek Wilderness date back more than five hundred years.

Oh—and in case you're wondering—George added, the name "Opal" was not out of special recognition for the creek's color, but rather a woman's beauty: "An early US Forest Service ranger (Elliot) saw Opal Creek and said it was almost as beautiful as his wife. So, he named it Opal Creek (it had been called Boulder Creek) for his wife."

Today, the popular trail requires a three-mile hike to reach Jawbone Flats. You may also choose to link with many other trails that reach across Opal Creek Wilderness or the adjoining Bull of the Woods Wilderness. The hike into Jawbone Flats is "fairly mellow with only two hundred feet of elevation gain in that whole distance," added Katie. When you arrive, you will discover rustic rental cabins that are available for an overnight stay (reservation only), an education center, a general store, and even a restaurant.

"It's a great place for families to bring little kids because we have all the amenities of home but you feel you're in wilderness," said Katie. "Many people stay here for a night, go out on a backpack trip, and come back and stay for another night." The Opal Creek Ancient Forest Center offers a varied curriculum suitable for adults and children about the values and the science of the land and water found in an old-growth forest.

Visitor Zoe Edelen Hare has returned each summer ever since she was a college student in the early '90s. She said the hands-on learning experiences bring the kid out in everyone: "It's serene and quiet—and completely off the grid so no one is looking at their cell phones, looking for text messages. It's nice to slow down, plus our children know that we're focused with them and not trying to do our own work. There's something about this place—it's magical and we like to come back here."

Katie agreed about the magic of the moments at Opal Creek. While it may take a bit more effort to reach, it is worth each step of the journey. "The reason our water is so clear is because the trees are still on the banks holding the landscape in place and all of this functions the way a forest is supposed to; it's not managed and that's becoming harder and harder to find."

For More Information

Where: Willamette National Forest office, 3106 Pierce Parkway, Springfield, OR 97477 and Opal Creek Ancient Forest Center, 721 NW 9th Avenue, Suite 236, Portland, OR 97209

Phone: US Forest Service: 541-225-6300; Opal Creek Forest Center: 503-892-2782

Watch the Episode: www.traveloregon.com/opalcreek

Paddling in the High Cascades
Wanderlust Tours

C entral Oregon's Cascade Lakes Highway is a path once taken, you'll never want to leave, but—you might try a summer detour! We did just that at Sparks Lake, twenty-five miles west of Bend and we found adventure on the water with Wanderlust Tours. Jeff Gartzke was our guide for an afternoon canoe paddle across Sparks Lake. We joined an enthusiastic group of folks who were sporting personal flotation devices (PFDs) and—with paddles in hand—each was eager and ready to go aboard canoes to see the lake from a different point of view.

Jeff noted that flat-water paddling is an easy activity that requires a short amount of practice time, especially on Sparks Lake: "Sparks Lake is one of about twelve lakes in this region that we have to choose from for our afternoon paddle trips. It is well over a mile in length from north to south and people are impressed by the scenery—it's as photo friendly as Central Oregon's high lakes can get."

At 5,400 feet in elevation, Sparks Lake is perfectly suited to a canoe adventure with awesome views of South Sister, Broken Top,

Sparks Lake, like many Oregon Cascade Mountain lakes, is perfectly suited to a paddling adventure.

and Mount Bachelor. Sparks Lake was formed more than ten thousand years ago when lava blocked the Deschutes River. In fact, a narrow channel—defined by volcanic rock shorelines—connects two halves of Sparks Lake. The lake covers approximately four hundred acres and it is no more than ten feet deep. We paddled, we smiled, and we laughed as we toured the lake as a slight breeze eased our downwind paddle.

After an hour or two, we arrived at a sprawling sandy beach. The site offered plenty of elbow room for a shoreside lunch and a cold brew to go with the expansive view of the lake and the surrounding mountains. It was a stunning setting not lost on our fellow paddlers, including local resident Mike Sawyer: "Oh—love it," he noted. "This lake is one of the reasons I live in nearby Bend and I enjoy coming out here as often as I can. I hike, ski, and boat—it's a wonderful place to live, work, and play."

Jeff smiled and agreed—he offered that the contrast of the rugged rock, broken by the soft, colorful beauty of the shoreline's wildflowers draws him back to Sparks Lake each week. "It's a true testament—a true trial—to find something in Central Oregon that isn't volcanic in origin; it's volcanic all around you. Any rise in the landscape, any hill around you is volcanic in one form or another and the scale of it all makes my work a dream job. This is my office right here. Can't beat it!"

For More Information

Wanderlust Tours
Where: 61535 South Highway 97, Suite 13, Bend, OR 97702
Web: www.wanderlusttours.com
Phone: 541-389-8359, 800-962-2862; Fax: 541-383-4317
Watch the Episode: www.traveloregon.com/highcascade

At Home on the Water
Lake Billy Chinook

When you leave Oregon's Cascade Mountains behind and Central Oregon's US 97 unwinds before you, enjoy a desert landscape of sage and juniper and then set your travel compass west of Madras, Oregon. It is where three east-side rivers—the Deschutes, the Crooked, and the Metolius—merge into a vast watery playground at Lake Billy Chinook. Many call Lake Billy Chinook at Round Butte Dam an oasis in the desert for once you arrive, it is water, water everywhere, framed by towering four-hundred-foot canyon walls at a popular destination that is also nicknamed "The Cove."

Ever since the completion of Round Butte Dam in 1964, this lake has been the drawing card for fishing, skiing, camping, and hiking. This is big water! The reservoir covers 3,997 acres and is as deep as 415 feet. Each arm of the lake is six to twelve miles long, creating more than seventy-two miles of shoreline at full pool. Gary Popp, owner of Cove Palisades Resort, said it's the only place in Oregon where you can "take your home on the water" through a unique partnership with Oregon State Parks. "Water sports are everything—folks come here for the water-skiing because we don't get cold weather in the summer and there are lots of places to go on these arms that aren't crowded. We offer more than thirty floating homes for rent, many are based right at the Cove State Park Marina, so it's easy to find us."

Lake Billy Chinook is more than seven miles long and you can spend a day aboard a comfortable houseboat—complete with all the comforts of home, exploring some seventy miles of shoreline that includes a stunning, jaw-dropping view to Kettle Falls. Many travelers make Cove Palisades State Park their vacation home. The park begins at the top of the rimrock above Lake Billy Chinook and is situated among towering cliffs that surround the beautiful lake. The grounds contain approximately

Cove Palisades Marina is the watery gateway to vast Lake Billy Chinook in Central Oregon.

three hundred campsites amid soft grass and timeless views and boat launches, one on the Crooked River arm and two on the Deschutes arm.

Oregon State Parks Manager David Slaght said visitors appreciate the full-service campgrounds, the general store, restaurant, and a full-service marina with rental services: "You have so much to explore at one destination: the high desert experience with the dramatic geology, the lava flows, the canyons, three distinct rivers that come together, and then the Cascade Mountains form a gorgeous backdrop." Not interested in camping? Rustic lakeshore log cabins are available. Yes, log cabins. Just the idea of them conjures up atmosphere: summer nights, the sound of the door slamming shut, the creak of the floors when you walk across them, the smell of the campfire outside. That is "cabin camping" in an Oregon state park. Most are one-room affairs, thirteen-by-thirteen with a six-foot porch and electricity, beds with mattresses, tables, and chairs. Some contain two rooms and sinks, refrigerators, and microwaves, even bathrooms with showers. Any of these relaxing abodes is a wonderful base for enjoying views of the mammoth four-hundred-foot walls layered with alternating bands of ash, gravel, and lava flows.

The most spectacular features of the canyon are the lava flows that erupted out of Newberry Volcano about a million years ago. They form the high, columned cliffs and also The Island, which rises to captivate your attention just across from Cove Palisades State Park. Water carved and wind eroded, the sun-browned canyon vistas are compelling and powerful displays of seven million years of geologic history.

Meanwhile, back at Lake Billy Chinook, Gary added that PGE (Portland General Electric) has made more than $6 million worth of improvements at campgrounds, boat ramps, and restrooms to make this destination more enjoyable. But he noted that it's the timeless qualities that people enjoy the most: "It's a chance to get away and reconnect with friends and family in a setting that takes the breath away."

You'll be coming back too—to seek out some sheltered cove, drop an anchor, and enjoy the ageless vistas across dazzling canyons. This lake has always had a special place in my heart. It makes me feel small in relation to life's bigger natural story, a feeling I don't get in many other places. Perhaps it's a serene intimacy and mobility you'll discover too when you enjoy a houseboating adventure on Lake Billy Chinook.

For More Information

Lake Billy Chinook Houseboats
Where: PO Box 1921, Redmond, OR 97756
Web: www.lakebillychinook.com
Phone: 541-504-5951 or 866-546-2939

Cove Palisades State Park
Where: Off US Highway 97, 15 miles southwest of Madras, OR
Web: www.oregonstateparks.org
Phone: 541-546-3412 or 800-551-6949

Watch the Episode: www.traveloregon.com/billychinook

Touchable History
Oregon Caves National Monument

Some of the best travel experiences across Oregon happen at places that offer teachable moments through touchable history. So it is at an iconic site in southwest Oregon that will put you in touch with geologic history that reaches back 250 million years. It's an above and below ground adventure at the Oregon Caves National Monument.

When you trek inside "Mount Elijah" at the Oregon Caves National Monument, you must go through a locked gate. It's just the other side of that gate that you discover it's a national parkland unlike any you've visited before. "Imagine what it may have been like here in the 1870s," said National Park Service (NPS) Ranger Sandy Gladish. "Elijah Davidson went into this cave to rescue his dog named Bruno. He thought the dog was in trouble because it had chased a bear into the darkness. So, Elijah did too and that's how Oregon Caves was discovered."

The half-mile-long trail through the Oregon Caves offers shadowy glimpses into a timeless world of mystery and adventure. Park rangers like Sandy Gladish can teach you much about the place that—despite its century-old national designation—remains surprisingly foreign to many visitors. "It's called 'Oregon Caves' because early explorers thought there were a lot of caves here," noted Sandy. "The name just stuck even though there's but one cave."

"Visitors tend to think the cave is all there is but there's a lot more—in the monument and the area around us," added George Herring, the NPS Monument's chief interpreter. He said that the 480-acre national parkland—established in 1909—offers miles of trails with stunning scenery of mountains, creeks, and waterfalls. "It really is an opportunity for folks to explore their own Oregon backyard and discover geologic complexity that parallels any other place on the planet. You also learn that a little bit of intellectual curiosity can go a long way toward experiencing a very different world."

The adjacent Chateau at the Oregon Caves provides a base camp to launch your adventures. It is a five-story wooden lodge built of locally milled lumber, plus massive hand-hewn Doug fir posts and beams. The Chateau at the Oregon Caves opened to the public in 1934 and the lodge's rustic simplicity (surprisingly, there are only twenty-three spacious rooms) provides a warm setting supported by down-home family comfort that's based upon a simple idea: "It is a cool cave with a warm hearth," chuckled Menno Kraai, the Chateau's general manager. "When you walk in the lobby, see a fire in the fireplace, and then gaze up to the large fir beams and posts, it all says Oregon!"

There are few distractions at the Chateau—no phones, radios, or TV contribute to a sense of isolation, but that's a good thing. The lack of distractions offers a wonderful chance to reconnect with your family or friends that makes the time here so fulfilling. The Chateau also offers a super cool Oregon Caves Coffee Shop that will also make you feel right at home. "Our counter is like a huge S-shaped serving tray," noted Laura Empems, the Chateau's hospitality manager. "Each person can be served from behind the long counter—plus the knotty pine paneling on the walls adds up to an experience that's like stepping back in time. People love that—and the milkshakes too."

Back down in the Oregon Caves, the temperature is a constant 44°F, so be sure you are prepared for the ninety-minute tour with a jacket, cap, and comfortable shoes. Don't forget a camera to capture stunning stalactites that drop from above and stalagmites that reach to the roof. "These form drip by drip by drip," noted Sandy. "They can take anywhere from a hundred to a thousand years to grow just an inch."

"The true adventure is coming up the highway, letting go of the present, and spending time in the past," added George. "You will relax here—nature doesn't give you any choice!"

For More Information

Where: 20000 Caves Highway, Cave Junction, OR 97523

Web: www.oregoncaveschateau.com

Phone: Oregon Caves: 541-592-2100; Oregon Caves Chateau: 541-592-3400 or 877-245-9022

Watch the Episode: www.traveloregon.com/oregoncaves

Passage into Paradise

Rogue River Jet Boat

I f travel is a state of mind, Oregon sure makes you wonder how one region can offer so much wide-ranging recreation and scenery—and how you will ever be able in one lifetime to experience it all. Even for the seasoned traveler, an endless supply of secret places is available for exploring. So, slow down and savor a once-in-a-lifetime experience this summer on a river steeped in legend, lore, and interesting characters and enjoy one of the most breathtaking boat rides into the Rogue River Wilderness.

The Rogue River is world famous and has attracted adventure seekers for decades, some as well-known as the river itself, like Zane Grey, the Western novelist who came to the canyon to write and even set one of his novels there. Once a lifeline of sorts for folks who lived along the river, boats have been used for more than a century to deliver food, supplies, and news from the outside world into the rugged canyon.

Now, they're lifelines of laughter and smiles that help folks reconnect with Oregon's outdoors. Speedy jet boats launch family excursions and recreation into a distant world away from the routines, noise, and general hubbub of city life.

In early morning—when the air is still and nature is waking up—Oregon rivers like the Rogue are a marvel. As daylight grows, people come out to play at Jerry's Rogue Jets and Rogue Mailboats along the Rogue River waterfront at Gold Beach. Jet boat pilot Jeff Laird keeps the century-old tradition alive as he launches our tour at 8 A.M. sharp—it's a 104-mile-round-trip journey into the Rogue River Canyon—the longest trip that's offered.

The journey was outrageous fun as Jeff deftly steered and throttled his thirty-two-foot-long specially designed jet boat, powered by three 450-horsepower engines. We plowed through white-water cauldrons, splashed and swung right, then left, over skinny shallows to avoid bulging boulders, and rocketed across two-foot standing waves. "Hang on, guys—should we go faster? Little bumpy here—whoo hoo!!!" Jeff shouted to us. Everyone onboard was wet and grinning with delight.

The jet boats can reach speeds of sixty miles per hour—but we motored along at less than half that speed in half a foot of water—it was shin-deep shallow and amazing. Then he throttled back the powerful engines and we slowly cruised through the deep shadows of the Rogue's calmer stretches. Cliffs and canyons are the rule along the river's course through the Oregon Coast Range, where eons of water and wind have eroded the exposed rock into smooth, otherworldly sculptures. Along shore, small waterfalls spout across rocky rims, slap a shelf here and there, and plummet into deep, swirling whirlpools.

Thousands enjoy easy access into the Rogue River Canyon each summer when they go aboard the popular jet boat tours.

Settlers arrived in the canyon of the Rogue River by the mid-nineteenth century, following the trails left by early trappers and miners. As I gazed up the steep forested walls, it was hard to imagine anyone scratching out a living in such remote terrain but as Jeff said to me: "Really, Grant, this part of Oregon is defined by its remoteness and rugged geography. It has never been an easy place to live—many have tried and failed—but there is something about this canyon that speaks to an individual's soul and says, 'Without trying, what's the point of living?'"

One of the pleasures of so much isolation is the abundant wildlife—a bald eagle may cruise by overhead; Canada geese may be seen shepherding their young from one shore to the other; an osprey might dive to catch its finny prey in the water. Even black bears are regularly seen strolling the shoreline.

It's fitting that so many critters are more at home in the canyon than any of us ever will be. Jeff told me that he had been leading the watery escape for Jerry's Rogue Jets tours for nearly twenty-five years. He is a jet boat pilot with family roots that run as deep as the river canyon. You see, his uncle is Jerry Boice, one of the men who started jet boat touring nearly half a century ago. "I get up every morning thinking 'Golly sakes, I get to go drive a tour boat for the day,' Laird said with a chuckle. "This 104-miler is the best trip for the rapids, the thrills, and the splish splash."

It is an awesome collection of wilderness: From forest hilltops that touch the sky to remote steep canyon walls that touch the hard charging white-water rapids, it's easy to see why Jeff comes to work each day. "How many guys get to do this? Look at the people out here—they're smiling and having fun—and a lot of people cannot say when they go to work they give people a smile. And that means something to me. It's really why I like my job so much and hope to keep at it for another twenty-five years."

For More Information

Where: Jerry's Rogue Jets, 29985 Harbor Way, Gold Beach, OR 97444.
(Forty-five minutes north of the California border on US Highway 101)
Web: www.roguejets.com
Phone: 800-451-3645
Watch the Episode: www.traveloregon.com/roguejets

Ready, Set, Fore!
Disc Golf

GETAWAY #62 – GREATER PORTLAND

There's a new way to "play a round" in the great Oregon outdoors but surprise: you don't need clubs, carts, or golf balls to play this round of golf but you may need to yell "fore" at the new and very first forest disc golf course set in an Oregon state park. Mike Phillips loves his "tee shot" so he carefully eyes the right line down the fairway—before he lets the disc fly to hit speeds of sixty miles per hour. Mike is a disc golfer, one of the best around and he has a bag of discs to prove it. He uses up to fourteen different discs in a round of disc golf and each has a specific purpose: "It's a bit like ball golf that way—if you need to hit that low shot, you use that 2-iron because you need the distance or maybe you need that high flop shot so you use a 9-iron or a wedge . . . it's the same thing with disc golf."

Mike is especially proud of the brand-new "mountain-style" disc golf course in a forested setting inside Stub Stewart State Park. That's no surprise—after all, he designed it! "It was like a dream come true. You always hope that you'll get to a point where you can help design a course or make a

Each disc golf "hole" is actually a chain link basket. Don't miss your shot or it'll cost you a "stroke."

The disc golf "swing" can take years of practice to perfect for accuracy and distance.

change to a course—but when I was invited to walk this terrain I knew this was a really nice place to put in a course."

The new eighteen-hole or "basket" course stretches across forty forested, hilly acres that presents a unique challenge to even the most experienced disc golfer. Park Ranger Steve Kruger noted that wasn't the original intent but changed with Mike's leadership and vision. "Originally, we thought let's put in nine holes of an easy level," said Steve. "Something that's basic, but Mike insisted that if you want people to come and make the park a destination, we needed to do more. He was right!"

Stub Stewart State Park has been a fine camping destination since 2007 and offers miles of trails for biking or hiking or horseback riding. The park includes a spacious campground plus rental cabins for folks who don't own a trailer or tent. The spectacular views are a fine complement to a state park that's an easy drive—less than thirty miles—west of Portland. Steve said that new forest disc golf course is the latest addition to the park's recreation scene: "We did our best to plan this and design it in a way that would flow naturally with trails to walk so that it isn't just a march through the woods."

Mike says much thanks is due to the all-volunteer effort from metro area golfers who belong to Stumptown Disc Golf—a club that helped build the course. Now, the word is slowly getting out about something special at Stub Stewart that is a lot of fun with many challenges. "This is a technical mountain-style, trail based course," said Steve. "I tell folks to play the trail, not the basket and play conservative."

"Disc golf is a sport for all generations," added Mike. "You don't have to be in perfect physical health to do it, doesn't require a lot of money, and it's available to anyone for the cost of buying a disc."

There is no fee to play a round of disc golf at Stub Stewart or any of the other Oregon state parks that offer courses, but you will need to pay a daily parking permit. Mike added that for little more than $20 you can purchase three discs (he recommends Next Adventure) that include a driver, a mid-range, and a putter discs.

For More Information

Where: Stub Stewart State Park is located on the east side of State Highway 47 between Banks and Vernonia, OR.

Web: www.oregonstateparks.org

Phone: 503-324-0606 or 800-551-6949

Watch the Episode: www.traveloregon.com/discgolf

Outdoor Tip: Passport to Adventure

You might also consider making it a family sport and if you do, consider a new way to discover outdoor activities just for kids who can also earn rewards. It's called Outdoor Seekers (www.outdoorseekers.com) and it gets youngsters outdoors for all the right reasons according to Amanda Rich, executive director of the Oregon Recreation and Park Department. "It gets down to kids' health—we're facing an obesity crisis in this nation and every little thing that we can do to keep kids active, actively engaging their minds, and their bodies will help. Outdoor Seekers will also instill in them a lifelong love of being outdoors and being active."

It is a passport to adventure noted Amanda—a checklist of sorts that can help your kids achieve ten activities: "Take a trail on a bike or a hike, go boating, try camping—or learn to swim," noted Amanda. "The possibilities are fabulous and lengthy."

Once a child completes the passport's activity, he or she has an adult sign off on it and when all ten activities have been completed, mail in the passport and receive an Outdoor Seekers' Award. "Kids love games—they love lists and they love having a goal," noted Amanda. "And they love prizes, so each child who submits an Outdoor Seekers' Passport gets a unique prize. And it is year-round too."

Supper from a Stream

Crawfishing

Trask River County Park, one of the easiest campgrounds to reach in Tillamook County, is a sprawling, forested affair with sixty campsites—and many of the sites are situated streamside. The park, open daily, is also a destination that's a bit of a secret, and except for holiday weekends, crowds are seldom the rule. You're likely to find plenty of elbow room at this paradise that is located high in the Oregon Coast Range.

The Trask River hides small pockets of cool water and Oregon Department of Forestry's Nathan Seable called it a "refreshing moment" near a county park that's often overlooked: "Trask River Park is a really golden nugget for recreation that is pretty much a full-service campground. There are no RV hookups, but there's running water and vault toilets and more of a family-oriented type camping area. A beautiful setting with a nice day-use area and you can get down and use the river."

The trail I like to travel is just four miles away—along the narrow winding ribbon of asphalt named Trask River Road. You'll know the spot: watch for bald eagles soaring overhead or midsummer wildflowers still showing off and a large trailhead sign that marks the start of a moderate hike called Peninsula Trail. Nathan added, "The Peninsula Trail is about a mile-long loop and it is on a unique geological formation of lava that bubbled up out of the earth eons ago. It became a hard basalt feature that the Trask River could not cut through, so it went around and created the peninsula."

Along the trail, watch for charred remains of burned out old-growth trees from the four major fires—collectively called the Tillamook Burns—that roared through this country in the last century. When you reach the river and the trail loop turns to take you back, you'll find picnic tables for a river shore lunch—the perfect place to linger for awhile. "It's a beautiful spot," said Nathan, "especially when the river's down in summer! There's a nice beach for kids to play along the river and people can fish too." While salmon, steelhead, and cutthroat trout swim about, take some time to explore the river's nooks and crannies for something else—this is where the crawfish live.

I have been visiting the Trask River each summer for more than forty years to explore the river's depths and catch small crustaceans called crawfish. My kids have grown up enjoying the area as well—sometimes with a mask and a snorkel so as to dive and catch the crawfish by hand—or with rod and reel and a chunk of bacon at the end of a line. Not long ago, my youngest son, Kevin McOmie, joined me for a visit on a blistering summer's day.

We used a small wire-mesh crawfish trap (readily available at any sporting goods store) baited with a can of cat food. We placed the bait inside the trap as an attractant. The crawfish walk inside through the narrow funnel-like openings at either end. Once inside they can't seem to find the way back out. We attached a rope to the trap, tossed it into a deep pool, and then tied the rope off to a tree.

"You can find crawfish anywhere along the river in summer," noted state fishery biologist Robert Bradley. "Walk out into any of the pools and even swifter water and start flipping over rocks and you'll find some pretty quick. Folks can catch them by hand or with traps; it's a bit like crabbing in the bay only on a smaller scale. It's an abundant resource that people can enjoy all summer long."

We tossed our trap into the inviting water and we spent the day lounging on the inviting beach. When the mood to move, or the heat of the sun, struck us—we would scamper into the river. My youngsters and I have always had a ball along the Trask River—diving, exploring, searching the river bottom's nooks and crannies, and rolling over submerged rocks to see what secrets the river held. Whenever a sizable crawfish (we'd made a vow not to keep any under five inches in length) appeared, the youngsters would carefully maneuver hands to capture the critter by its head, just behind its two impressive and substantial pincer claws. Catching crawdads by hand is fun sport and a delightful way to beat the summer heat.

No angling license or shellfish license is required to catch crawfish—and the limit is generous: One hundred crawdads per person per day is the daily limit. Crawfish or crawdads or just plain "dads" are a creepy crawly kind of critter that kids love to catch and they taste good too.

We often prepare our catch using my good friend Birt Hansen's Basic Crawfish Boil recipe (see page 189). The taste of fresh-cooked crawfish is sublime—a very mild shrimplike taste that's somewhat delicate. The taste, the setting, and the adventure offer a stark contrast to the broiling sun during the heat of summer—a perfect cap to a day's adventure that your family will want to try soon. Crawfishing and summertime confirm what you may suspect: you're never too old to be a kid again—especially during the dog days of summer.

Where: Trask River Park, 25455 Trask River Road, Tillamook, OR 97141

Web: www.co.tillamook.or.us/gov

Phone: 503-842-4559

Watch the Episode: www.traveloregon.com/ORcrawfish

Birt Hansen's Basic Crawfish Boil

This recipe relies on a handful of simple ingredients and serves up to 4.

2 quarts water	½ cup pickling spice
1 cup vinegar	4 bay leaves
½ cup salt	2 to 3 pounds crawfish

Bring the water, vinegar, and seasonings to a boil, then add the crawfish. Cook no longer than three to four minutes. Overcooked, the crawfish become rubberlike and flavorless.

Spread out a sheet or two of newspaper on a picnic table, dump out the steaming crawdads, and dig in. Grab the tail section, pull it away, and simply peel off the tail shell—everything else will pull right out. Same with the claws—crack them open and pick out the meat.

This is hands-on eating at its finger-licking finest—and that's best with youngsters who really get into their meals. Enjoy with a twist of lemon!

Huckleberry Hounds
Willamette National Forest

The beauty of the Oregon lifestyle is that such an amazing variety of adventures awaits to satisfy your appetite for life, in more than one spin of the word: not just an outdoor adventure but tasty treats too. The Cascade Mountains can satisfy your needs for exploration and adventure in so many ways: perhaps aboard a white-water raft where thrills, chills, and spills wait at each turn . . . or maybe with a rod and reel and the chance to land a trophy with each cast. Or perhaps it's something far simpler that can be found down a quiet forest service road in the Willamette National Forest where a bounty of berries is ripe for the pickin'.

US Forest Service spokesperson Jennifer O'Leary said that late summer is prime huckleberry season: "A wonderful activity to enjoy with family or friends. It's really great to see visitors out there enjoying themselves and tasting a little bit of Mother Nature."

It is what I call "Huckleberry Hound" time for my family and friends and we couldn't be more pleased with this time of seasonal change in the forest. It's a favored time of year because no permit is

Plump and juicy huckleberries grow in patches that are easy to find in the Willamette National Forest.

required and there are no personal harvest limits either. We take what we can use near the Twin Meadows area inside the Detroit Ranger District of the Willamette National Forest.

Jennifer offered timely advice to the newcomer: "Check in with us at the ranger office—get a map, then explore some of the easy to reach roads where the huckleberry patches are located. If you see a huckleberry bush by the side of the road, chances are good there's more right there, so get out there and look."

There are nine species of berries in the forest, but two dominate this area: one is large and sweet, the other more red and tart. We have no trouble finding plenty of bushes full of berries that are a bit like candy drops as I often eat more than I pick. The berries are plentiful in areas of the forest that provide a sun–shade mix. Lift up a branch and expose the underside and you'll find an easier chore of picking the berries, especially if you have both hands free.

While in the area, we also stopped along the Santiam River where the Oregon Parks and Recreation Department has converted long-popular North Fork Santiam Campground from a day-use site to an overnight campground. Park manager Bob Rea said, "It's great to have a place to come to off the river and camp in a tent. We also added a group picnic shelter and a visitor can also make a site reservation. We have converted picnic sites and actually remodeled them to tent sites."

There is a 2.5-mile-long trail through the park and the best part is that more than a half mile of the parkland includes river frontage. Bob noted, "It's very peaceful and quiet and there aren't very many sites—the overall experience that people have there is very satisfying."

Soon, we are kitchen-bound with our bounty to try a favorite recipe called Huckleberry Crisp. It's a simple recipe (see page 193) that works well with the tart berries and best of all, it can be assembled and cooked in less than one hour. A delicious reward for time well spent in the great Oregon outdoors.

For More Information

Where: Willamette National Forest, Detroit Ranger Station, 44125 North Santiam Highway SE, Detroit, OR 97342
Web: www.fs.usda.gov
Phone: 503-854-3366; Fax: 503-854-4239
Watch the Episode: www.traveloregon.com/huckleberryhounds

Huckleberry Crisp

Serves up to 6.

⅓ cup sugar	1 tablespoon lemon juice
2 tablespoons cornstarch	1 cup huckleberry or blueberry juice
¼ teaspoon cinnamon	4 cups huckleberries (slightly sweetened)
¼ teaspoon nutmeg	Topping (recipe follows)
¼ teaspoon salt	

Preheat oven to 400°F.

Combine sugar, cornstarch, cinnamon, nutmeg, and salt in a saucepan. Add lemon and huckleberry juices and stir until smooth. Cook over low heat until thickened and clear, stirring constantly. Stir in huckleberries and pour into a greased baking dish. Sprinkle topping over the huckleberry mixture. Bake for thirty minutes or until topping is crisp and golden brown. Serve warm or cold.

Topping

⅓ cup butter	2 tablespoons flour
1 cup brown sugar	3 cups corn flakes

Melt butter in a saucepan. Combine sugar and flour and add to melted butter. Cook, stirring constantly over low heat for three minutes. Add cornflakes, mixing quickly until they are coated with syrup.

Climbing Giants
Willamette National Forest

H igh above the Willamette Valley in the Willamette National Forest, follow the roadway that traces a trail along Fall River, near Lowell, Oregon, and you could discover adventure that's guaranteed to take you to new heights. I met a group of climbers along this roadway near Fall Creek Reservoir. As I discovered, they were a small corps of climbers that was a breed apart from typical rock or mountain climbers. Just like rock climbers, these folks used gear that included harnesses, ropes, mechanical ascenders, and even helmets. A hardy collection of people had gathered to meet guides with the Eugene-based Pacific Tree Climbing Institute (PTCI) who don't climb tall mountains; rather they ascend Oregon's tallest trees.

Jason Seppa, co-owner of PTCI and a lead guide in my adventure, coolly showed each of us the correct way to wear the harness and how to handle the ascenders, the main mode of movement up the giant trees. He also explained to us why wearing our helmets was so critical: "If you hear someone shout 'Headache!' Don't look up! Headache means something is coming down—maybe a little branch, or somebody's dropped his water bottle. Sometimes that can happen, so wear it at all times." The team had gathered to climb three of the tallest giants in the forest. Trees that had been nicknamed "The Three Musketeers" because the trio of six-hundred-year-old Doug fir had grown so closely together.

Robb Miron, Seppa's partner in PTCI, explained the advantages of climbing these big old trees: "They are really climber-friendly with a lot of limbs and a lot of architecture. When you're up in them, it's the kind of a feeling that you get being inside a grove of trees." PTCI operates under a special use permit from the US Forest Service and their climbing techniques and equipment do not damage the trees. Jason and Robb called it "eco-friendly" climbing as they teach both newcomers and the experienced how to reach for the tallest heights of the trees without hurting the trees they climb.

They employ the same equipment and skills that each had learned on their jobs as full-time arborists in Eugene, Oregon. Jason explained: "People see all of these ropes (each climber has his own dedicated line that's been secured in the top of the tree) going up into space and don't really know where the ropes end—it's quite mind-blowing for the person to see as they walk up to the tree." The trained arborists turned their attention to recreation climbing six years ago and agreed that the forest has much to offer people.

Usually, that begins by overcoming any doubts or fears of heights. After all, the goal is to climb perhaps 250 feet or more above the ground. "It's interesting," noted Robb. "You get up into the canopy and you can't see the ground anymore but it's almost like the height gets easier for many people. You are so focused on what's in front of you—the tree itself and then the physical act of climbing, you don't really think about the height."

Ah, the climbing technique! Now, that technique does take some time to master. First, it required a "jug," or thrust, with my left hand that was firmly holding on to one of two mechanical ascenders. That move was quickly followed by a solid stand up move on my two feet that had been resting in two looped straps that were attached to the ascenders. With my right hand, in yet another ascender, I picked up the excess rope and tightened the line. That procedure was repeated over and over and allowed me to make my way up the tree.

I felt a bit like an inchworm as I watched more experienced climbers take to the task with relative ease. No doubt about it, I was the slowpoke in this group of climbers! Approximately halfway up the tree—at nearly 150 feet—I discovered that Jason and Robb had set up a base camp of sorts as a half a dozen "tree boats" were set up and waiting for us.

Tree boats are fabric hammocks, approximately seven feet long—that were tied off onto nearby branches. The hammocks provided a "rest stop" and I could easily lie down or sit down inside of one—before moving farther up the tree. I discovered they provided a well-earned rest for I was flat-out bushed by my efforts. I felt I earned my reward of a rest in a tree boat. It was heavenly.

I wondered if I had established a new PTCI record for taking so long to get but halfway up the giant tree. "Oh no, not at all," noted Jason with a smile. "Each person takes his or her own time—there's no rush at all." He added that men are often in too big of a hurry and miss the sights along the way, while women often prove better climbers than their male partners. "Oh yes," he noted. "Women bring a lot better climbing technique to this than the men. More fluid and less muscling—guys like to muscle things up while women have more finesse and seem to sneak right up nice and smooth."

Once climbers reached the end of the line, approximately 280 feet off the ground, the payoff was nothing short of spectacular. There was a genuine rush of energy and excitement at the doing of the thing and the unmatched view of the surrounding forest. "A sea of green," said Jason. "As far as the eye can see—nothing but treetops. It's quite cool." Rob noted that the view close at hand was equally impressive too: "Oh my, so much vegetation that you'd never expect—salal, ferns and mosses and lichens—a real variety of flora that you can never appreciate on the ground because you wouldn't know that it even exists way up here."

When it was time for us to return back to ground, mechanical descenders made the journey down incredibly easy. I simply held on to the rope in one hand and held the device in the other and with a quick release of its latch, I gently slid down the rope at a controlled speed. I decided that it was much more fun going down the tree than it was going up.

Robb estimated that he'd led many hundreds of clients up and into big old trees over the years. He said that people really liked climbing The Three Musketeers and everyone he'd ever taken up has a newfound respect for the giants of the forest. "Oh, it's the sense of accomplishment, the sense of doing something that they never thought they could do. And then it's the closeness that you feel with nature. Basically, anyone that comes with us on one of these trips is amazed one way or another."

For More Information

Pacific Tree Climbing Institute
Where: 605 Howard Avenue, Eugene, OR 97404
Web: www.pacifictreeclimbing.com
Phone: 541-461-9410
Watch the Episode: www.traveloregon.com/treeclimbing

New Way to Get Around Oregon
Siltcoos River Canoe Trail

There is something special about seeing the great outdoors from a river's point of view. I am filled with wonder and surprise on each new river adventure, especially on a waterway that reaches from freshwater to the ocean like the Siltcoos River Canoe Trail in the heart of the Oregon Dunes.

The outdoor life doesn't get much simpler than a kayak, a paddle, and a PFD (personal flotation device). We joined local paddler Marty Giles of Wavecrest Discoveries who said you need little more than those items plus a spirit of adventure to travel the Siltcoos River Canoe Trail. Marty noted that the nature of the Siltcoos River is little current and no rapids along a three-and-a-half-mile-long protected water trail that can be paddled in half a day. "It flows through the heart of the Oregon Dunes National Recreation Area," said Marty. "People come from all over to experience thirty-two thousand acres of sand, forest, rivers, and lakes amid the only temperate sand dunes in North America."

The Dunes NRA stretches more than forty-two miles from Florence to Coos Bay and it is an Oregon landmark for outdoor recreation. You may well wonder just where all the sand came from too. "It came from the mountains," said US Forest Service (USFS) spokesperson Gayle Gill. "The mountains in the Cascade Range—thousands and thousands of years ago glaciers melted and carried the debris—sand sediments—to the ocean and deposited them out there. There are no rocky headlands to prevent the sand from coming back out of the ocean and so the waves and wind pushed it back up on the land and that's what we have today."

Many visitors plan vacation time at one of the oldest parklands in the state, Jesse Honeyman State Park, just south of Florence. Camping in the park's campground reaches back nearly eighty years to the days of the CCC (Civilian Conservation

Organization is an important first step in the preparation for a paddle trip on the Siltcoos River.

Corps) that was made up of thousands of young men from the East Coast who built the park in 1933. Our starting point was the USFS Lodgepole Wayside; a day site along the Siltcoos River and just a stone's throw from Honeyman State Park.

Yet along the Siltcoos River it felt a million miles away from human hubbub and noise. The river zigs and zags sharply at low tide and many of the river bends are framed by huge sandbanks. At ebb tide, we watched for logs and branches that were silent and sobering reminders that we had to negotiate on an adventurous trail. "It courses from a narrow freshwater stream environment out to the estuary and close to ocean," said Marty. "The character of the riverway changes quite a bit—like most coastal streams there will be a lot of branches and logs and woody debris in the stream."

Cyndy Williams and her husband, J. C. Campos, had never done anything like this trip before, but they loved each minute of it. The couple traveled from their home in Portland to be our guests on the daylong adventure. As the pair paddled, they soon discovered that the Siltcoos River offered intimate moments where nature's touch restored the soul. "Ohhh, I am hooked," noted J. C. with a smile. "Kayaking is now one of our new choices to get around Oregon."

Before long, our downriver journey slowed across a much wider waterway with tall sedge grasses that seemed to wave us along from shore. We noticed important warning signs along the estuary shore too—plus, roped areas that marked a beach closure in effect from March 15 to September 15. It's an important area to protect nesting sites for small shorebirds called snowy plovers that are endangered species.

We were soon three miles from the start and in the heart of the estuary—it was a view that offered sneak peeks across the sand of the crashing ocean surf. We also noted varied shorebird species that were probing the muck of the marshes—often they were right by our sides. It is the sort of adventure that will set your clock back—guaranteed! Perhaps to a time that will leave you refreshed and ready for more adventures. The Siltcoos River Canoe Trail is open anytime.

No permits are required to paddle the Siltcoos River Trail but a US Forest Service Northwest Forest Pass (available for day or annual purchase) is required at Lodgepole Wayside. Central Coast Watersports in Florence provided our boats, paddles, and PFDs—they even delivered to our launch site in the Lodgepole Recreation Site and picked them up at the end of our trip.

For More Information

Oregon Dunes National Recreation Area, Reedsport Visitor Center
Where: The midpoint of the Dunes along US Highway 101 in Reedsport, OR
Phone: 541-271-3611

Wavecrest Discoveries
Where: PO Box 1795, Coos Bay, OR 97420
Web: www.wavecrestdiscoveries.com
Phone: 541-267-4027

Central Coast Watersports
Where: 1901 US Highway 101, Florence, OR 97439
Phone: 541-997-1812 or 800-789-3483

Watch the Episode: www.traveloregon.com/siltcoosriver

Digging into Oregon's Past
Digging Fossils in Fossil

O regon is home to a treasure trove of interesting places and fun activities that can reveal much about our region's past. In fact, one Eastern Oregon town offers fascinating lessons in prehistory, that—with a bit of imagination and some handiwork—can transport you to a quite different Oregon. In Fossil, Oregon, all you need are some simple tools, keen eyes, and curiosity to learn more about the state—as you dig into Oregon's past.

Eastern Oregon's gigantic landscape holds on to memories; old homestead sites where families once worked the land and carved out their livelihoods across the high desert. Time has passed most of them by and what often remains today are small reminders in a big country that are worth a pause to consider.

Fossil, Oregon, is worth more than a pause. Especially if you enjoy history, like to get your hands dirty, and really dig buried treasures! "You take a rock, crack it open—and there's a fossil or two," noted Wheeler School District Superintendent Brad Sperry. "It's that simple! Our entire area contains fossils. So, it's really a matter of how much work and time you wish to spend digging then slicing open shale rocks that determines the quality of the fossil that you collect."

It's a much different slice of outdoor life for the visitors who stroll through the back gates at Fossil's Wheeler High School—pass under the goal posts of the school's football field and then take a step back in Oregon history. It's the only public fossil dig area in Oregon that offers surprises with each handful of dirt and rock that you turn over.

Brad added that the area has been known to the locals for years: "Oh yes, it's been kind of a local secret, the community has known of it and they come up and kick around in the rocks to pick up a fossil or two. About eight years ago, we were discovered and today, there are even websites dedicated to the Fossil Field—lots of folks come to visit."

Today, the fossils that you dig reveal a much different scene in this part of Eastern Oregon. In fact, thirty million years ago the region was more akin to today's Oregon Coast Range Forest—a temperate rain forest with ancient firs and cedars and ferns and even prehistoric insects. All were covered and trapped by ancient mudflows born of volcanic eruptions that were a common geologic feature in this part of Oregon. All of it adds up to a stark contrast to the high desert sage and juniper country that surrounds Fossil in the twenty-first century.

Just down the street, the new Oregon Paleo Lands Institute (OPLI) will teach you much about the fossils that you collect. Anne Mitchell, the Institute's director, said the OPLI provides a new way to look at the high desert. "Many people come out to Fossil and say, 'I want to dig up a fossil.' Now, when they actually get here, they start learning about the fossil's context in history. Our center was designed to be sort of a hands-on, get a little dirty and comfortable with ancient history location and I think it helps people see that history is real and not just something to read about in books."

Brad noted that fossil digging isn't free—the district appreciates a small donation—and he emphasizes that there's little need to take more than a handful of the fossils. He'd rather see more people coming back again and again instead of loading up by the bucketful. He also said that simple tools, like a hammer and chisel—plus, a bucket—are all you need to get started. "It's all about kids and families and the excitement of finding fossils and realizing they're thirty million years old. It is like Christmas morning and seeing what Santa brought you. Well, take the rocks, crack them open, and suddenly it's Christmastime. You never know what you're going to find!"

For More Information

John Day Fossil Beds Visitor Center
Where: 32651 State Highway 19, Kimberly, OR 97848-9701
Web: www.nps.gov
Phone: 541-987-2333

Oregon Paleo Lands Institute
Where: 333 West Fourth Street, Fossil, OR 97830
Web: www.paleolands.org
Phone: 541-763-4480

Watch the Episode: www.traveloregon.com/diggingfossils

Oregon's Striking Azure Beauty!

Crater Lake

C rater Lake, in the southern Oregon Cascades, is a paradise for those who savor scenic driving, camping, hiking, and wildlife watching. The lake's translucent surface and dark, cold depths make for a scene of striking beauty. It is a place of moody moments, and like countless visitors I am overwhelmed by its size and awed by its sublime beauty. Its brilliant blue is magical, even enchanting, and yet its history speaks of ancient and fiery times.

The lake has been a national treasure since 1902, when Congress declared it a national park to be "dedicated and set apart forever as a public park or pleasure ground for the benefit and enjoyment of the people of the United States." That declaration, following seventeen years of lobbying by William Gladstone Steel, ensured forever that the 180,000 acres of surrounding hills and mountains, volcanic peaks, and vast evergreen forests would be protected forever.

I have always experienced timeless moments along the thirty-three-mile Rim Drive around the lake. This two-lane road has more than twenty scenic overlooks to stir the imagination about the power and fury of the incredible events that occurred here seven thousand years ago. Up until a few years ago I had always visited this setting of unparalleled beauty as a side journey following my fishing interests to another watery jewel not far to the north, Diamond Lake. But when I went aboard one of several forty-foot tour boats that motor across Crater Lake, I was able to admire this massive caldera of a burned-out mountain from quite a different point of view.

Ages ago, successive eruptions of magma built up impressive Mount Mazama to an estimated twelve thousand feet (about the height of Mount Hood). When the mountain cooled, glaciers cloaked its flanks and carved out deep valleys. About 6,800 years ago, the mountain erupted with lava and magma shooting toward the sky. The mountain collapsed, leaving the bowl-shaped caldera in its place. Over the ages, the bowl filled with snowmelt and rain and became a lake.

Our recent visit explored the lake from a water level point of view on the Crater Lake Boat Tour—an up close look at Oregon's striking azure beauty. Many people begin their visit at Crater Lake Lodge—the stone and timber destination for nearly a century—where folks will grab a bite, relax, and unwind—even spend the night and soak up the gorgeous scenery that lies some two thousand feet below.

It is distant scenery for sure so grab your day pack, lace up hiking boots, and don't forget water and a camera for if you want a closer view of Crater Lake, you must hike the trail to Cleetwood Cove. The seven-hundred-foot elevation drop on the Cleetwood Trail is done in a series of switchbacks but it doesn't take long to reach the boat dock where Captain Rick and Ranger Dave will welcome you aboard.

Hikers reserve a spot in advance to step aboard one of the eight daily Crater Lake boat tours. The boats seat up to forty-eight passengers and sport names like *Rogue*, *Klamath*, and *Umpqua*. "Mount Mazama's eruption was one hundred times as powerful as the eruption of Mount St. Helens in 1980," according to park ranger Dave Harrison, who hosted our two-hour voyage across the six-mile-wide lake. He added, "Today its ash lies scattered across eight states and three Canadian provinces." As we slowly trolled the azure water, all eyes of our two-score party were stunned by the size of the lake and the six-mile distance from shore to shore—a gigantic scene you cannot grasp from the high rim.

Dave noted that Crater Lake—when it was Mount Mazama—was taller than Mount Hood. "It is so calm and serene and peaceful out here today but that peace belies the violent nature of the birth of this place," said Dave. The two-hour tour motored near the rugged lake shoreline and offered unique points of view.

Dave noted our wonder and added, "When you look up the sides of the crater wall, you're actually looking at the insides of the mountain that started forming about four hundred thousand years ago. The different colored layers, the milky white, tan, and dark gray that you see, those are the ages of the lava as the mountain grew taller."

He called the lake a window on time at places like the Devil's Backbone, a rocky spine created as surface cracks allowed lava to ooze up and then freeze. It is now resistant to erosion from sun, wind, and water. It took five hundred years for the Mount Mazama caldera to become a lake—fed by forty-four feet of snowfall that produce thirty billion gallons of water—each year. He added that the azure blue color is in part a reflection of the sky but the two-thousand-foot depth and clarity of the lake contribute to the rich color too.

As we wrapped up our journey, Dave left us with this lingering thought: "It's good to protect places like this and watch the natural processes of life continue without human interruption. Many people drive to the lake, but never take time to explore it from the water—in fact, it's surprising how few people know that boat tours on Crater Lake are also part of this special recreation scene."

Visitors wishing to reach the shore of Crater Lake will need to hike the Cleetwood Cove Trail, two miles round-trip. Located on the north side of the lake, it is the only safe and legal access to the lake. Boat tours of the lake depart from Cleetwood Cove several times each day and operate from late June through mid-September. Travelers may stop at Wizard Island and take a later boat back to the dock. Bring water, a warm jacket, and your camera. If you hike, wear closed-toe shoes and bring plenty of water, sunscreen, and mosquito repellent. Toilets are available at both the trailhead and the boat dock area.

It's the immensity of the lake, the surrounding land, and what happened here thousands of years ago that prompts a respectful and contemplative silence that lasts long after the boat has returned to the dock. I was surprised to learn that less than 1 percent of Crater Lake visitors actually make the trek to Cleetwood Cove to experience the boat tour. That really is a shame because the trip offers an unmatched educational experience and stunning lesson on the geologic history of the Northwest. There are other overnight options beyond Crater Lake Lodge that include two National Park Campgrounds. You could also consider the nearby Joseph Stewart State Park Recreation Area and Campground.

For More Information

Where: From I-5, State Highway 138 east to the North Park Entrance (June-October)

Phone: 888-774-2728; Fax: 303-297-3175

Watch the Episode: www.traveloregon.com/craterlake

Swiss Alps of the West
Wallowa Lake State Park

I am a big believer in the adage "Our lives are but houses built of memories." It certainly holds true for me! Yet, strangely, I have the strongest, most lasting memories of meeting people and visiting places and experiencing adventures that unfortunately just didn't last long enough. Often, my fondness for a particular time and place has been the result of an escapade into a very distant, very wild place that demanded a great deal of planning and preparation. The Wallowa Mountains in far northeastern Oregon is such a place.

When artist George Keister searches for inspiration, he doesn't look far beyond his front step in northeast Oregon. George uses brushes and oil paints to capture the special places he's been lucky enough to visit in a career that spanned nearly four decades as a state wildlife biologist. He developed a keen eye and appreciation for the vast eastern Oregon point of view and now he paints it. "It is all so big and seems to go on forever, but when you actually start to paint it you need some kind of relief on the canvas. I can't just paint sagebrush and make it too interesting—that's often where the wildlife come in."

George paints the wildlife that live in the wild nooks and crannies of eastern Oregon. He said that too many people don't make time to see the region: "Too many people think they're in eastern Oregon when they get to Bend. In fact, they are just starting to enter it. I really like Wallowa County for that—it's big, it's beautiful, and you have to come here, not go through here."

One place to see and enjoy that "big, beautiful country" is at a state park that will capture your heart: Wallowa Lake State Park at the southern edge of Wallowa Lake near Joseph, Oregon. State Park Manager Todd Honeywell said that visitors will find plenty of recreation in a year-round campground that offers more than two hundred

The towering Wallowa Mountains make you feel small when you're boating across Wallowa Lake.

sites for tent or trailer: "It is a destination park! Everyone comes here because they want to—it's not a place you just happen to hit on your way somewhere else. Boats, fishing, water-skiing—you name it, we have it on the lake."

Wallowa Lake State Park's boat launch is free for anyone to use and has courtesy docks available for boats as well. In addition, there is no day-use fee so you're free to come in, sit on the beach, enjoy it, or go fishing. That's not all—a recent addition to the parkland scene is the newest site at the north end of the lake, a sixty-two-acre parcel of protection.

The Iwetemlaykin State Heritage Site is a grassland with stunning views of the Wallowa Mountains. Pronounced Ee-weh-TEMM-lye-kinn, the name translates to "at the edge of the lake." The property is adjacent to a Nez Perce National Historical Park, site of Old Chief Joseph Gravesite and Cemetery. Oregon Parks and Recreation Department Park Ranger Madeline Lau said that the area is the ancestral homeland of the Joseph band of the Nez Perce tribe. It is a sacred place to the native peoples who helped secure its protection in partnership with Oregon State Parks. "This park has a much more peaceful vibe," said Madeline. "It is meant for walking, experiencing nature, and ideally—thinking about the Nez Perce history in this area and how important this land was to them."

This state park is adjacent to Wallowa Lake Village, home to several commercial lodges, restaurants, cafes, and other amenities, such as bumper boats, canoeing, bike rentals, and miniature golf. The nearby Wallowa Pack Station is the oldest continuous

The Mount Howard Tram ride provides a spacious perspective on Wallowa Lake and the surrounding countryside. This trip is a must when you visit the area.

packing business in northeast Oregon, offering a variety of guided rides from hourly to ten-day vacation pack trips for those who seek adventure on horseback.

With the opening in 1970 of the Mount Howard Tramway—the steepest in America—Wallowa County added one of its most popular attractions. Rising 690 feet a minute to an elevation of 3,700 feet, the tramway will take your breath away. The exciting trip to the top of the mountain allows you to enjoy the view as the four-passenger gondola rises above Wallowa Lake Village and the azure blue waters of Wallowa Lake. During this spectacular ride, you get a view of the Eagle Cap Wilderness and its rugged peaks. Upon arriving at the upper terminal, you can explore the summit area and enjoy the extensive variety of alpine plants and vegetation along any of the many trails. Interpretive signs and information help you make the most of your walk. The tramway manager, Kevin Almas, told me, "It's your chance to look down at a real pristine area. From below, you just cannot see the entire valley, but way up here you can see everything for miles around."

The walk to the Wallowa Valley overlook is about a quarter mile and takes most people between fifteen and twenty minutes one way. It serves up a breathtaking view of the valley where Chief Joseph and his people spent their summers. The communities of Joseph, Enterprise, Lostine, and Wallowa are visible. The summer and fall season typically begins at the end of June on the lower elevation trails and runs to the end of November.

Nearby, another historic structure is worth your time for a visit: Wallowa Lake

Lodge—the oldest private hotel at the lake that dates to 1923. Like the nearby state park, the lodge is a convenient walking distance to varied activities that the entire family will enjoy.

The Eagle Cap Wilderness with bare granite peaks and forested ridges and U-shaped glaciated valleys characterizes this enormous wilderness area of nearly half a million acres. All of it is accessible to visitors who are willing to take the time and explore a corner of Oregon full of wonder and surprise. "It is the kind of place that takes a dedicated effort to get into because we're at the end of the road," said local resident Steve Larson. "But when folks come here—almost universally it's, 'Oh my gosh—this is a gorgeous place.' Because it really is!"

For More Information

Wallowa Lake State Park
Where: Off State Highway 82, 6 miles south of Joseph, OR
Web: www.oregonstateparks.org
Phone: 541-432-4185 or 800-551-6949

Wallowa Lake Tramway
Where: 59919 Wallowa Lake Highway, Joseph, OR 97846
Web: www.wallowalaketramway.com
Phone: Summer: 541-432-5331; Winter: 503-781-4321

Iwetemlaykin State Heritage Site
Where: Off State Highway 82, one mile north of Wallowa Lake on the
    south end of Joseph, OR
Web: www.oregonstateparks.org

Watch the Episode: www.traveloregon.com/wallowalake

September

Take Aim!
Oregon Archery

There is a recreational resurgence of a sport that is as old as human culture and while many say it never really disappeared, archery appears to be in fine form and more popular than ever in Oregon. At its simplest, all you really need is a stick, a piece of string, and a shaft of wood to discover the world of archery.

John Strunk dreams of carving the perfect bow from the perfect piece of wood. He gently draws a knife blade across the bark of a vine maple stick and paper-thin curly-Q strips of shaved maple rise, fall, and float to the floor. As John carefully crafts his next tool from the six-foot long, lanky stick of wood, it's clear that the Tillamook County resident has a master bow maker's touch. "When I start cutting out a bow, my hunt, my thoughts, my dreams are all generating at the same time," said John. He added, "If you really try you can build a bow just like the Native Americans."

For nearly forty years, John has tried and succeeded in creating everything he needs just like native people might have: the bows, the arrows, quivers, and broad heads. The natural materials he prefers for bow making include bamboo, maple, osage, and the long-popular and gorgeous yew wood: "Yew is probably one of the most used woods in archery in the northern hemisphere," he said with a smile.

The native Oregonian said his passion for the bow was born as a kid—watching movies like Robin Hood that starred the-then popular Hollywood actor Errol Flynn. "I love to shoot a bow just to see an arrow fly and it gives me more pleasure to do it with a bow that I have made," declared John. He's a longtime hunter who is among the best in the country at building bows in a form called traditional or primitive archery.

The retired Tillamook schoolteacher not only excels at building the bows and arrows, but at shooting with them too. He admitted that an evening doesn't go by when he leaves the shop behind and steps into the backyard to shoot arrows. "You need to train the muscles that are needed for shooting and that is done only by shooting lots of arrows. To me, that's the essential love affair that I have with this sport. If I'm not using what I create, then I lose interest in it."

By all accounts, thousands of folks have renewed interest in this ancient sport that puts each individual in control of their actions. At Tigard's Archers Afield—one of Oregon's largest indoor shooting ranges—twenty-eight lanes are jammed with youngsters learning how it's done.

Manager Kris Demeter said that young imaginations are fueled by movies like *Brave* and *The Hunger Games* whose main characters discover independence and self-reliance with a bow and arrows. "We have many teenage girls coming in that want to resemble or be like the main characters they see in those two movies. They want to wear the back quivers or shoot the longbows—it's remarkable," noted the longtime manager. Kris is an accomplished archer and she has been the archery instructor at Archers Afield for the past twenty-seven years. Newcomer Gabe Bolden said that he learned something new his first visit: "I learned that instead of standing flat square facing the target, it's best to turn for a better aim—it's true."

Back at John Strunk's Tillamook workshop, he agreed that the learning never stops, and that's a good thing. It keeps the sport fresh, engaging, and exciting. He remains motivated to build more bows and shoot more arrows. "It becomes a passion and that's what it's all about for it helps to build lifelong friendships too—I've many brothers in archery. Who couldn't have fun doing this?"

You can reach out to John's Spirit Longbows to learn more about building bows and arrows. He teaches classes in the craft throughout the year. Traditional archery is more popular than ever and you can find clubs and shooting ranges across Oregon to give it a try. If you are interested in learning how to shoot modern bows, try the Oregon Bowhunters Assocation.

For More Information

Archers Afield
Where: 11945 SW Pacific Highway, #121, Portland, OR 97223
Web: www.archersafield.com
Phone: 503-639-3553

Spirit Longbows
Where: Tillamook, OR
Web: www.tradbow.com
Phone: 503-842-4944

Watch the Episode: www.traveloregon.com/archery

Out 'n Back Adventures
Willamette Valley Wanderings

My television reports entitled "Gas Tank Getaways" have long been a favorite of mine for their convenience and lasting enjoyment. The unique out-'n-back adventures won't break the bank on auto fuel, and they are the kind of exciting activity in which the journey can afford as much pleasure as the destination. I'm especially fond of the trips that breeze along some of Oregon's finer back roads on a crisp late September afternoon, when summer's glorious colors have faded and an amber glow wraps the land while the seasonal bounty is harvested from Willamette Valley farms.

Perhaps you'll get as much of a kick out of this picture as me when you travel high on the spine of a ridgeline to find two spectacular views for the price of one stop at Bald Peak State Park. At nearly 1,700 feet in elevation, Bald Peak offers a miles-wide checkerboard perspective on Willamette Valley farmlands to the east. On a clear day, you can pick out three Cascade peaks, including Mount St. Helens, Mount Hood, and Mount Jefferson. If you step a hundred yards to the west and glance over to the Tualatin

Enjoy a breathtaking view of the Tualatin Valley from atop Bald Peak State Park.

Valley, you'll also see the rising Coast Range just beyond. In a soaring grove of Douglas fir, take your pick from dozens of picnic tables scattered here and there. To the east of a vast parking area, stroll across the open grass meadow that serves as the peak's namesake. This marks the perfect site for an October afternoon picnic lunch, though there is no drinking water available in this park.

From atop Bald Peak, a wavy ribbon of asphalt carries your four-wheeled land schooner south to Dayton. From Dayton, stay on State Highway 221 for approximately eight miles and pull into Maud Williamson State Park, where enormous Douglas firs shelter the picnic sites and a rough-hewn post-and-beam timber shelter can be reserved for larger groups. This is a park that's entertained families since 1934, when the Williamson family donated the land to Oregon. (Note: That's the family's whitewashed home that still dominates the scene.) Maud Williamson is a wonderfully shaded recreational oasis. The park is equipped with toilet facilities; volleyball and horseshoes are available; plus there's lots of room to roam. The ease of access from State Highway 221 makes it another ideal site for a quick lunch stop.

The park is pleasant, but there's more for the curious just around the bend and a quick dash down an intersecting lane to the Wheatland Ferry dock. This is where the *Daniel Matheny V* river ferry drops her steel gate, unloads her passengers, and quickly takes on more for the short ride across the broad Willamette River. There was a time when ferry travel was a common and necessary experience along the Willamette River, but not anymore. Now there are but two other river ferries (nearby Buena Vista and Canby) that work from one side of the river to the other.

The flat-bottomed *Daniel Matheny V* is based at a once-functioning pioneer wheat port, but it is far from a nostalgic tourist attraction. It's all about the business of transporting vehicles and commerce: an average of six hundred cars and trucks a day, and during peak periods commuters and farm trucks may wait as long as twenty minutes to make the five-minute crossing. A ferry has operated here since 1844. The *Daniel Matheny V*, the newest, was delivered in 2002 and has onboard computers and a diesel generator that has eliminated the need for the overhead electric lines that once powered the ferry. While auto drivers will have to pay a small fee for the short journey from shore to shore, bicyclists and pedestrians still ride for free.

Once you've landed on the Willamette's western shore, it's only a matter of a mile to reach the entrance to rambling Willamette Mission State Park: 1,680 acres of fantastic picnic opportunities and many group sites for larger crowds, making it a long-favored destination for family reunions. You'll find a wide variety of natural settings and accommodations for varied recreation at this day-use park (no overnight camping allowed, but open from dawn to dusk daily; small entrance fee charged during the peak of tourist season—Memorial Day to Labor Day—larger fee to reserve group picnic shelters). Plus, nearby Mission Lake is ideally suited for gentle canoeing (no motors allowed). Eight miles of trails wind throughout the park with an incredible number of native birds, plants, and wildlife. This parkland also offers many photo opportunities, including one of the oldest trees in the state. A massive cottonwood tree stands 158 feet high with a canopy that spreads more than 110 feet wide. The circumference at the trunk is more than 27 feet, and the limbs are as big as most tree trunks. The gnarly bark resembles plowed furrows that stretch hundreds of feet into the air. Some estimate the tree dates back to 1735. Taking a moment to stand beside it and feel its age is a worthy pause.

You may wish to consider the role this historic area played in Oregon's early political and religious development too. Willamette Mission is named for the site where in 1834 pioneer Jason Lee established the Oregon Territory's first Methodist church. Although nothing remains of the original buildings, follow the well-marked trail to an interpretive plaque that explains Lee's role in early Oregon. It's a peaceful place with a fine wooden bench on which to sit while taking special note of a rambling pink rose bush that grows near the plaque; it descends from the original bush that was planted near here almost 170 years ago.

For More Information

Bald Peak State Park
Where: Near Newberg, State Highway 219 north 4 miles to Bald Peak State Road and then 5 miles to park.
Web: www.oregonstateparks.org
Phone: 800-551-6949

Wheatland Ferry
Where: From I-5 take Brooks exit and drive west to Wheatland Road.
Web: www.co.marion.or.us
Phone: 503-588-7979

Watch the Episode: www.traveloregon.com/fallwanderings

Fishing for Kings
Tillamook Bay

September is prime time for "king fishing." King Chinook salmon, that is! There is a simple reason that they are called "kings": after all, the big fish can tip the scales at fifty pounds or more. And if you're eager to catch a king, you arrive at the Garibaldi docks an hour before sunrise. Longtime Oregon fishing guide John Krauthoefer told our huddled group of anglers: "It's the early bird who gets the worm, men! This has become such a popular fishery that if you wait and go late, you might miss the bite."

By mid-September, thousands of salmon begin migrating through dozens of West Coast estuaries like Tillamook Bay and then swim into their home rivers. As we motored out of the marina, John noted that it had been a wet and wild weather week and that several big storms had pumped up a huge ocean. As we approached the ocean, we watched huge swells rise and fall—sometimes fishing boats would briefly vanish as the swells passed by. The bar was closed—no one would be heading out onto the ocean today.

Birt Hansen, a longtime fishing partner, had joined John and me on Tillamook Bay where scores

Fishing guide John Krauthoefer shows off a thirty-pound king Chinook that he caught from Tillamook Bay.

of other anglers had also gathered—we were excited, anxious, and ready for action. After all, low tide was about to turn to flood and it might serve up the biggest of all the salmon species called king. "It's a perfect tide for fishing out along the jetty," noted John. "There's a small exchange. What those fish do is smell that outgoing Tillamook water and because the current isn't very strong, they'll come in against that tide. So, we'll fish the slack into the flooding tide."

John quickly baited up the rods and reels with plug-cut herring. John's a big believer that a plug-cut herring makes the best bait when fishing for Chinook. He makes a bevel cut with his razor sharp knife just behind the herring's head to make the bait spin when it's trolled in the water. He explained: "This is their (salmon) natural feed out in the ocean and they'll eat it like candy. You just have to get it in front of one. That's the big trick. So just slowly drop down it down to the bottom. When you hit the bottom, bring it back up about two, three cranks of the reel."

We dropped our lines over the side and John began a slow troll with the tide. As the tide turned to flood, signs of salmon life began to appear as nearby anglers hooked up. It happened to us too! "Get him, get him," John yelled. Suddenly, I had my hands full with a hard-charging king that had decided to head back to sea. John put his motor in gear and followed the salmon. With a wry smile, he noted, "They're strong and full of muscle and they let you know that they're on the other end of the line."

After a twenty-minute tug of war, the gleaming twenty-pound salmon came to the net and it was scooped aboard. "A beauty! That's really a pretty one and they don't get any nicer than that," noted John. "The only thing nicer is we got to get the gear back in the water and get some more." John added that a big ocean, coupled with a forecast of more squalls and storms, means that anglers must be on guard against a dreaded fishing disease: "Don't get salmonitis!" he said with a chuckle. "That's a disease where you get so focused on fishing that you forget about your surroundings. This area of the bar can be dangerous. You can get in trouble if you don't pay attention at all times. Things change out here very quickly."

It can be a challenge to fish along the jetty—where the swells and the waves and the tide can combine to change conditions in a heartbeat. We wore our inflatable PFDs (personal flotation devices) at all times. John would not give us—or any of his passengers—any choice. For him, the angler's safety is personal. "These are self-inflating vests and we wear them all day in my boats. I had a friend drown a few years ago and if he'd had one on, he'd be alive today. They're very comfortable and you don't even know you've got them on."

Sport anglers catch more than twelve thousand king salmon on the bar, the bay, and the five rivers that flow into the bay on their way to the sea. So, special rules are in place to protect the kings from overharvest. An angler can keep one king per day and

Smoking the Catch

It's always a challenge to catch a big salmon, but now that I had landed a dandy, twenty-pound chrome bright salmon, what to do with the catch? I didn't have to travel far to discover one delicious idea!

Karla Steinhauser likes to say she hasn't met a salmon that she doesn't like—to smoke—the old-fashioned way. Nearly half a century of experience in the Tillamook County village of Rockaway, Oregon, has led her to use alder and vine maple in a smoky fire. Through the years, she has prepared tons of sushi-grade salmon, sturgeon, cod, and albacore tuna with a simple cure of two parts kosher salt and one part brown sugar. She cuts the fish into numerous small chunks and places each on racks inside her famous wood smoker.

I joined her in the smoking room as she pulled a fresh batch of golden hued salmon and tuna from the mammoth wood smoker that once had a life as a stainless steel crab cooker. But Karla had a better idea for the piece and thought that if the cooker was turned on end it would make a better smoker. She was right!

"I basically taught myself—the fish has to be done in the thickest part of the fish—I pick up each piece and look for color and feel for firmness. It's a touchy sort of thing but forty-six years of experience lets me know when the time is right to take it out."

She learned her way around a kitchen from her Norwegian grandmother and her business savvy father and Karla's Smokehouse has been a fixture on the north coast since 1964. "My dad always said that during the Depression there were two businesses that never go broke—the beer joints and the banks—so I thought, I don't drink, so food is the way to go because people have to eat. I wanted a business that I controlled and one where I wasn't likely to lose my job."

So, the college graduate (she attended Portland's Washington High School and Lewis and Clark College) who double majored in art and biology created a "beachy" life for herself—one that offered independence and self-reliance. This year, she decided the time had come for a change! She wanted to slow down a bit and thought it would be good to share her secrets in a book: *I Am Karla's Smokehouse.*

"I always wanted to pass on what I knew to the public, which is ironic because when I was young, customers scared the dickens out of me. I was so scared of people that I asked the hired help to wait on the people. I was so shy and I had to overcome that. It took a lot of time, but eventually I did and writing a book was much the same for me, a big challenge!"

I Am Karla's Smokehouse is an enjoyable and easy to read text that offers practical how-to techniques in every phase of fish smoking. The many photographs are by local photographer Don Best and show detailed, step-by-step pictures of filleting varied fish species, the proper application of the cure, and the fish's appearance at the end of the smoking time.

The book also offers Karla's own colorful art of whimsical moments that make you smile. "I make myself look ridiculous with a long spiked nose and a great big belly and skinny legs. I am really a satirist and make fun of myself. It is expressing the real me to people and giving them the proper techniques. I want to be a teacher!" So stop in and say "Hello!" Chances are good that Karla will be there with her friendly smile and easygoing manner as she tends the smoky fires. It's a warm and welcoming place where "class" is always in session.

For More Information

Where: Karla's Smokehouse, 2010 US Highway 101, Rockaway Beach, OR 97136
Web: www.karlassmokehouse.com
Phone: 503-355-2362

five per season from Tillamook Bay or its rivers. In addition, anglers can also keep a hatchery coho salmon.

Our luck soon changed too! John's rod doubled down from another fresh king salmon. "Oh, just let him run if he wants to run," noted Birt. "That fish was in the ocean five minutes ago so it's full of fight." The battle was on as another twenty-pound king charged down to the bottom. After twenty minutes, the shimmering silver Chinook came to the net and I lifted it aboard. "That's as pretty a king as the last," noted John. "What a beauty and it's funny; after you've fished for years and years, your knees still shake when the fish is in the boat. It's a great experience."

While Birt enjoys the fishing, he admitted that there are other reasons to go fishing for kings in Tillamook Bay: "The attraction to me is really the outdoors—just watching nature around you—the varied bird life and other wildlife that live here. Plus, the smell and sounds of the bay and the nearby ocean's pounding surf—all of it creates lifetime memories."

For More Information

Where: Firefighter's Guide Service, PO Box 141, Tillamook, OR 97141
Web: www.oregoncoastfishingguide.com
Phone: 503-812-1414
Watch the Episode: www.traveloregon.com/kings

Dinosaurs with Fins
The Giants at Bonneville Fish Hatchery

It is a fact of Pacific Northwest angling life that few fish species swimming in our rivers or streams can match the massive size and strength of the prehistoric fish called sturgeon. Sturgeon can exceed ten feet in length and weigh more than four hundred pounds, so few would argue that the fish provide a terrific angling challenge. In summer, one of the best places to try your luck with hook and line for catch and release sturgeon fishing is the Columbia River estuary near Astoria. I like to call it "fishing for a dinosaur": the fish species known as Columbia River sturgeon. (Oregon fishery managers have shifted away from sturgeon retention to primarily a catch and release fishery.)

A slate-colored morning rises across the powerful Columbia River. The otherwise drab gray sunrise touched the shore and only dully lightened the dark skyline as Joe Salvey of Fish Hawk Adventures motored his boat away from the placid port at Astoria, Oregon. Joe is one of the regular Oregon fishing guides who takes newcomers and experienced anglers alike across the lower Columbia River. The anglers who joined us for this adventure included Leroy Howe, Ed Bruser, longtime fishing partner Trey Carskadon, and the father-son team of Richard and David Parker.

Each anticipated an exciting day of angling fun for a fish species as old as time. You see, sturgeon have been swimming across the planet's waters for more than two hundred million years—long before the age of dinosaurs. Joe noted that we had much to look forward to: "Right now, the sturgeon fish are coming in out of the ocean to eat the anchovies so it's a good time of year to catch a big one."

Joe is a fishing specialist who knows just where to be on a fast falling tide in the vast salt chuck near Astoria. The fish that live here are big—so is the gear: nine-foot rods, heavy duty reels loaded with sixty-five-pound test line, large hooks that held sand shrimp or whole anchovy for bait. All of that terminal gear was held on the bottom with eight ounces of lead weight.

As he smoothly cast each of our lines to create a half-moon shaped array of baited lines whose rods were firmly mounted in rod holders, Joe noted that we were in the right place at the right time: "We don't get a lot of small fish down here—in fact, the average fish is usually four to four-and-a-half-feet long—and we've certainly come to sturgeon central for there are lots of fish in this part of the river." I glanced over to Trey Carskadon who was intently watching his rod tip dance—down-two-three-four—up-two three-four—in a quick time motion, like an Irish jig. "Trey!" shouted Joe. "Get ready! It's a fish bite." Trey's rod danced the two-step one more time before he reared back on the arcing graphite rod, firmly setting the hook in the fish. He left no doubt to all of us who watched that his sturgeon was firmly a fish on! "That's a big fish right there," noted Joe.

That much was certain as the line played out from the sturgeon that seemed to have one thing on its mind—get back to the ocean—and fast! Trey held his ground and let the fish run away from the boat for twenty, thirty, forty yards before he slowly worked the sturgeon back toward the boat. He told me, "Right here in the Columbia River is the largest population of white sturgeon on the planet. Biologists figure that the population is about one million fish below Bonneville Dam." But the fact is, sturgeon fishing wasn't always so popular.

Trey said that while the ancient fish have been swimming in the Columbia River for thousands of years, most Pacific Northwest anglers have looked down on them until recently. "Around the late 1980s, when our salmon fishery slowed down a bit and suddenly sturgeon fishing became a go-to fishery. People caught on to the magic of catching these wonderful fish."

"Nice and easy, Trey," coached Joe. "Don't forget to breathe. That's a good fish." It was a huge fish too—easily four feet long—perhaps much longer—and perhaps reached forty pounds—or more. Joe's net dipped as Trey pulled the rod back and the fish slid into the mesh—"in the bag" as they like to say. "Good fish!"

As the morning tide reached full ebb, each angler in the boat had similar opportunities to repeat what Trey enjoyed: hooking and releasing sturgeon. My turn came as my fishing rod doubled over and throbbed down hard. I wrestled it from the rod holder and held on for dear life. "Oh, it's a nice one, Joe," was all I could mumble as I prayed the hook would hold tight.

"Oh, look at the size of that one, Grant! Biggest one of the day," shouted Joe. Finally, time and patience held as I brought the large sturgeon to the side of the boat. Joe estimated the weight at nearly forty pounds. "Wow! Now that's some kind of sturgeon!" I noted with a huge smile.

There were plenty of smiles and plenty of sturgeon to go around as we all agreed that the sturgeon's strength was unmatched. Ed Bruser, another longtime angler and frequent client on board Joe's adventures, may have summed it up best: "I always describe it as standing on the side of the freeway and hooking the back of an F-350 doing seventy-five miles per hour. It's exciting to catch these fish."

Sturgeon live in rivers but also migrate to the ocean. You can see them alive and well at the Oregon Department of Fish and Wildlife's (ODFW) Bonneville Fish Hatchery in the Columbia River Gorge. Bonneville Hatchery has long been a popular

Herman the Sturgeon, a nearly ten-foot-long specimen, is the star attraction at Bonneville Hatchery.

destination for good reason. You see, as far back as a century ago the state-run facility raised thousands of baby fish for release. But this was a time long before roads, so the railroad was the only way to transport baby fish to reach horse and pack trains that would trek into distant Oregon lakes and streams.

It's an Oregon fish hatchery with a front row seat into prehistory. Greg Davis, ODFW's Bonneville hatchery manager, told me, "You are literally face to face with really big sturgeon; as close as six inches away, separated only by a thick piece of glass. We consider it our little aquarium." Greg noted, "There isn't another opportunity that I know of in Oregon where you can view a sturgeon quite like this—underwater—it's a unique opportunity to see a large ten or twelve-foot-long sturgeon up close and personal."

Two windows of one-inch-thick Plexiglas are all that separate 450-pound Herman the Sturgeon from his adoring fans at Bonneville Hatchery in the Columbia Gorge. Herman is a nine-foot, ten-inch-long white sturgeon, probably seventy years old, and a member of a fish family dating back some two hundred million years. The Oregon Department of Fish and Wildlife, working closely with the Oregon Wildlife Heritage Foundation, designed the "Home for Herman" to give him room to move about in a natural setting while allowing visitors to stay dry while watching him below water level.

The pond measures thirty feet by one hundred feet and is about ten feet deep, and unless you're a Columbia River fisherman, you've never been able to see a sturgeon so well, or to learn about their biology from well-designed information panels located near the windows. For the most part, these giants of the Northwest are bottom dwellers, and their pea-size eyes don't allow them to see much in the murky depths of a river, so they rely upon four hairlike projections called barbels that are located at the ends of their snouts. These help the fish find food and feel their way along the river bottom.

Instead of scales, sturgeon have tough skin and rows of bony, diamond-shaped plates along their lateral sides and down their top sides or dorsals. The plates are called scutes (pronounced skoots), and biologists think of them as a sort of fish armor. It seems that in prehistoric times sturgeon were entirely covered by these scutes for protection against even larger predator fish. Sturgeons also have upturned, sharklike tails and skeletons largely made of cartilage and less of bone. Sturgeon historically migrated throughout the Columbia River basin to the Pacific Ocean and can grow to twenty feet, weigh a thousand pounds or more, and live for more than a hundred years.

The first reference to a sturgeon named "Herman" occurred in 1925 at either the Bonneville or the Roaring River Hatchery near Scio. The very first report of a sturgeon named "Herman" occurred in 1935 when a former game commissioner raised the fish to be shown each year at the Oregon State Fair. This Herman was stolen from the Roaring River Hatchery in the middle of the night. Other "Hermans" have fulfilled the role since then.

These days, Bonneville Hatchery raises eleven million salmon, steelhead, and trout across a facility that's a most amazing parklike setting. "It's a great tribute to our ground staff," said Greg. "The grounds are beautiful—flowers and gorgeous plants throughout and it's a fine place to spend a Saturday afternoon and it's close to Portland." Best of all, it is also free! Since 1998, the Sturgeon Exhibit has given up to half a million visitors a year the chance to see a species seldom seen so close. "We hear oooh's and ahhh's all of the time from the visitors," added Greg. "Folks are so impressed to walk up and see something that huge that is slowly swimming past them—almost seeming to eye the visitors as they pass by."

But let Bonneville Fish Hatchery be just the start of your journey to other gigantic discoveries in the Columbia River Gorge. As you travel east on the interstate highway, make time to stop, learn, and experience rich lessons in natural and cultural history at the Columbia Gorge Discovery Center and Wasco County Museum in The

Dalles. Since 1997, the center has been the showcase setting and interpretive site for the National Scenic Area in the Columbia River Gorge. The Discovery Center's awesome entrance will captivate and leave you spellbound.

Spokesperson Roxie Pennington said, "We're perched on one of the most phenomenally beautiful scenic outlooks in the Gorge. As you walk inside our entrance and gaze up and through the pillars, you are drawn out of the glass wall to see the distant Klickatat Hills and even more sky than most people see every day." Spokesperson John Connolly added, "The Discovery Center is far more than dramatic scenery—the center links people to Oregon's rich cultural histories too—framed by the beauty and immensity of it all—it's a beautiful area to come celebrate and it's right out our backdoor."

For More Information

Fish Hawk Adventures
Where: 33896 SE Elm Street, Scappoose, OR 97056
Web: www.fishhawkadventures.com
Phone: 503-349-1411

Bonneville Hatchery
Where: 70543 NE Herman Loop, Cascade Locks, OR 97014
Web: www.dfw.state.or.us
Phone: 541-374-8393

Columbia Gorge Discovery Center and
Wasco County Museum
Where: 5000 Discovery Drive, The Dalles, OR 97058
Web: www.gorgediscovery.org
Phone: 541-296-8600

Watch the Episode: www.traveloregon.com/dinosaurswithfins

All Hands on Deck
Newport

The Oregon coast is a place where carefree moments are easy to come by and can make you feel young all over. One place in particular—Yaquina Bay at Newport—offers a perspective to the marine world that's unique and educational. Don and Fran Mathews own and operate Marine Discovery Tours (MDT), and the centerpiece of their ecotourism business is *Discovery*, a sixty-five-foot boat that's as much a floating science laboratory as it is a retired fishing craft. Marine Discovery Tours specializes in trips that teach visitors more about the ocean, the estuary, and all of the marine life that can be found there. "We have travelers come from all over the world," noted Fran. "And they're here to find the real Oregon coast. Well, we can offer that—we have our beautiful four-thousand-acre Yaquina Bay and twelve miles of Yaquina River too—plus—the big blue Pacific Ocean is just off Newport's front step."

Fran's husband, Don Mathews, is a former commercial fisherman who ranged across the Pacific all the way to the Bering Sea before settling at Newport. He noted, "After all of my travels, it makes me feel quite grateful that I'm able to work and live and play on the Oregon coast." Who wouldn't feel grateful on a sun-kissed day where a rising tide found skipper Don steering *Discovery* across the bay for a typical two-hour exploration of the estuary. Fran observed that her "class," thirty-three folks of all ages from all across the country—had one thing on their minds: "Oh, people just want to do stuff—and so we have them pulling crab pots, pulling plankton nets, visiting with our naturalist, chatting with Don in the wheelhouse, and even driving the boat."

The Mathews have been guiding visitors across the bay for fifteen years. They were the first to try their hands at ecotourism in Newport and it has really taken off for them—and even for longtime local residents who learn something new. "We have Oregonians who live on the coast who've never been out on the ocean," said Fran.

Hands-on adventure with Marine Discovery Tours includes learning how to catch fresh Dungeness crabs from Yaquina Bay.

"And it's such an eye-opener for them to see home from the opposite direction instead of always being on land and looking out."

Steven Mulvey, the MDT's official onboard naturalist, added that it's also an experience that puts people to work—but in a fun way! "All hands on deck for hands on science," said Steven. He retrieved a thirty-foot length of rope floating off the starboard side of the *Discovery*. The rope was tied to a submerged crab pot. As he handed the rope to one of the guests he said, "Pull, pull, pull!"

Soon the trap appeared at the surface and Steven hoisted it aboard. Inside the crab trap, a half-dozen Dungeness crabs scurried across the wire mesh bottom. "Okay folks—we hit the jackpot—lots of crab here—who wants to hold a Dungeness crab?" he yelled to the crowd. Several tentative hands went up and each person had a chance to hold and examine a crab up close as Steven explained, "A female Dungeness will release about a million eggs per crab per season. Now, that's productivity! The ocean affects everything. It affects the climate. It affects our food—where our food comes from—and so it is really important to protect it and understand it."

Fran watched the activity on the back deck and added, "Our best day everyday is to get people out on our boat and let them feel like they own a part of all of this. Because we really do! Look at this beautiful waterway. This belongs to all of us—don't you think we should learn all we can about it?" Nearby, there's another destination that may help you to answer Fran's question.

I am a big believer that learning more about the places that I visit is critically important to appreciating all that Oregon has to offer. So, in Newport I regularly stop in at the Hatfield Marine Science Center (HMSC). Located on the south side of Yaquina Bay, just off US Highway 101, the center is one of the best bargains of the entire area. Hatfield MSC is a professional science base that is the home for scores of scientists linked with Oregon State University.

The exhibit areas of the center are open to the public and admission is free, although donations are accepted and appreciated. The center is like a window to the ocean with exhibits that display the varied marine species that are found just off Oregon's coastal shore. Bill Hanshumaker, HMSC's education director, explained, "I think the animals are the big attractor, and my challenge is to enhance the learning that takes place with hands-on activities, talks, lectures . . . we're helping expand the knowledge of the people that walk through the door and I promise—you will not be bored!"

For More Information

Marine Discovery Tours
Where: 345 SW Bay Boulevard, Newport, OR 97365
Web: www.marinediscovery.com
Phone: 800-903-BOAT or 541-265-6200

Hatfield Marine Science Center
Where: 2030 SE Marine Science Drive, Newport, OR 97365
Web: www.hmsc.oregonstate.edu
Phone: 541-867-0100

Watch the Episode: www.traveloregon.com/marinescience

Hidden Treasures
Wolf Creek Inn State Heritage Site

In Southern Oregon, history runs as deep as the forested canyons where the early miners hit pay dirt in Oregon's early days of gold mining. It's a landscape marked by "Forgotten Dreams and Hidden Treasures" at an Oregon state heritage site that makes you feel right at home called the Wolf Creek Inn.

The Wolf Creek Inn was made for the road weary. It was built in 1883 and remains the state's oldest operating hotel. Over a century ago, it was a highlight stopover on a twelve-day stagecoach ride between San Francisco and Portland that transitioned to the railroad and then the automobile. The Wolf Creek Inn established a tradition of comfort and service that continues today.

The Wolf Creek Inn—located just off I-5, less than twenty miles north of Grants Pass—is operated by Mark and Margaret Quist, who fell in love with the scenery, the location, and the history. "Oh, it was a hard life back then," noted Mark. "Rough—real rough, hard work and long days and this place was built specifically for travelers on the road." Margaret added with a smile, "You're staying at a park, but you don't have to use a tent." The Quists have operated one of Oregon's landmark properties for the past couple of years and say the door is always open and anyone can stop in and look around.

As the oldest active hotel in Oregon, the site offers nine rooms that cater to visitors from all over the world. Guests have included celebrities, the rich and the powerful who needed an escape and often found it on the nearby Rogue River. In fact, in the early days of the twentieth century, anglers discovered that the Rogue's waters held big trout and exciting white-water rapids. So dudes signed up for thrilling river trips that provided daylong white-knuckle adventures and the allure of big fish. At the end of the trip, the inn provided a warm meal and a soft bed.

Mark said that little has changed through the decades. "Clark Gable and

Carol Lombard often came to Wolf Creek in the 1930s and stayed in one particular room on each visit. Robert Redford spent some time here during the filming of the fly-fishing scenes of *A River Runs Through It*." The spacious inn was acquired by the state of Oregon in 1975 and the agency embarked on a four-year multimillion dollar remodel. The historic building has nooks and crannies worth exploring: in fact, there is the Jack London room—a tiny enclave where the famous author boarded for over a year back in 1911—while a resident of the inn, he wrote several short stories and a novel.

The arched entry to Wolf Creek Inn welcomes visitors with a certain charm and down-home comfort. It's a place that can set your clock back and put you at ease.

In those days, men and women socialized in separate parlors, each room complete with piano and a warming fire. Mark added that the women would stay in a separate parlor, "Because the men were doing things the women didn't want to be a part of—drinking and smoking. All of the rooms are furnished in antiques, so it's like stepping back in time."

In fact, a small museum on the second floor shows off photos from the bygone past that hint at a lifestyle that seems so foreign today. Yet it is history worth exploring at another nearby state park property just up the road from Wolf Creek Inn. "Golden, Oregon, was never really a town—more like a mining camp," noted Oregon Parks and Recreation Manager Anna Krug. Golden was a booming place in the 1850s when millions of dollars in gold was dug or power-washed out of nearby Coyote Creek. At one time there were as many as twenty-five buildings including several homes, a general store, a blacksmith shop, a school, and a church.

Remarkably, four buildings remain standing at the Golden State Heritage Site today. It's a state park that you can visit anytime. "The Golden Church is especially worth your time to visit," added Anna. "It really is the iconic building for Golden; religion and family came first! You can walk up onto the porch and it's like—well, it is stepping back in history—there's wooden pews, a pulpit up front, and the glass windows are historical glass and make you feel as though you are stepping into the golden days of Golden. The experience really gives you that sense of history and of place."

Back at the Wolf Creek Inn, there's always a place for you at a dining table where delicious meals are served throughout the day before you stroll across three acres of landscaped grounds complete with a historic orchard. Mark said that many trees in the orchard are more than 130 years old: "The history of homesteading is that you put down your roots and usually that meant you put in an orchard. It was the simplest and easiest thing you could do to provide for the future." Margaret added that Wolf Creek Inn is a state heritage area that belongs to everyone in Oregon: "This is their inn, this is their park, and that is what we try to bring to it. It's what we enjoy the most: to preserve the inn and the history that it has for all to enjoy."

For More Information

Where: Wolf Creek Inn, 100 Front Street, Wolf Creek, OR 97497
(¼ mile off I-5 at exit 76)
Web: www.historicwolfcreekinn.com
Phone: 541-866-2474

Golden State Heritage Site
Where: Coyote Creek Road, Golden, OR
Web: www.oregonstateparks.org
Phone: 800-551-6949

Watch the Episode: www.traveloregon.com/wolfcreek

Vanishing Wilderness
South Slough Estuary

The beauty of Oregon's coastal ports is that they shine like faceted jewels during an endless Northwest summer. I favor these quaint ports of call as I have a passion for traveling through them. I believe that's because at each turn there's a unique adventure waiting to be revealed.

A lonesome coastline swings southwest of Coos Bay and offers one of the most spectacular getaways in the Pacific Northwest. The Cape Arago Highway (State Highway 240) leads you along the south shore of the bay, through the suburban community of Barview, across South Slough, and along the southern arm of Coos Bay to Charleston. This village by the sea is a simple and friendly commercial and sportfishing port just inside the entrance to Coos Bay, and it is home to small shops, restaurants, charter sportfishing, a Coast Guard station, and the fascinating Oregon Institute of Marine Biology.

Two miles west of Charleston, the roadway winds over a forested ridge, then approaches the Pacific Ocean at Bastendorff Beach, a great stretch of sand extending south from the bay's entrance.

Bastendorff Beach County Park offers a beach stop my family never misses for an extended visit. It is a spacious eighty-nine-acre park that sits on top of a hill overlooking the Pacific Ocean and has been a regular destination for McOmie family gatherings because of its fifty-five secluded and quiet campsites. You'll find a grass-covered play area for kids, fishing and fish-cleaning facilities, a basketball court, and horseshoe pits. This is a beautiful place to camp or spend the day because beach access is nearby. A clear view to Coos Bay's entrance is had atop the park bluff overlooking the beach. The park is open year-round for RV or tent camping, with dune, lake, and ocean access. Campsites are available on a first-come, first-served basis. The RV sites have electricity and water. There are handicap-accessible restrooms and warm, coin-operated showers.

You will want to make time to travel five miles farther up the Seven Devils Road to visit a piece of Oregon coastal paradise that's been preserved since 1974. It is a pristine corner of the coast known as the South Slough Estuarine Research Reserve (ERR), a sanctuary that encompasses more than 4,400 acres of upland forest, 115 acres of riparian habitat, and eight hundred acres of tidelands that have been federally protected since 1974. The site includes an interpretive center that is open to the public each day and houses exhibits, a video viewing area, a small bookstore, and facilities for formal lectures. An outdoor amphitheater located near the interpretive center serves as an area for presentations and also as a resting place for hikers. Together, the displays put you in touch with a rare piece of Oregon coastal environment according to the center's Deborah Rudd: "It is undisturbed, it is not developed, and you do have more interaction with wildlife here. It's quiet! It's peaceful! And you can picture what life was like many years ago across this southern branch of greater Coos Bay."

In fact, hiking is the most popular way to explore the reserve. Recently my family was fortunate to join South Slough ERR's resident director, Tom Gaskill, for a half-day adventure on the Hidden Creek Trail and to learn more about this relatively untouched corner of the state. The trail is a 2.3-mile round-trip hike, and it follows Hidden Creek from the interpretive center to the estuary's edge. The trail descends three hundred feet to a boardwalk, which winds through freshwater and saltwater marshes, with the option of stopping at an observation platform or continuing to the water's edge.

As we strolled, Tom showed us how estuaries form where freshwater flows from the land and mixes with the tidal flows of saltwater from the ocean. Tom pointed out that estuaries have a higher productivity than most other ecosystems on Earth. Hidden Creek flows through the ground to a narrow stream channel before expanding into a freshwater swamp of red alder and skunk cabbage. It is lush and inviting and abounds with wildlife species including deer, elk, soaring bald eagles, plentiful waterfowl, and myriad shorebirds.

"One of the reasons South Slough is particularly inviting is because it is fairly pristine," said Tom. "It has high-quality marsh and tide flat that are largely unaffected by human activity. As a result, we have been the center of scientific research since our inception over twenty-five years ago."

In fact, more than three thousand youngsters trek this trail each school year to gain a better understanding of natural science. As Tom explained all of this, I was reminded how rare clean, undeveloped estuaries have become in Oregon. In fact, up to 70 percent of the state's coastal wetlands and marshes have been diked, then drained, then filled—and as a result, lost forever. The Hidden Creek Trail fills your senses with an appreciation for something very special in Oregon.

Note: During the summer, guided tours on the water are available. While the South Slough ERR does not offer boats for rent, it will provide a trained interpretive guide to describe the natural and cultural history along the six-mile tour and a shuttle vehicle to transport drivers (participating paddlers) back to their vehicles at the put-in point. All participants are responsible for their own safety equipment, boats, and vehicles.

The preserve is open throughout the calendar year, but Tom said some seasons offer unique surprises for the hardy traveler. "I'm a birder, so for me this time of year in fall is the beginning of the most exciting part of the season. We have flocks of waterfowl that pass through here and a lot of the overwintering forest birds too—there are many species that we never see here during the summer, so it's exciting in the winter months to see some of these migratory species that spend summers in Alaska and Canada but they're here for the winter."

"It is a beautiful place whatever season you come to visit," added Deborah. "You will be amazed and it will be worth your effort to come find us."

For More Information

Where: South Slough Reserve, 61907 Seven Devils Road, Charleston, OR 97420
Web: www.friendsofsouthsloughreserve.org
Phone: 541-888-5558

Bastendorff Beach County Park
Where: 63379 Bastendorff Beach Road, Coos Bay, OR 97420
Phone: For information, 541-396-7759; for reservations, 541-396-7755

Watch the Episode: www.traveloregon.com/southslough

Summer Passage
Deschutes River Steelhead

When you travel east from Oregon's lush Willamette Valley, be on the lookout for a silver lining in the high desert. You may find it when you board a jet boat to travel up the Deschutes River and cast lures for silver-sided steelhead!

When you talk summer adventure, the Deschutes River is a rite of passage for anyone who calls the Pacific Northwest home. Since 1968, fishing guide Bob Toman has been steering anglers to the right spots on the Deschutes River. He knows the river's nooks, crannies, and holding areas where the big fish live. "There are hundreds and hundreds and hundreds of spots to fish," noted the longtime angler. "Even though it can seem a crowded river at times, there's always a place to find that you can fish—and there's fish in all of them."

It didn't take long for fisherman Kevin Kaseberg to prove Bob right! No sooner had Kevin cast his lure into the river's current when a hard charging eight-pound steelhead flew across the river with the lure locked in its jaw. The gleaming fish made several determined runs before Kevin was able to slide it up the riverbank. Bob said he has lost track of the number of anglers he has helped to discover the Deschutes and all of them love the river's fishing reliability: "One of the good things about the Deschutes is that the steelhead bite all sorts of things. If you get a strike and miss it or see one boil at your fly, stay right there, and give it a half dozen more casts—you'll get 'em."

Kevin and Patty Kaseberg enjoy the fishing and the dramatic scenery that the ribbon of river provides as it courses more than a hundred miles through the high desert to reach the Columbia River. "The scenery truly is wonderful," said Kevin. "And it is great to get out and enjoy it." Patty added, "It's like stepping out of the world into a peaceful, beautiful, and restful place. It's really kind of a magical place."

It may be magical! Anglers are each allowed a generous three-hatchery steelhead limit a day and they usually catch them, while all wild fish must go back. Bob offered this piece of advice that he's earned from decades of fishing the river: "Well, I move and I move a lot! That seems to work because most of the fish get hooked in the first little bit when you start casting at a spot. So if you stay and pound, pound, pound the same spot for hours at a time, you don't get as many."

"The "moving" part is a bonus and the reason I like to travel with Bob. It's my chance to drink in that special central Oregon scenery that is framed by vistas of wide-open spaces, my chance to reconnect with childhood memories of times and places that helped launch my angling passions more than half a century ago. The timeless Deschutes River offers big surging rapids that churn to their own rhythms and challenge boaters who must pass through safely; it's a place only the experienced dare travel.

"It is a very technical river," noted Oregon Department of Fish and Wildlife (ODFW) Biologist Rod French. "That's especially true for power boaters. It is a big river with lots of volume and lots of ledges and you need to know where to go. You need to have some know-how here because you can get yourself in trouble in a hurry. Unless you're experienced with that or been up it several times or with someone who has, it's very difficult

Kevin Kaseberg (left) and Cobey Pentecost are big believers that summer steelhead provide the heart-pounding thrills that anglers search for on the Deschutes River.

to read." You should wear a PFD (personal flotation device) when you're going up the river too. The Deschutes has several Class 3 white-water rapids and it's the law to wear one when you're underway.

If you travel to the Deschutes River, consider a longer stay at Deschutes River State Recreation Area that's located near the river's confluence with the Columbia River. "This time of year, it's the fishing that draws the crowds," noted Bruce Meredith, an Oregon Parks and Recreation Department park ranger. "The fishing has been phenomenal and people are scrambling to find spots. At other times of the year folks come for bike riding, horseback riding, hiking, and camping. There's always something to do. We have thirty-two sites with electricity and water, plus new shower facil-

Written on the Rocks/Deschutes River Scenic Byway

Long a drawing card for rafters, kayakers, and fishermen, the fast-flowing, foamy Deschutes River will toss you up and down its big rapids better than any carnival ride at the county fair. Just two hours from Portland, the Deschutes beckons and refreshes, but you don't have to get airborne or water-soaked to enjoy the river. Another, more peaceful route to travel was once a rail bed and is now a national backcountry byway.

Managed by the Bureau of Land Management, the byway is a direct route to solitude that begins near Maupin, Oregon. A gentle gravel road winds more than forty miles through an ancient basalt-rimmed canyon along the lower Deschutes River. Fifteen day-use sites and overnight campgrounds are found along the way.

I travel this way a couple of times a year to admire the geology of the Deschutes Basin. In the rocks you can see an amazing record of the volcanos that erupted across this landscape millions of years ago. At many places along the byway, canyon walls close around and tower over you.

Pull into any campground and take a short hike to a canyon wall. Look up and discover what at first seem to be insignificant variations in the rock structure, but then understand that they tell a story. For example, geologists call the cracks in the rocks "joints," and they tell the story of the rock's heating and cooling and stresses and tensions.

Much of the Deschutes Basin geology is unmistakable columnar basalt, which formed as molten lava cooled, solidifying joints and columns from the bottom up. Many of the columnar basalt cliffs are hundreds of feet high. As the sun dances across their surfaces, the shadows lengthen and cast an eeriness on the place, especially early in the morning or late in the day. I feel a certain wonder when visiting places like this, where the geology is worn so well on the landscape's sleeve that a drive will set your clock back—and you'll be the better for it too. I find the timeless quality reassuring.

When in Maupin, don't forget to stop in at the Oasis Cafe. The McLucas family has been serving up their famous down-home comfort there for more than thirty years. My favorite meal includes their platter-sized cheeseburger, plus a strawberry shake so thick I have to scoop it out with a spoon. As you enjoy your meal, admire the collection of old family photos chronicling life along the Deschutes; some of the pictures stretch back to the early days of the twentieth century.

ities. We also have an additional sixty sites for tent camping or dry RV camping. So there's something for everyone!"

"It's kind of an oasis," added Bruce. "Folks are used to the desert's dry landscape and they come here to find that it's lush and beautiful and right next to the river. It's a parkland that takes their breath away."

Bob says it's a bit of all that—plus, the chance to catch big steelhead—that brings him to the Deschutes River each summer. And if you cross paths with Bob in summer, chances are you'll find his sidekick Cobey Pentecost nearby too. Cobey said that he had been his granddad's "steelhead student" for the past three summers. He is one lucky youngster and he is good fisherman too. No surprise, really! The young angler is learning the river from a living legend who knows the water and fishing strategies like the back of his hand.

"A couple weeks ago I told my grandpa, 'I never catch any fish' and he said—'you're not fishing with confidence,'" noted the smiling youngster. "So Grandpa gave me a whole speech about staying confident no matter what happens and not ten minutes later, I caught a fish. So I am confident all the time."

Patty agreed and added that there is much to love about steelhead fishing on the Deschutes River: "I tell folks that once you have caught one, you're hooked and you'll be back. The Deschutes is simply irresistible." If you go, keep this in mind: a Deschutes River Boater Pass is required for all folks who travel the river in a motorized or nonmotorized watercraft. In addition, there's approximately sixteen miles of graveled road on the east side of the river that is open to the public. The roadway is perfectly suited for hiking or for a mountain bike ride to access fishing or camping along the Deschutes River.

For More Information

Bob Toman Guide Service
Where: 18721 Southeast Semple Road, Damascus, OR 97089
Web: www.bobtoman.com
Phone: 503-705-3959

Deschutes River State Recreation Area
Where: Seventeen miles east of The Dalles on I-84, take exit 97.
Web: www.oregonstateparks.org
Phone: 541-739-2322 or 800-551-6949

Watch the Episode: www.traveloregon.com/deschutessteel

Paddling the Season
Tualatin River

GETAWAY #78 – GREATER PORTLAND

Fall colors are a sure sign of the fast-changing seasons and you can make fun adventure both afoot and afloat when you explore the wonder of nature along the Tualatin River. Brian Wegener, the Watershed Watch coordinator for Tualatin Riverkeepers (TRK), said that canoe paddling "puts him in touch with his neighborhood."

"The Tualatin is a great place for beginners," noted the longtime conservationist, because most of the year there is little or no current. There's not much traffic on the river either and as you can see, at this time of year, it is carpeted with the golden leaves of the ash trees that fall on the river."

The Tualatin River is born high in the Oregon Coast Range and it flows nearly a hundred miles through the heart of fast-growing Washington County on the western edge of the Portland Metro area. "The river drops a foot and a half over a thirty mile reach," added Brian. "So, there's no gradient to speak of—and it's a great place for blue herons, green herons, bald eagles, and ospreys."

Brian and the small party of friends who joined our paddle trip near Sherwood, Oregon, are all members of the Tualatin Riverkeepers. The organization centers its activities on recreation and protection of the watershed. It is a grassroots conservation organization that puts the paddles of their members into action to help the river.

For example, on a recent fall afternoon, scores of volunteers gathered and walked the talk of caring for the stream. They gave up their time to pick up boatloads of trash from the river's shoreline. "Garbage of all kinds," noted Brian. "Lawnmowers, garbage bags, plastic, all sorts of stuff—even a thirty-year-old car chassis."

Tarri Christopher, a longtime TRK member, added "This is the source of our drinking water, so it's important for us to keep it clean. We take a recreational aspect and we turn it into an educational component too." Paul Whitney, another longtime

Riverkeeper, agreed with the conservation aspect of their group and added that paddling puts his mind at ease as the fall colors come into their own. "My blood pressure drops and I can feel the calmness with each paddle stroke. I consider it undiscovered wilderness that most people in the Portland area aren't aware of . . . maybe you don't get the diversity of colors that you do in New England but it's certainly a show of yellows and oranges."

The most common trees along the river are Oregon ash and when they drop their leaves, it's as if a bright yellow carpet had been laid down across the water's surface. It is really beautiful! Not only on the river, but ashore at the Tualatin River National Wildlife Refuge where many people stop in at this time of year to gaze across more than a thousand acres of protected landscape near Sherwood, Oregon.

"It's a gem and it's an unusual situation where people can take a bus and go to a wildlife refuge, noted longtime paddler and Metro Councilor Carl Hosticka. "When you get out on this river, you see you're out in nature, but you go only a mile in any direction and there's the city and people and development. It's a remarkable contrast and the sort of place that may leave you wondering, 'Why haven't I been here before?'"

The refuge was established in 1992 and it opened to the public in 2007. It is vast for an urban wildlife refuge at more than a thousand acres. The site is best enjoyed on the Refuge Trail: a mile-long, wheelchair accessible ribbon of wonders that skirts the wetland's perimeter and follows the river too. There are plenty of stops along the way including a river overlook where you may spy waterfowl during the fall and winter seasons. It is a fine place to escape the city rush for the rush of wings.

Tarri noted that most people who live in Washington County, one of the state's most populous counties, don't even know about the river that they live near. "And that's okay because we love to introduce folks to it. The refuge offers that opportunity and the Riverkeepers really encourage people to visit it." Brian added that he and other members (there are nearly one thousand Tualatin Riverkeeper members) are pushing hard for more river access closer to the refuge so more people can explore—mile by mile—the river's beauty and adventure. "When you're out on a day like this and it is so quiet, you can't really see much human influence—it sure feels like what it must have been two hundred years ago."

For More Information

Where: Tualatin Riverkeepers, 11675 SW Hazelbrook Road, Tualatin, OR 97062

Web: www.tualatinriverkeepers.org

Phone: 503-218-2580; Fax: 503-218-2583

Watch the Episode: www.traveloregon.com/fallcolors

Connections with Our Past
Historic Cemeteries

History runs deep across Oregon with fascinating, colorful, and surprising stories. Perhaps the biggest surprise for most folks is that Oregon's Pioneer Cemeteries are heritage sites and offer a kind of window to the past. Lone Fir Pioneer Cemetery is as much a celebration of life as it is a resting site. Frank Schaefer, chair of the Friends of Lone Fir said, "This cemetery was established before Oregon was a state, so we have mayors, politicians, policemen, firemen, criminals, and the pioneers who came from the east to the west—all are here."

It's a pioneer cemetery in the middle of Oregon's largest city and it recently made big news when National Geographic announced that it is one of the "Top Ten Cemeteries" in the world. The site dates to 1846 and it boasts remarkable ornate architecture, gigantic trees, and famous people. Frank added, "That combination makes it very unique and very special."

Lone Fir Cemetery holds on to its heritage in unique fashion according to Metro's Rachel Fox: "It's our keynote cemetery, a thirty-acre arboretum that's loved by the community." Metro manages Lone Fir's parklike setting that wasn't always so rich with natural beauty. More than a century ago, the cemetery was largely barren with just a scattering of trees including the namesake Doug fir that's now 150 years old. "We have a unique variety of trees and habitats within the cemetery and it actually serves as a community park," noted Rachel. "I call this place the 'family album' of Portland and that's what sets us apart. Even though it's a place set aside for remembrance and there is death here, it's full of life and it's a comfortable, warm place to visit."

Kuri Gill, Oregon State Parks and Recreation's Heritage Cemetery Program manager, agreed and noted: "These places give the long history of the community—the surrounding community, so it's very local history and people appreciate that." There are more than 750 Oregon Pioneer Cemeteries that have been officially documented, according to Kuri. There may be another five hundred that have not been identified yet. Many like Washington County's small Harrison Pioneer Cemetery have volunteers like Judy Goldmann who take care of them. Kuri added, "We encourage people to do that in a friendly way with good stewardship to really go out and be in the cemeteries. Of course, be respectful when you're there, but it's great to have people here because it protects the sites from vandalism."

Judy has no family in Harrison and yet she's been tending the site over thirty years. She is proud to take care of the past: "Oh yes, to preserve it and to make it known that there were these people who came way before and built the foundations of what we now have in this beautiful land."

Just off Stafford Road near Lake Oswego, the Oswego Pioneer Cemetery is a beautiful hillside setting, but when you dig a bit deeper you discover a story you've likely never heard. The story of the iron-workers who worked, lived, and passed on in long-ago Lake Oswego. This was a time long before it was

Lone Fir Cemetery is the final resting site for many of Oregon's famous and infamous citizens.

known as a suburban residential community. Local historian Susanna Kuo of the Lake Oswego Preservation Society, explained: "They had the water power, they had the forests for charcoal, and they had the iron ore. It all added up to a promising business plan in the 1800s."

The Oswego Pioneer was once a company cemetery and it was a part of a company town. Workers came from across the country to work at a so-called "Iron Plantation" that was located in what is now downtown Lake Oswego—right next to the Willamette River. "The company owned the post office, a general store, and they built cottages for their workers," noted Susanna. "They platted neighborhoods and they operated the cemetery for nearly forty-two years." They mined the iron ore from the nearby hills, smelted it, and cast the molten iron into all sorts of items—including pipes that delivered Bull Run water to Portland residents.

Susanna added that the mining work was dark, dirty, and dangerous. "They had zero safety equipment and it was very hard work with twelve-hour shifts. The furnace ran around the clock because you don't turn off something that's 2,800°F and expect to relight it and get full power the next morning."

A new Heritage Trail is underway that will link the important historic industrial sites with the Oswego Pioneer Cemetery where ninety ironworkers are buried. Information plaques will tell the largely unknown story. In fact, you can check out an original iron foundry furnace too. It rests intact and restored by local folks at George Roger's Park in Lake Oswego. Steve Dietz, member of the Lake Oswego Preservation Society, added: "The furnace and the stack for the furnace have gone through a recent rehabilitation and restoration and it is now a one of a kind in Oregon."

That's the nature of Oregon's Heritage Pioneer Cemeteries—each offers unique stories and they are open to visitors too. Oregon State Parks managers ask that when you visit, be a good steward and become a fan—visit the cemeteries in your community and if you see vandalism, report it. Be sure to check out information about Lone Fir Cemetery's famous Halloween night event on October 31. The cemetery is lit from 6 P.M. to 10 P.M. when more than a hundred volunteers will offer guided tours across the grounds in an annual event called the Tour of Untimely Departures.

For More Information

Oregon Commission on Historic Cemeteries / Kuri Gill
Where: 725 Summer Street NE, Suite 3, Salem, OR 97301
Web: www.friendsoflonefircemetery.org
Phone: 503-986-0685
Watch the Episode: www.traveloregon.com/historiccemeteries

Century Farms

The seasons are changing—that's what the calendar says—but there are other signs of fall as harvesttime for Oregon's abundant and locally produced fruits and vegetables kicks in—especially noteworthy at longtime family markets that are also distinct Century Farms.

You can meet some of the friendliest folks—people like Gerry Frank—down on the farm: "People come from all over to E.Z. Orchards because they know that this is a place that offers the freshest food. We're really lucky—we're in eating heaven here in Oregon country." Gerry Frank's knowledge of Oregon's people and places may be surpassed only by his appetite for locally grown products like the fresh corn and peaches he enjoys at

E.Z. Orchards near Salem, a family owned farm-market that's been in business for more than a century.

Few can boast of a love affair quite like the one that Gerry Frank has with his home state. It's a deep, long-lasting and passionate affair that comes through clearly when you thumb past the cover of his new book, *Gerry Frank's Oregon*. "It's Oregon's stores, restaurants and hotels, attractions, and interesting lore about various communities," he said. "The book also includes places for kids to go and a lot of my family history—all of that stuff."

The sort of "stuff" that's been Gerry's bread 'n butter in his Sunday *Oregonian* travel column and his radio and TV reports through the decades. He is an Oregon man for all seasons whose roots reach back seven generations—linked by birth and profession to the famed Meier and Frank family retail business. But Gerry insists that it was his twenty-six years on Senator Mark Hatfield's staff that really put him in touch with the people and places of Oregon: "We hit every nook and cranny in the state and I got to know Oregon very well," he said with a smile.

Bauman's family farm stand take great pride in the motto: "From the field to the table doesn't get any fresher."

So, you should not be surprised to learn that some of Gerry's favorite places to visit are Oregon's unchanged and timeless regions. "Oh, I love to drive along the southern Oregon coast that stretches from Bandon to Gold Beach. It is my favorite part of the state for the uniqueness of the geography, the natural beauty, and so many friendly people—there's nothing in the world like that."

Gerry is also a self-proclaimed chocaholic and he has been the sole judge of the chocolate cakes competition at the Oregon State Fair for the past fifty-three years. In addition, his popular restaurant in Salem, called Konditorei, is where pastries, pies, and cakes rule the counters, although these days, book signings often rule the dining area. Gerry couldn't be more proud of his new effort and hopes the book prompts many to say: "Gee, Gerry, I didn't know that!"

That takes us to what Gerry calls one of the most interesting and least known Oregon

Department of Agriculture programs called Century Farms. In addition to E.Z. Orchards, he likes to encourage folks to visit Bauman's Farm near Gervais. It's a working farm and market and it provides a glimpse into an Oregon lifestyle that should be prized and supported.

"The Bauman farm has been operated by the same family for more than a hundred years," noted Oregon Parks and Recreation Department Heritage Conservation spokesperson Kyle Jansson. "When Century Farms like the Bauman's invite you to come out, they are sharing some of the strong values that come with the tradition of being close to the land. It's a special opportunity and should be enjoyed."

Brian Bauman is a fourth-generation member of the family that began farming the fertile land in 1895. Today, Brian operates the business end of the market place where visitors purchase fresh produce that's grown on the land. "People come in and want practical information," noted Brian. "For example, they want to know 'when the corn was picked, this morning?' Yes, I tell them—this morning and it's great."

Bauman's grows scores of different fruits and vegetables across hundreds of acres and all of the produce is sold in the family's full-service market shortly after the daily harvest. Brian said that he is proud of the fact that the family farm is part of the Century Farms program. He credits the family's blending of tradition and an entrepreneurial spirit that has allowed their operation to endure. "We must be doing something right for a hundred years to continue doing business," added Brian. "My name is on the products and I want to make sure that it's good."

Gerry Frank couldn't agree more! Century Farms represent something lasting and solid and prove that the Oregon spirit is alive and well—family tradition is too. He said he enjoys encouraging visitors to explore and visit uniquely Oregon people, places, and activities. "I really do love this place—it's all so alive and well and we have such abundance and that's a good and important thing to see and experience."

For More Information

Gerry Frank's Konditorei
Where: 310 Kearney SE, Salem, OR 97302
Web: www.gerryfran+konditorei.com
Phone: 503-585-7070

Bauman Farms
Where: 12989 Howell Prairie Road NE, Gervais, OR 97026
Web: www.baumanfarms.com
Phone: 503-792-3524

Do You Have Chanterella-Vision?

Mushroom Hunting

Longtime chef and local restaurateur and all-around Oregon adventurer Leather Storrs figures it's simple: if you want to harvest wild mushrooms, learn their habitat. In the Tillamook State Forest—where sun and shadow dance through the towering Doug fir trees while Leather's well-trained eyes are fixed down close to the ground where there's a culinary reward. "Ohhh, there we are—chanty number one—it's always good to get off the dime early," exclaimed Storrs with a hearty laugh.

Chanterelles have a golden-orange hue and their chalice shape make them hard to spot—but their allure is a woodsy flavor that's hard to resist. Since 1999, the gorgeous fungi have been Oregon's official State Mushroom. "As soon as you see the first one," noted Leather, "there is this chanterella-vision that allows you to see that unique sort of peachy-orange color, but with the weather change and the alder leaves turning yellow on the ground it's getting trickier."

Chanterelles are not the only mushrooms in the forest. Leather, an experienced mushroom hunter, said that there are dozens of other mushrooms that grow here and most are none-too-friendly to people and many are downright dangerous. "When you're doing it without knowledge and confirmation, there's no reason to take any chances. I learned in culinary school an old saying: 'There are old mycologists and there are bold mycologists, but there are no old, bold mycologists.'"

Leather Storrs may not be an old, bold mycologist, but he is one of Portland's finest chefs. His restaurant, the Noble Rot, set in Northeast Portland, is where Leather has mastered the art of cooking a wild chanterelle recipe that can be served with many other foods. He cleaned approximately one pound of chanterelles— he never washes them in water but prefers to clean them off with a soft rag or brush—and he also prefers smaller, button-sized mushrooms. Leather then proceeded to slice them lengthwise; he likes to preserve their overall shape and size as much as possible.

The wild chanterelles hit an oiled (olive oil) pan with a "bounce, sizzle, and snap." Leather added, "Chanterelles are one of those things that really depend upon a hot pan. While the mushrooms cooked, Leather finely diced one large shallot. When the mushrooms were nearly done, in went the shallots and two chunks of butter. And more: "I've some big beautiful parsley here that I will chop and add near the end of the cooking time along with a small amount of lemon juice."

Meanwhile, from out of the oven, Leather pulled a cracked egg that was nestled inside a rich, grainy bread. It was warm and toasty and called Egg in a Hole. Soon, he smothered the dish in the richly cooked chanterelles with a recipe that serves up to four. "That's one way to treat a chanterelle ragout," noted Leather. "Not only is this a dish of the place and seasonal, it's also virtually free." Leather is a big believer that the meals that you contribute to are the most rewarding—that is, the ones that connect you to the source of your food. "There's something exciting and magical that comes about when you find it, prepare it, and then share a meal with friends and family," said Leather. "I don't think it can get much better."

The Oregon Department of Forestry allows you to harvest up to one gallon of wild mushrooms on state forestlands, but any more than that, you are considered a commercial picker and must buy the $100 permit at any state forestry office. Leather stressed critical safety points if you choose to head into the forest at this time of year. First, pick only mushrooms that you know are safe. If you don't know, go with someone who is experienced and does know, or take a mushroom identification class. He suggested the Cascade Mycological Society. Leather also suggested that mushroom hunters who are in unfamiliar territory stay close to the road and never out of earshot of the road traffic.

For More Information

Where: Leather Storrs @ Noble Rot: 1111 E Burnside, 4th floor, Portland, OR 97201

Web: www.noblerotpdx.com

Phone: 503-233-1999

Watch the Episode: www.traveloregon.com/mushroomhunting

A Walk on the Wild Side
Wildwood Recreation Site

You'll enjoy hiking trails, crimson-colored fall leaves, and spawning salmon in an educational backdrop at an overlooked recreation area not far from Portland. You'll want to bring your camera to capture the steady stream of color along the Salmon River that flows through the Wildwood Recreation Site near Welches, Oregon.

Many parts of the Cascade Mountains demand a slower pace. You simply see more when you leave busy campgrounds behind and let quieter, wilder moments surround you. Those moments are easy to come by down the many trails inside the Wildwood Recreation Site near Welches, Oregon. A site that may have you wondering, "How is it I've never heard of this place or visited it before?"

After all, the Salmon River is born from glaciers atop Mount Hood and it is Oregon's last undammed river that flows unhindered from the mountains to the sea. It cuts a beeline through more than five hundred acres of designated public recreation land at Wildwood. Adam Milnor, a Bureau of Land Management recreation specialist, said that most people who are in a big hurry to reach Mount Hood or Central Oregon and overlook Wildwood. "Mount Hood beckons to everyone who lives in the Portland area and that's understandable; it's a hugely popular draw. But it's also a mistake not to pull in and see what this site has to offer. We have such a great place for families to introduce their children to the outdoors with a rushing river, salmon, and fantastic trees in a beautiful forest."

The trails that wind through Wildwood are marvelous opportunities to explore the parkland. The Wildwood Wetlands Trail is a one-mile loop of gravel and paved footpaths that gives you access to the heart of a vast wetland area where many different wildlife species live. Observation decks extend into the wetland at a number of locations and allow closer inspection. Don't be surprised while hiking the boardwalk to see blue herons, mallards, teals, turtles, or any number of small songbirds. Pay special attention to the many interpretive signs that describe the wetland habitat and the critters that live there.

"A wetland ecosystem is something you have to really see up close to get really fascinated with it," noted Adam. "Building this structure really allows you to get up close and personal to it in a way that you wouldn't otherwise." There are more than one thousand feet of the boardwalk on the Wildwood Wetlands Trail that was built four feet off the ground to keep hikers' feet dry and limit access onto the sensitive wetlands. Beginning in mid-October, the boardwalk area explodes to life with a show of brilliant reds, oranges, and yellows from vine maple, big-leaf maple trees, and alder trees.

The Cascade Streamwatch Trail is a barrier-free and paved, three-quarter-mile trail adjacent to the Wild and Scenic Salmon River. Interpretive displays describe points of interest. The most remarkable highlight of this trail is a stream-profile viewing chamber where you gain an underwater "fish-eye" view of a small stream and salmon habitat. The chamber—ten years in the making—drops twelve feet below the water surface and allows you to see through two large windows more than twelve feet across and seven feet high where "baby" salmon live.

I enjoy just watching the behavior of the three- to four-inch salmon fry and how they use logs, branches, and even rocks to hide. As a bug floats on the current, a fish jets out and picks it off, then retreats back to its shelter. "We love the fish and we want to protect the fish," noted Donna Hansen, Wildwood park ranger. "If visitors go to the river and they come at the right time of year, they actually get to see fish too. The salmon spawn throughout the Salmon River from October through November. People like to see that."

The park is open from 8:00 A.M. to sunset from mid-May to early November. However, during the off-season, you may park at the gate and access Wildwood and Cascade Streamwatch by foot, walking the entrance road to the trailhead or other facilities.

For More Information

Where: Forty miles east of Portland just off US Highway 26 near Welches, OR
Phone: 503-622-3696
Watch the Episode: www.traveloregon.com/wildwood

Crazy for Dungeness
Crab Class

When you try something new, it pays to go with the pros! That's what more than thirty newcomers recently discovered when they signed up for the Oregon Department of Fish and Wildlife's (ODFW) "Crab Class," a course from the agency's menu of adventures called Outdoor Skills. Instructors, biologists, and volunteers teach and assist students in the varied Outdoor Skills courses. Crabbing is a popular recreation that requires some skill and knowledge, so the agency developed the day-long course to encourage participation.

ODFW spokesperson and instructor Mark Newell said that the students get all of the gear and assistance that they might need for a day of fun and excitement at Yaquina Bay in Newport. "We want people to care about the environment and the only way to get them to do that is to get them out enjoying it. That's what 'Crab Class' does for many students." Mike Hoge and his son, Jerrad Hoge, came all the way from Silverton to pick up pointers on the crabbing recreation. "I did it a little bit as a kid," noted Mike. "But I didn't really have any instruction, so I thought some good lessons would help and I'm glad we came today."

The students kick off the affair at the South Beach State Park Activity Center, just south of Newport. Instructor Brandon Ford presented the basics of crab biology and explained the trapping techniques and the rules and regulations of the sport. The session was followed by a short drive to Yaquina Bay Marina where the hands-on action began. The first order of business was how to place the bait inside the crab trap or rings. The bait of choice for the day's adventure: chicken!

Jennifer Erickson said that she didn't mind the tradeoff of chicken for crab. In fact, her husband, Steve Erickson, traveled from Portland for the chance to learn something new about a seafood they really enjoy eating for dinner. "It's really fun to go out with experts," she noted. "To be coached and helped along the way before doing it on our own just seemed to make a lot of sense to us. Plus, crab is so tasty—that's a bonus." Once the students were comfortable with the gear, it was time to toss the traps from atop Yaquina Bay Pier that juts hundreds of yards into the bay. The pier is open to fishing and crabbing anytime.

Students learned how to measure a crab to make certain it's legal (only twelve male Dungeness crabs are allowed and they must be five and three-quarters inches across the back) and how to tell the difference between the two species of crab that are present in Yaquina Bay: Dungeness crabs and red rock crabs. "We show them how to crab from the pier," said Brandon. "But we also take them out on the bay in boats to drop traps in several places that our biologists have scouted. We try to take folks to the best places in the whole bay." The traps were checked, the crabs were counted, and then it was time to cook. It was a fine way to round out the day's adventure.

Each student in the class must purchase an ODFW Shellfish License. The course costs $40 for adults and $10 for kids under eighteen. Students are provided with instruction, plus all of the gear including bait, traps, and PFDs (personal flotation devices). "It's a real good deal," added Brandon. "That's especially true at lunchtime because no one goes away hungry from the class."

For More Information

Where: Oregon Department of Fish and Wildlife, 3406 Cherry Avenue NE, Salem, OR 97303

Phone: 503-947-6000 or 800-720-6339

Watch the Episode: www.traveloregon.com/crabbing101

Outdoor Tip: Cooking Your Catch

Fall is a time of seasonal change when the weather can turn on a dime from fair skies to wet, windy, and downright crummy. But on those wonderful "blue hole" days when the sun plays a peek-a-boo game, I like to take advantage of every opportunity for a new adventure.

When you're lucky enough to go fishing with a good friend who knows the water well, you're sure to learn something new. That's especially true when the Columbia River is under your keel and carries you toward new adventure. Steve Fick first explored the Columbia River estuary as a kid, so he knows his way around the vast waterway where the river meets the sea. He and his longtime friend Jim Dickson intended to teach this greenhorn how to catch his supper from the sea.

For Steve, the first lesson is simple enough: always wear a PFD (personal flotation device). He insisted it's a personal lesson in life and safety: "You always wear it, Grant, because if you fall overboard, particularly with heavy rain gear on, it's very difficult to survive. The water is always cold and can sap your strength in a matter of minutes."

We left the snug harbor at Hammond, Oregon, and slowly motored the short distance downriver to an area just off Clatsop Beach. Steve had prepared five large crab traps with varied baits—a strategy he often used to "see what the crabs prefer." Sometimes he'll use turkey legs, chicken wings, shad, or salmon carcasses—even a can of tuna for crab bait. Anyone say, "lunchtime?"

"Oh yes, a can of tuna fish is perfect bait!" exclaimed Steve. "All you do is perforate the can so that the scent comes out—you can also buy canned sardines or mackerel too—both work well. As long as they have a high oil content, it seems to fish well—the scent is what draws the crab into the pot."

Each Oregon crabber must carry an Oregon Department of Fish and Wildlife Shellfish License. Each crabber is allowed to use up to three crab traps. We timed our trip to fish our traps the last hour of the incoming tide and through the high slack period, often the best crabbing time. Steve said it's the safest time to crab in the estuary: "There is no reason to be out here on the ebb tide—that's the outgoing tide. It can be the most dangerous part of the tide cycle and this river can change so fast. You just don't take chances out here."

Steve said that each trap should "soak" for fifteen to twenty minutes—that allows enough time for the crabs to locate the bait and enter the trap. Each crabber is allowed a dozen male crabs apiece, and in Oregon they must be five and three-quarters (5¾) inches across the back. Females are protected to preserve the breeding population of crabs. A crab gauge or other measuring device is essential gear since some crabs miss the mark by only a hair's length.

Jim and I pulled in the last of the five traps. "Oh, man look at that," I shouted. "It's the mother lode and I think they're all legal." Steve showed me how to safely hold each crab so not to get pinched. "Watch me, Grant—see how I place my thumb on the underside and my other four fingers across the back. You can hold it safely and not get pinched. This is a dandy crab. That's great!"

Within a half hour, we had landed and checked each of our traps and we were fortunate to retain eighteen legal Dungeness crabs, plenty to go around for our small but hearty crew. As much fun as it was to catch these crabs, the best part was yet to come when Steve motored back to the dock in Astoria and we carried our crustaceans up to his shop to learn the proper way to cook our crabs. Steve dropped a pound of salt into ten gallons of boiling water and then placed each crab into the pot. The crabs must cook approximately twenty minutes and then Steve chilled our catch on ice.

I asked Steve what he enjoyed most about the adventure that's just off his front doorstep: "Oh, it's simple and everyone can be involved in it. It's easy to catch a dozen crabs per person with lots of action for kids. And—you never really know until you pull the pot up what you got . . . you know, and that is fun!"

It is a lot of fun and continues in the kitchen where Steve shares three of his favorite Dungeness crab recipes. "You can do a lot of different things with crabmeat—you can make a chowder, fritters, salads, sandwiches—so many different things. You can mix it with fettuccine, other seafood, so it's very versatile."

Recipe number one was new to me and is called a Stuffed Crab Sandwich.

Steve cut four sandwich rolls in half to make eight sandwiches. He then mixed one cup of grated Swiss cheese with two cups of crab and added one teaspoon each of Worcestershire sauce and lemon pepper before he mixed in one cup of mayo and a half-cup of sliced black olives. The mixture was then stuffed into each half of a hollowed-out sandwich roll. Steve spread a generous amount of grated Parmesan cheese across the top of each roll and slid the tray of sandwiches into a 375°F oven for seven to ten minutes. "This is a filling dinner," he noted. "You need to be in the mood for something rich and robust—it works well on a cold winter's night."

While we waited on the sandwiches, it was time for recipe number two that Steve called the Fick Crab Cakes. Steve began with a pound of crabmeat—he added one egg, one cup of Panko, one cup of mayo, and a couple of teaspoons of mustard. A generous cup of diced yellow onions and a tablespoon of seafood seasoning followed and the ingredients were mixed and formed into approximately twelve small cakes. The cakes were placed in a fry pan with a quarter inch of hot peanut oil with Steve's words of caution: "You don't want to overcook these or you'll get pieces of crab cardboard and that doesn't taste too great."

Steve's recipe number three is called Crab Louie Salad and it is one of his favorites because he can make it as elaborate or as simple as he likes. He insisted, never ever hold back on the crab. He used it atop a bed of sliced lettuce and then again atop all the other ingredients. Salad fixings include sliced white onions, cucumbers, celery, sliced olives, tomatoes, a sliced egg, and a cup of shredded yellow Cheddar cheese. It made for a grand salad that serves up to six. "It's a light meal," he noted. "But it can be a heavier meal if you want it to be with the ingredients—especially the cheese." Our seafood feast was topped off too—with a glass of Oregon white wine (Steve prefers Pinot Grigio) and a local microbrew.

The table was set for a couple of kings who volunteered as official "Getaway Food Tasters": Jim Shores and Birt Hansen. Each was eager to sample our efforts and offered their reviews: "Excellent, excellent, excellent and what surprised me was so many ways to fix it," said Jim. "The taste is something you don't get in upper Minnesota where I come from, so let me say that and I love Oregon crab."

Birt nodded in agreement and then with a chuckle he offered, "This all looks outstanding for Jim and me, but what are you guys going to eat? There won't be any left over for you." It was a perfect way to round out a Dungeness crabbing adventure and then bring the day's activity full circle: from the estuary to the dining table.

Bonney Butte Raptors
Mount Hood

On a clear day, the view from Bonney Butte onto the southern flanks of Mount Hood is brilliant and awesome. Raptor specialist Dan Sherman said that his camouflaged blind is the "best seat in the house. Well, there aren't many offices that have a view out a window like this one. I look straight in front toward Mount Hood and then off to the west as well, and as I look, I pick out all the little black dots."

Dan is part of HawkWatch International's Raptor Banding Team and those "little black dots" will take your breath away when they become big raptor birds that soar right overhead. Sometimes they do more than soar—they also attack.

That's what happened when a large red-tailed hawk swooped in to Dan's site and with its razor-sharp talons became entangled in a fine mesh fabric called a mist net. The net panels surrounded a feathered nonnative prey called a lure. Dan wasted little time removing the big broad-winged raptor. He carefully bundled up the bird's legs, talons, and wings and held it close to his chest. "Most red-tails are not biters," he noted. "But occasionally you'll get one that will lunge at you. I am sure that if I stuck my finger in its face it would bite it. Well, that was the hard part, now let's process her."

Dan and fellow team member Jade Ajani quickly and quietly weighed, measured, and banded the captured bird. "It can be pretty exciting when you're working with hawks," whispered Dan—a twelve-season veteran at the stunning locale of Bonney Butte. He added with a smile, "These birds can really make the adrenalin flow!"

Bonney Butte is on a ridgeline that runs north and east of Mount Hood toward the Columbia River. It is a place where the raptors would rather soar than flap their wings. "The birds are migrating south and looking out for other birds," noted Jade. "They look to see if other birds have good lift from thermal updrafts that are created off the ridges. Plus, you often have westerly winds that hit the ridges and create the lift—that is what the birds are after—saves them energy to soar or glide rather than fly."

Dan jerked a cord that lifted the lure and another sharp-eyed raptor was decoyed into the mist net panels. Speed is everything in the capture and banding process. Not only to free the trapped raptor and catch more, but if stranded too long, the predator can easily become the prey of another soaring raptor. The team will capture scores of raptors on any given fall day and usually half a dozen species are represented. Some, like a sharp-shinned hawk that Jade held tight prior to release, sported a razor-sharp beak. They are fascinating birds that are rarely seen so close.

A half mile away, several volunteer observers were perched on a rocky outcropping of the Bonney Butte ridge. HawkWatch International's Adam Baz said that the ever-watchful volunteers count every raptor species they can from one of the most remarkable view sites in Oregon. "We can see seven and sometimes eight different mountains from up here—that view coupled with the amount of hawks that come through here make it a really incredible place to work."

Hawkwatch International has been monitoring, trapping, and banding hundreds of raptors since they began operation atop Bonney Butte in 1994. Their record of raptors has helped to contribute a new understanding of birds that travel from the Arctic to Central America. The site's geography makes it a first-rate laboratory. "The diversity of species we get here is astounding," noted Adam. "On any given day we will see every species of hawk in the area, plus eagles and falcons too. It is amazing!" It is also open to visitors every day. If you come—bring water," added Adam with a chuckle. "The weather changes quickly up here too, so a rain jacket is a good idea. A camera, binoculars, and hiking boots are must-haves as well."

I hope you make time to visit Bonney Butte for there's simply no other place like it in Oregon. If you go, know that the drive is long, the road is extremely rocky, and the site is remote. Be prepared and allow for a two-hour trip from Portland. HawkWatch International continues the capture and banding and observation work at Bonney Butte through October.

For More Information

Where: HawkWatch International, 2240 South 900 East,
Salt Lake City, UT 84106

Web: www.hawkwatch.org

Phone: 801-484-6808 or 800-726-4295

Watch the Episode: www.traveloregon.com/bonneybutte

It's for the Birds
Oregon Birding Trail

There's a new way to explore Oregon and this one is really for the birds! But it's designed for people—especially folks who like to explore new destinations where half the fun is in the getting there. The first Willamette Valley Birding Trail is a new partnership between varied birding groups and Travel Oregon. It offers people a chance to explore 130 legitimate birding sites in a region that is home to 70 percent of the state's population.

Joel Geier and I recently met at William L. Finley National Wildlife Refuge where he told me that variety is the spice of his birding life along the new Willamette Birding Trail. "They're such fascinating creatures; they're feathered and for me, they have a little more variety than mammals."

Joel knows his birding game well! After all, he's a longtime member of the Oregon Field Ornithologists. His organization along with several others including Travel Oregon joined to identify 130 birding trails in the Willamette Valley. "We've set it up as twelve different loops in the valley so that if you live in one of the communities in the valley, you can go out on a weekend and visit a loop that includes ten or twelve different sites."

It's easy to locate a trail online. A click of your mouse takes you inside one of the dozen different loops where you'll find directions to the sites plus photos of the species that you'll see along the way. "On each of those loops," noted Joel, "there will be sites that you never thought about visiting before and you'll be surprised that they are pretty special places."

Sallie Gentry and Molly Monroe agree that the new Homer Campbell Memorial Boardwalk at Finley Wildlife Refuge near Corvallis is one of those special places where you can go birding. "The boardwalk is on pretty level, even terrain and there are two benches along that they can rest if they get tired," said Sallie. It's an astonishing wheelchair accessible trail along seventeen hundred feet of elevated boardwalk that leads to an observation blind overlooking a small pond that attracts many different birds. "It is a magnet for wildlife," noted Molly. "We'll have thousands upon thousands of ducks and geese and swans here within the next few months."

Sallie added, "We're kind of a little-known secret right now, but I think we're going to become more well-known because there are such excellent wildlife viewing opportunities here and you can get relatively close without disturbing the wildlife." Not only wintering waterfowl, but also raptor species like bald eagles make the Finley Refuge their winter homes. "It's one of the easiest birds for most people to identify so it's fun for them. Often, you just look out on a tree line of snags and say, 'Oh, there's an eagle perched right there.' Eagles are good because they're well-known by most people and their recovery from near extinction is such a success story."

If you're eager to learn more about birding, but you're not sure how to get started, Sallie said that there is good news for the casual first-time visitor during the fall season. "Many people come here and don't realize the wealth of birds that they may find on the refuge and so lack some basic tools. We've developed 'family kits' that include everything one would need here. Check out binoculars or a field guide, take it with them out on the hike or drive the auto route and just bring them back at the end of the day. It's really a great deal!"

All agree that wildlife viewing along the new Willamette Birding Trail is just the ticket to see Oregon from a different point of view. "Oh, I think it's a huge deal!" exclaimed Molly. "Birding is a growing pastime—and it is one that brings a lot of enjoyment to a large variety of people of all ages."

For More Information

Where: Travel Oregon Salem Office, 250 Church Street SE, Salem, OR 97301
Web: www.oregonbirdingtrails.org
Phone: Joel Geier: 541-745-5821
Watch the Episode: www.traveloregon.com/valleybirding

Golden Nugget of History

Sumpter Valley Dredge State Heritage Area

Northeast Oregon's Powder River is a small, cool, quiet, and refreshing stream, but not so long ago, it was a river under siege. It's a landscape where monstrous gold-dredging machines ravaged the river valley floor. Square-bowed and built of steel and wood and iron, three giant dredges lifted and sifted the terrain, reaping a golden harvest worth $12 million during the peak of the Depression era. Today, it is a park that holds on to history and takes visitors aboard to see and touch the past at the Sumpter Valley Dredge State Heritage Area in Sumpter, Oregon.

I hope you will be as awestruck as I was when you come face to face with the Sumpter dredge, whose massive boom bears seventy-two, one-ton buckets. Rella Pfleeger-Brown is the assistant park ranger and guides visitors aboard the dredge. She pointed out how the buckets moved like the chain links of a chain saw, bored into the riverbank, and carried loose rock back into the dredge's hulking interior. "When you stroll into the heart of the dredge—it's as big as a barn and filled with gears and belts, winches and pumps—where the rock passed through steel cylinders, separating rocks by size."

Water and sluices separated the gold from the sediment and the spoils from this process were discharged behind the behemoth as it moved across the valley. Nine tons of gold in nineteen years! If you are lucky, you may meet some of the men who lived the history, like brothers Wes and Paul Dickison who grew up in nearby Baker City. In 1947, the two teens worked on the dredge for the highest wages around: $1.35 an hour. "OSHA [Occupational Health and Safety Administration] would have shut this thing down the very first day they stepped on it," noted Paul. "There were all kinds of hazards: cables, open gears that weren't guarded. And if the power went out—watch out!"

Wes recalled that happened twice. When the electric power that ran the dredge failed and everything stopped on the night shift: "We didn't have lights," said Paul. "We didn't have nothing and it was the spookiest place you'd ever been in your life. All these pumps running, pipes running, water running, mud everywhere, and boom—power went off and it was coal black. You'd hear a splash over here, splash over there—something there—real spooky!"

But the lure of golden profit (the dredge made more than four million dollars in profit) was strong, and repairs were made quickly so operations could continue. It's the noise they remember most! The dredge operations were so loud you couldn't talk, so a bell system was the only way to communicate. Signals were written on the wall—long and short rings—that helped the three-man crew communicate across the massive floating machine.

Jerry Howard's father was a winchman in the 1930s who operated the dredge from three stories up in the winch room. He had a commanding view of the entire operation. Inside the room, handles moved cables that moved the buckets down below that gouged out the ground. "I can still hear the rocks hitting the tailings," noted Jerry. He recalled bringing lunch to his father and said it was a real boyhood adventure to go aboard the dredge. "The digging of the bucket line was something—seventy-two buckets going round and round twenty-four hours a day. It dug up a lot of land."

The Sumpter dredge ravaged the Powder River Valley for miles around and all these decades later, the tailings undulate like snakes across the valley. They are lasting reminders of a bygone era for sure, yet time has a way of healing the land: trees and other vegetation are slowly coming back along the river. Ranger Rella added that it remains an important Oregon story that she enjoys sharing with park visitors. "The telling of Oregon history is an important mission for Oregon State Parks. By virtue of the dredge's presence in the valley, many visitors ask those questions and then you can teach them about that time. It really does provide the opportunity to share that chapter of Oregon's past—and it's really fun—it's really fun."

For More Information

Where: Off State Highway 7, 30 miles west of Baker City, OR
Web: www.oregonstateparks.org
Phone: 541-894-2486 or 800-551-6949
Watch the Episode: www.traveloregon.com/sumptervalley

Communities That Flock Together

Jackson Bottom Wetlands Preserve and Fernhill Wetlands

GETAWAY #86 – GREATER PORTLAND

"Whatizthat?"

"Whatizthis?"

"Wherezitfrom?"

"Wherewegoinnow?"

"Huh? Mr. McOmie, huh? Whatizit?"

Field trips are interesting affairs! I call them my "Whatizit?" trips—the times when I volunteer to lead groups of youngsters on an outdoor adventure to teach them more about the natural world, times when my energies are tested to the max, as a somewhat uncomfortable knot develops in my neck from the quick swish panning this way or that to answer all of their questions.

"Mr. McOmie, Mr. McOmie, whatizthatbird, whatizthatplant, whatizthatfish?"

Yet I love to teach young people about the great outdoors! I started my professional life in a classroom, and I always considered my jump into television broadcasting but an expansion of the class size. But the truth be told, television audiences can never be reached in the same way. There's a special moment when you can see that lightbulb of new knowledge click on in a youngster's eyes, followed by a nod and a knowing smile. That's my reward for time outdoors.

Two of the friendliest places in the Portland metro region to see what's new in the great outdoors include Jackson Bottom Wetlands Preserve and Fernhill Wetlands. Situated on the southern doorstep of one of the fastest-growing communities in Oregon, Jackson Bottom stretches across more than seven hundred acres near Hillsboro in Washington County. While a mere eight miles to the west—as the crow flies—Fernhill Wetlands—on the southern edge of Forest Grove—invites wildlife and wildlife viewers alike.

Jackson Bottom Wetlands Preserve

Jackson Bottom offers varied wildlife habitat of marshes, meadows, ponds, and Douglas fir and ash tree stands that in turn attract all kinds of wild animals—especially birds: from waterfowl to blue herons to raptors such as hawks and eagles.

Jackson Bottom was little more than a dumping ground for decades throughout much of the twentieth century. The open meadow areas were often grazed over by cattle, and even local businesses would dump all manner of waste and debris on the land. The attitude reflected a simple philosophy of "out of sight, out of mind." That attitude began changing in the early 1970s when people saw that wetlands, marshes, and other so-called marginal lands might deserve a different perspective. That is, these places are important, and if wetlands could be restored, wildlife could be helped too.

An ambitious project and partnership began at Jackson Bottom in the 1980s using water supplemented in the drier summer by treated wastewater from the nearby Clean Water Services wastewater treatment plant. The landscape was sculpted with bulldozers into pondlike areas and filled with the treated wastewater, which helped restore the wildlife habitat. The water became even cleaner as it was filtered through native grasses and sedges, bushes, and trees, and then returned to the nearby Tualatin River.

Is it working? Absolutely! A measure of that has been the dramatic increase in populations of wildlife, such as frogs, turtles, great blue herons, and waterfowl that nest in the cattails and sedges. In winter, the remarkable sight of several bald eagles is great testimony to the wetland's value. In fact, not only wintering bald eagles, but also a nesting pair, have made Jackson Bottom their home for nearly two decades. While it was once rare to see a bald eagle, more often than not, you'll see one or two or more—perched like ornaments in tall trees from one of several viewing platforms that have been strategically placed across the Jackson Bottom Wetlands Preserve. With their bold white caps and tail feathers, the big raptors are unmistakable. And the eagle nest is gigantic and hard to miss. Each year the pair of adult birds has added more sticks and branches to their nest, so that today the five-foot-tall nest is very distinct.

Aside from the designated view sites, you are encouraged to hike at Jackson Bottom, perhaps by strolling down the Kingfisher Marsh Trail to enjoy the sights and sounds of the thousands of Canada geese that winter on the preserve. Or step inside the six-thousand-square-foot Jackson Bottom Wetlands Preserve Education Center to discover classrooms and interpretive exhibit areas highlighted by a full-sized bald eagle nest that was rescued and moved indoors from a giant cottonwood tree that was about to fall down. Another successful outreach program is the weekly "Lunch with the Birds," when you can visit with one of the preserve's staff members for an hour or two, learn more about the wildlife and the preserve, and almost always see some pretty amazing wildlife. Jackson Bottom Wetlands Preserve is a very special place that's exploding with amazing educational opportunities—and it's all there for your exploration and enjoyment.

Fernhill Wetlands

It's really remarkable to watch the parade of birds on winter vacation at Fernhill Wetlands near Forest Grove, Oregon. Some, like ducks and geese, are passing by on their migration routes, but others like to linger and, it seems, just plain loaf among the grasslands, marshes, and wetlands at Fernhill. Fast on the tail feathers of the annual waterfowl migration are the raptors, such as the ever-alert bald eagles roosting high overhead in a stadium stand of cottonwood trees on the south side of the hundred-acre wetlands. "They will be on prey lookout at Fernhill Wetlands until spring," whispered my bird-watching partner, Rob Stockhouse, during one of my first visits to the site on a fine November morning in the late '80s. Even more special, according to the retired Pacific University botany professor and wetlands educator, is the fact that Fernhill was created by people for animals. Together, public and private interests—including several neighborhood groups and schools, Clean Water Services (CWS), and the City of Forest Grove—have transformed a series of wastewater lagoons into a wildlife paradise.

Canada geese arrive by the thousands at Fernhill Wetlands each fall—they linger here until March and then return to subarctic breeding and nesting grounds.

Rob and I hiked the easy path through the wetlands and enjoyed a front row view of the expansive ponds containing more than a dozen species of ducks and Canada geese. As we slowly approached one of the ponds, a flurry of feathers rose in the sky, and we stopped in our tracks to watch an amazing drama unfold. In hushed tones Rob told me, "Watch this! Notice that bird's feathers are mottled black, brown, and white all over. It's a young bald eagle, and he's hunting for his breakfast, but not very well."

We hunkered down near a cattail stand and gazed across the water as the youngster made repeated strafing runs across a flock of ducks too scared to fly. But the eagle wasn't having much success. Each flyby went for naught as he dove, sharp talons

Walk Slowly, Pause Often

Each of us loves to explore the wide-open spaces of the Northwest. There we can find elbow room to stretch out and play. We admire these places for their scenic beauty, but they are much more because of the wild animals living there. Once you've learned a bit about wildlife and their habits—where they live, what they eat, where they sleep, and so on—you'll always have something to look for and to think about.

Animals are often threatened when crowded by humans, even though humans may mean no harm. Sometimes it seems wildlife want to say "Don't get too close!" From a tree branch, a bird watches a person approaching; when the person gets too close, the bird takes flight. So be sure to keep a comfortable distance away from those critters you chance upon.

Though you don't need to be a hard-core camper to go critter crazy, binoculars help plenty, and a camera is a good option too. Wearing the proper clothes is also important: Street shoes on muddy trails will spoil a fun adventure. It's best to be prepared for changeable weather and challenging terrain.

Encounters with wildlife usually last but a heartbeat, so be ready when animals appear. First, find the right spot for viewing. Stay in your car at those locations that don't invite you to hike and explore. Go slow and be patient, quiet, and attentive. Wherever you go, be gentle on the landscape: Take memories, a few pictures, and leave only your footprints behind.

extended to grab his prey, but when he was just inches away the ducks would scatter or dive below the surface. As the big bird passed over, the ducks would rise, catch a breath, give a quack, and prepare to dive again. After ten minutes of this, it seemed clear to me this game of "catch me if you can" was in the ducks' favor. They were simply too nimble for the huge eagle.

Rob noted, "Young eagles spend an amazing amount of time and energy trying to catch moving prey, and they just don't do well at all. They can't maneuver those big wings and their long bodies quick enough to catch the lightning-fast ducks. Usually they'll flush a flock off the water and wait to see which birds don't fly or dive. That's a dead giveaway of an injury, illness, or old age. Those are the birds the eagles will catch. That's really what they rely upon out here where nature's at work."

The Forest Grove community has really been at work too. They have made a difference when it comes to encouraging wildlife to make their homes near a populated town. "It's a refuge that's about as grass roots as it gets," Rob explained. "You cannot believe the pride this community has in what's been created here. It's an important site for the critters for sure, but it also serves as water storage to help prevent floods."

Recently, the City of Forest Grove sold the Fernhill Wetlands to Clean Water Services and CWS is now in the midst of a major $12 million renovation of the property. The new changes will affect how wastewater is treated throughout Fernhill's 748 acres. Centerpiece in the project is building a man-made wetlands and Japanese garden at its wastewater treatment plant. The project expands the capacity of the Forest Grove Wastewater Treatment Facility by naturally cooling and reconditioning the treated water before it flows into the Tualatin River.

Approximately three acres have been graded to simulate a natural wetlands, complete with channels where the water will snake through plants. Around one thousand tons of boulders have been trucked in, the largest weighing nearly seven tons. About five hundred trees and tens of thousands of native plants have been planted. And two arched wooden footbridges have been installed at the transition between the new and existing wetlands. Although the garden is intended to serve as a peaceful respite for visitors, it has a practical side too. The plants will help cool and add important nutrients to the treated wastewater. And some of the boulders have been piled up to create a waterfall that will add oxygen into the water. The new area is projected to open to visitors in early 2013.

Countless hours and thousands of dollars have been contributed to make Fernhill a wildlife draw. Native trees, bushes, and other vegetation have been planted by students and citizen volunteers. Habitat logs and stumps have been placed throughout the marsh to provide more diversity to the landscape. Nesting platforms and birdhouses have been set up in the nooks and crannies of the marsh and are always used in spring. More important are the countless volunteer hours contributed to rid the marsh of nonnative blackberry vines and canary grass. The gravel trails weave through the wetlands and allow easy strolling. Don't forget your binoculars or a spotting scope either! You'll want them handy for the many bird species that can be easily seen.

For More Information

Jackson Bottom Wetlands Preserve
Where: 2600 SW Hillsboro Highway, Hillsboro, OR 97123
Web: www.jacksonbottom.org
Phone: 503-681-6206

Fernhill Wetlands
Where: The intersection of SW Fernhill Road and Tualatin Valley Highway, Forest Grove, OR
Web: www.forestgrove-or.gov
Phone: 503-992-3200

Watch the Episode: www.traveloregon.com/jacksonbottom

Wilderness As Close As Your Own Backyard

Oxbow Regional Park

Sometimes the best travel secrets are very close to home! Oxbow Regional Park offers one of the richest outdoor experiences in the entire metro region where you can walk through stands of eight-hundred-year-old trees, watch big, brawny Chinook salmon return every year and gaze at petrified trees that are seemingly frozen in place. "It is a place where there's life on every scale and it's such a wonderful park to spend time," noted Karen Mathieson, a volunteer naturalist and longtime park visitor.

It's hard to believe that a wilderness-like setting can be found only a stone's throw from Portland, but it's true. In fact, you could say Metro's Oxbow Regional Park is right in Portland's backyard—and it is so special. Becky Lerner, another volunteer naturalist, said that Oxbow offers "an ancient forest trail where the trees are hundreds of years old—long before the city of Portland was imagined. I think that's really special."

Dan Daly is the Oxbow Regional Park naturalist who said that the park's twelve-hundred-forested acres offer plenty of elbow room plus key features with something for everyone. "Oh, a beautiful three-mile hiking trail that will take you through an ancient forest and also along the banks of the Sandy River. We have camping year-round, fishing year-round, and then recreational opportunities with classes in photography and skills like wildlife tracking. There are a lot of diverse activities in this park."

Gary Slone is a park volunteer and expert who teaches wild mushrooming classes. He said that the hands-on educational opportunities really put folks in touch with the parkland. "A park like Oxbow, so close to Portland, is a real gift; it's a wild place and a natural place." Oxbow Regional Park is also a natural for hikers who would like to explore the Sandy River Gorge for surprises that are slowly revealing themselves—one winter storm at a time.

You see, a stand of really old Doug fir and cedar trees—covered by a mudflow that hit the Sandy River in the late 1700s—is slowly revealing itself, according to Dan. "The stumps and snags have been excavated by recent high water events as the Sandy River bounces between the valley walls. The river is undercutting the banks, digs out the sand and leaves these ghostly looking trees standing straight up and down—they are at least 230 years old." Then there are the spawning salmon—often easy to see in the river's shallows—their spawning activity is constant against a backdrop of dazzling big-leaf maples and vine maples that show off brilliant yellow and crimson-red. It can be a stunning show for the visitor. "It's nature's drama at its finest," noted Dan. And all of it is waiting for you—anytime.

Karen noted with a smile, "This park is in our backyard and part of that whole idea of being 'wild in the city.' People think that if you live in a city like Portland that you leave nature behind, but Oxbow shows you can actually have both. It is great to have a place that's all wild like this." If you like to play outdoors, consider working there a little bit too through Metro's Nature University, a twelve-week class for folks who want to become volunteer park naturalists. The course runs from late January through early April. The class is perfectly suited to people who love nature and want to share their knowledge, experience, and enthusiasm with others.

For More Information

Where: Sandy River Gorge / Metro Oxbow Regional Park
Web: www.oregon.metro.gov
Phone: Metro Parks: 503-797-1700
Watch the Episode: www.traveloregon.com/oxbowpark

Access for All

Wheelchair Destinations

Most of us never give our travels or adventures into the great Oregon outdoors a second thought. Why should we? After all, for most of us there are countless exciting opportunities for varied adventures and destinations with few barriers to get in the way. But what if the challenge of simply getting there was huge, even monumental—so much so that it was far easier to just throw in the towel and stay home never to experience Oregon's many sights and sounds at all?

John Williams would like to change that perspective. John is a familiar voice to many in the Rose City. After all, he was on the rock radio scene for more than thirty years. But interestingly, when the radio studio went quiet, there was another sound that John preferred—the sounds of the wild!

John likes to be where the flocks are; it's a passion that he's owned since he was a kid. "I was always full steam ahead," noted the radio broadcaster on a recent trip to William L. Finley Wildlife Refuge near Corvallis, Oregon. "A normal childhood and I tried everything and even some things I shouldn't have," he said with a hearty chuckle. John had polio as a child—he didn't walk until he was four—but his family and their Northwest adventures always made John feel right at home—whether in leg braces or in a chair—the polio never slowed him down. "I wanted to be able to compete so I started playing wheelchair sports like wheelchair basketball when I was fourteen. I played that until I was fifty—but two shoulder surgeries told me it was time to get off the basketball floor."

But outdoor adventures like fishing, hunting, and boating came easy to someone eager to explore a love for the Northwest outdoors. Recently, John figured he could do more to help others too fearful to head outdoors. He produces a new TV program called *Wheelchair Destinations*. "I wanted to actually show people how accessible a

An avid outdoorsman his entire life, John Williams says his greatest joy is sharing his adventures with folks who roll on wheels rather than walk.

destination is! There are plenty of websites, plenty of books that talk about it, but no one has actually shown people how accessible a place really is when you get to it."

So far, he has compiled twenty-six, three-minute segments that center on places and activities for folks who roll on wheels rather than walk on two legs. His travels and specialty reports have taken John from the Oregon coast to the Cascade Mountains and include a visit to famous Timberline Lodge to find just how accessible the old lodge is for folks in wheelchairs. "Even I didn't realize how accessible a place it is," said John. "They've done some exceptional retro work up there: parking lots are very accessible and you can go in on the bottom floor through wide automatic doors. They've retrofitted with elevators, but they've not changed the integrity of the original building and I think that is very important." He's visited many prized local sites and critiques them too, offering a visual story of the good, the bad, and the not so friendly wheelchair access.

For example, John takes viewers to the popular Portland destination at Washington Park Rose Garden: "You actually see me huffing and puffing up a hill and if you see that on video, see what I'm going through, then you will have a good idea of what to expect and help you decide whether you want to go there yourself." Williams gave high marks to the recent retrofit of the famous Oregon State Park Vista House—for many it is considered the gateway to the Columbia River Gorge: "They have installed an elevator to take you from the bottom floor to the top floor but you don't see the machinery at all when you enter—it comes out of the floor! It was truly engineered properly and hasn't destroyed the integrity of the original building. I think they did a terrific job!"

John added that there are other notable travel destinations across Oregon that are wheelchair friendly too. For example, explore the North Fork Nehalem River's disabled angler platform, where salmon and steelhead are always on the bite. Or the John Day Fossil Beds National Monument where you will find a raised wooden boardwalk that allows folks a close-up view to 60 million years of geologic history. Finally, check out the Wildwood Recreation Site's Cascade Streamwatch Trail. The paved path takes you along the Salmon River for more than a mile and even puts you nose to nose with baby salmon in a tributary stream near Mount Hood.

Back at Finley Wildlife Refuge, John and I enjoyed the Homer Campbell Memorial Trail: a seventeen-hundred-foot elevated boardwalk that courses through an oak and wetlands area and eventually ends at a view blind. Here, you can duck in out of bad weather and the blind overlooks a pond that is favored by waterfowl and eagles. "They've done a real good job out here with a cement apron in the parking area that makes the wheelchair rolling easier and connects to the boardwalk that takes you clear out to the marshland. It's very impressive. You'll have no problem in a wheelchair—it's good stuff!" Williams adds that Oregon and especially Portland lead the nation in accessibility . . . that's something more people in chairs should embrace: "I really want to show folks what a beautiful part of the country we live in so they will get out of the living room and head out for travel across Oregon."

For More Information

Where: Wheelchair Destinations, 20225 SE 40th Street, Camas, WA 98607

Web: www.wheelchairdestinations.com

Phone: 503-936-0737

Watch the Episode: www.traveloregon.com/accessibleOR

Feathery Invasion
Sauvie Island Sandhills

Each fall, a feathery invasion drops in to Oregon's fields and wetlands as a quarter million Canada geese arrive on fixed wings with a rowdy chorus. At the Sauvie Island Wildlife Area, look closely and listen carefully for another bird species that stands head and shoulders above the crowd. Sandhill cranes are hard to miss and it's not just their three-foot height and six-foot wingspan, noted Assistant Wildlife Area Manager Dan Marvin. "This is the spot! This is it as far as opportunities to view sandhill cranes goes in the Willamette Valley. The most popular places to look for them on the island are the agricultural fields."

It's not only their distinct size, but adult cranes also have a striking red color across their faces. "Adults have a bright red crown—a bright red forehead really—and the chicks don't have that. In fact, the chicks look a lot paler in the face." There's an even more distinct feature according to Gary Ivey—Oregon's sandhill crane expert. He said that the sandhill sounds are unlike anything you've ever heard: "Well, it's kind of a loud trumpet that has kind of a trill to it. You can hear it from a long way off and the flocks use it as a contact call. Often, when they are migrating you will hear that call—even when they're almost invisible so high up. Once you hear the sound you never forget it."

The big birds fly to Sauvie Island from as far away as Southeast Alaska and British Columbia and they spend the winter lounging across the refuge grounds. The peak of their arrival is mid-October when up to four thousand birds show up on Sauvie Island. Most continue flying farther south, but approximately a quarter of them stay here all winter long. The best time to see them is during the early morning or late afternoon when birds are actively feeding in harvested grain fields.

Be sure to bring good optics too—either binoculars or a spotting scope—each will make a big difference enjoying the view to the birds. The "view" to all Oregon wildlife has recently improved according to Rick Hargrave—a spokesperson for the Oregon Department of Fish and Wildlife. He said that a recent survey showed nearly two million people spend more than a billion dollars each year to travel and watch Oregon wildlife. "We knew right then that we needed to get something out there that will make viewing a little easier for folks to enjoy and also highlight the wildlife that the department oversees and manages."

The new interactive Oregon Wildlife Viewing Map will help you see more of Oregon's fish and wildlife species. It is a Google-based map that details 235 great places to see wildlife in the state. It will help you discover where to see bald eagles or sage grouse or migrating snow geese. It will point you to good sites to view Oregon's largest mammals including migrating gray whales or high desert antelope or Rocky Mountain elk.

Rick said the map's sites reach into each corner of the state. "The state agency manages fish and wildlife for the people of Oregon and we want people to understand the connections between wildlife viewing, conservation, and the habitat. Without an emphasis on all of those, you're not going to see the variety of wildlife that we have in this great state." You've plenty of time to enjoy the sandhill show and hear their haunting calls. Sauvie Island Wildlife Area is their winter home through winter and the colorful birds will return north to their breeding and nesting grounds in April.

For More Information

Where: Sauvie Island Wildlife Area, 18330 NW Sauvie Island Road, Portland, OR 97231
Web: www.dfw.state.or.us
Phone: 503-621-3488

Oregon Wildlife Viewing Map
Web: www.dfw.state.or.us

Watch the Episode: www.traveloregon.com/sauvieisland

Down by the Old Mill Stream

Thompson's Mills State Heritage Site

There's simply nothing like what you'll find "down by the old mill stream" at Thompson's Mills State Heritage Site. When Park Manager Doug Crispin tells the unique tale of Oregon history at one of the newest state park properties, the nineteenth century comes to life. It is history that dates back more than 150 years to a time when leather belts wrapped wooden wheels to move augers and elevators carried grain that gave life to the earliest settlers of the Willamette Valley. It was a time when the Calapooia River produced hydropower that moved all manner of machinery at Thompson's Mills near Shedd, Oregon.

Martin Thompson owned the mill for much of its life and even built a Queen Anne–styled cottage next door. But it was the gleaming whitewashed grain silos and the towering five-story mill that marked the site for miles around. Doug said that Oregon State Parks and Recreation Department was so impressed with the treasured landmark that they bought the mill, the cottage, and the surrounding property a few years ago. "Every time I walk through this mill and see the axe marks on these original timbers, it comes alive to me. I just marvel at the craftsmanship, the hard work, and the ingenuity of our pioneer ancestors. Plus, the fact that it still stands today."

Restoration efforts at the site continue and offer hands-on exhibits that show you how tons of grain were moved and then milled with giant limestone millstones. It's a remarkable site with many hidden nooks and crannies according to Doug, who added it is "the sort of place that demands exploration." Thompson's Mills flour was shipped across the country—even to China and Europe. Parts of the process offer homespun memories for visitors who recall the double-life of cotton flour bags. "They were recycled and made into aprons," noted Doug. "Or tea towels by thrifty farm wives during

Grinding grain into flour is one of many hands-on experiences that keeps history alive at Thompson's Mills State Heritage Site.

the Great Depression and World War II. Folks were recycling the old flour bags long before it was fashionable—back then it was simply more practical."

It's a site that holds on to history and it is even more amazing when you consider that it was all built by what Doug termed "saddle back engineering."

"All of this—the mill, the cottage, the machinery—was built and put into place long before GPS, long before aerial photography, laser levels, or any modern technological help. These people figured the whole thing out by cruising the neighborhood on foot and on horse." It's a wonderful step back into an earlier time and place that's pretty much like it was—and that makes it all worth a visit.

For More Information

Where: One mile east of Shedd, OR on Boston Mill Drive

Web: www.oregonstateparks.org

Phone: 541-491-3611

Watch the Episode: www.traveloregon.com/thompsonmill

Rowing Through History

The All-Oregon Boat

When you sit between the oars of the all-Oregon boat, a classic craft called the drift boat, you will slide across rapids, slip past boulders, and leave all of your troubles behind. For local boatbuilder Ray Heater, you also touch Oregon history. "Oh, the drift boat is really a special type of boat the represents the state of Oregon. That has always attracted me—why don't I build something else? Because I'm a fisherman and I love to float rivers and I've never seen a craft that can perform as well as this simple boat."

Ray builds wooden drift boats in his Welches, Oregon, shop, a business called Ray's River Dories. He's the last to make a living by cutting, drilling, and hammering Doug fir and cedar into boats that take people down rivers. Ray's career spans more than four decades and it has been built upon a boat design that's all Oregon. As he and I recently stood admiring a pair of boats currently under construction in his shop he told me: "These are steelhead drift boats that can go in the back of a pickup and they really are a part of a tradition that began a century ago."

Drift boats were spawned on the McKenzie and Rogue Rivers in the early twentieth century and at first, the boats hauled supplies. By the 1940s anglers paid big money to fishing guides like Woodie Hindman who would take fishermen, called dudes, down rivers to catch fish. Ray noted, "It's really a floating platform for your camping and fishing gear—that's really what it's all about." Ray added that the all-Oregon boat was distinct because it safely rode atop the waves. "Oh man, they can provide a piece of ballet—water ballet! Those guys between the oars would just dance across those waves with the oars—it's a rush, a real rush . . . I mean I like to fish, but I like to run that white water."

Ray is not alone in his quest to protect and preserve the all-Oregon boat. He

The all-Oregon drift boat was designed to tackle white-water rapids and allow anglers easier access to remote rivers.

explained: "People will say, 'You should write something down about this.' And I say, 'Oh boy, that's going to be a tough one for me, I'd rather build a boat than write about one.' Well, then along came Roger Fletcher, who walks into my shop one day and says, 'I'm writing a book about the river boat. I thought, 'You are the man.'"

Roger never thought of himself as the man to save a chapter of Oregon history—he just likes the shape and feel and history of wooden drift boats. He builds them too—models—that are scaled down versions. "They basically require the same technique of a person building a traditional drift boat—just smaller. There isn't anything fancy about it, but when you look at the lines of a McKenzie River drift boat, there isn't a prettier set of lines."

Roger has had a love affair with drift boats since a boy. Today, he is the author of a new book called *Drift Boats and River Dories*, that tells the story of the earliest boats that were developed for Oregon rivers. He calls the drift boat design a "unique contribution to the boating world" and adds that few people know about them, although they've likely seen them and perhaps been lucky enough to even fish in one. "It's the crescent shape. And fellows like Hindman, Veltie Pruitt, and Prince Helfrich who designed and originally built them—they all fell in love with the design because it assumed the crescent shape of the waves. Plus, people fell in love with the ride." And who wouldn't? Today, drift boating's popularity has spread throughout the land. The all-Oregon boat can be seen on rivers across the country, wherever there are rivers waiting for adventure.

Now, thanks to Roger Fletcher, more people will know of the boat's important past. "My hope," he added, "is that more people will see more of these traditional and highly functional and beautiful boats out on the rivers. It's tough not to fall in love with this boat. If a person hasn't been in one—gets in one, has a day's experience in one—he'll be back." Each spring, there is an annual gathering of wooden drift boats and their builders on the banks of the McKenzie River. It is held at Eagle Rock Lodge and offers newcomers a chance to learn more about the boats and their lasting place in Oregon boating history.

For More Information

Ray's River Dories
Where: PO Box 19954, Portland, OR 97280
Web: www.raysriverdories.com
Phone: 503-244-3608

River's Touch
Where: 2353 East Ellendale Avenue, Dallas, OR 97338
Web: www.riverstouch.com
Phone: 503-559-0204

McKenzie River Wooden Boat Festival
Where: 49198 McKenzie Highway, Vida, OR 97488
Web: www.thecentralcascades.com

Watch the Episode: www.traveloregon.com/ORboat

Secrets in the Sand
Float Wizards

As the fall season surf floods and ebbs, beachcombers wander, seeking treasures from the tides—something to help them remember the moment. In the Lincoln City area, folks may cross paths with local resident Wayne Johnson—a self-proclaimed "float wizard" who makes certain that beachcombers have something special to find. "The fact is it's kind of undercover work that I do. First, it's hidden and I try not to be seen by anyone. And then I hide something colorful and prized too. I like that part of it a lot."

Like a secret agent, Wayne stealthily moves among sea-strewn logs and lush beach grass to hide beautiful, colorful glass floats. Wayne said that he and a

The colorful glass floats that you create at Jennifer Sears Studio are beautiful treasures that you can take home.

dozen other float wizards hide up to seventy glass floats along eight miles of Lincoln City beaches beginning each October and continuing through May. "We want them visible and yet hidden enough so that it will be difficult for anyone to see them at first glance—we want it to be a challenge to find them," noted Wayne.

Nearby at the Jennifer Sears Glass Art Studio in Lincoln City, you can see the challenge that it takes to create a glass float—in fact, you can even learn how to do it yourself—with the help of local artists like Kelly Howard. Kelly noted, "People always say, 'anyone can watch the glassblower but we never get to try it.' Well, here is the chance to do just that. Try it, you may get hooked on it."

Glassblowing is one of those activities that may leave a huge smile on your face just like it did for my youngest son, Kevin McOmie. He joined me on a recent coastal adventure and he was anxious to try his hand at glassblowing. Kevin, an accomplished art student who specializes in painting and drawing, had never tried anything like glass art before. But he soon got the knack of it and with Kelly's patient demeanor and easy-to-follow instructions—he was deeply into the art of glass within fifteen minutes.

First, Kelly pulled a glob of molten glass from the 2,100°F furnace. The material glowed yellow and red hot from the heat. She showed Kevin how to roll it and then apply color with other small pieces of glass. "Okay—Kevin, just blow and we'll expand the glass into a float—look! That's amazing, isn't it? You're doing great." Kelly coached as Kevin blew into a long rubber hose attached to the end of a five-foot-long hollow rod. The glass globe at the other end magically grew into a fiery globe. Kevin noted, "It really is fun! But you have to keep an eye on it—it's using a lot of skills all at once. In the end, I think I've created something really awesome that I'm going to remember for a long time."

The Jennifer Sears Studio is one of several glass art houses in the central Oregon coast area that's participating in the glass float project. Each float is like a moment of fiery magic that's captured in a heartbeat and leaves you spellbound. Kelly added, "To see something get made and then realize that you had a hand in creating it, especially something made out of glass—well, it really is mesmerizing and different." Back on the beach, Wayne Johnson insisted that glass floats provide great adventure for folks who get to try something new. "Whether you craft one with your hands or pick one up off the beach, it's like holding a beach treasure . . . something special from the Oregon coast." The glass float project continues along Lincoln City beaches through the Memorial Day holiday weekend.

For More Information

Lincoln City Visitor Center
Where: 540 NE US Highway 101, Lincoln City, OR 97367
Web: www.oregoncoast.org/finders-keepers
Phone: 541-996-1274 or 800-452-2151

Jennifer Sears Art Studio
Where: 4821 US Highway 101, Lincoln City, OR 97367
Phone: 541-996-2569

Watch the Episode: www.traveloregon.com/sandsecrets

Restoration—An Acre at a Time
Ladd Marsh Wildlife Area

I t was truly a chance encounter with wildlife artist and La Grande resident Jan Clark whom I met while traveling to the Foot Hill Road Viewpoint within the Oregon Department of Fish and Wildlife's Ladd Marsh Wildlife Area. Jan arrived in the area more than thirty years ago and never left. She fell in love with the scenery, the wetlands, and the wildlife and now she paints it all—every chance she gets. "Well, I simply love the scenery with the Wallowa Mountains in the background," noted Jan. "Plus, it's usually just quiet out here, really quiet—except for the birds."

In the silence—broken only by the rough sound of her brush across the canvas—it felt as though you could reach out and touch the wetlands, the wildlife, and the history of the Grande Ronde Valley. State Wildlife Biologist Cathy Nowak said that fifty years ago you would not have seen much bird life or much wildness because it had all disappeared. "At one time, the valley had about forty thousand acres of wetlands in it," noted Cathy. "But that was before settlement—by the 1950s, there were just a couple hundred acres that had not been drained for agriculture. So, the chance to see any wildlife was a pretty rare event in those days."

That began to change when the first Wildlife Area Manager Bill Brown developed the Oregon Department of Fish and Wildlife's (ODFW) Ladd Marsh Wildlife Area (named for nearby Ladd Creek). Brown's first purchase was nearly three hundred acres. Today, there are more than six thousand acres and half of that is in wetlands and marshland. Today, ODFW Ladd Marsh Manager Dave Larson noted that the site is the largest protected marsh in northeast Oregon. "At one time we had a lot of support from the hunting community, but now that we are opening up the wildlife viewing and a new auto tour route, we're seeing a lot more support from folks who travel here to look at wildlife. And they come from all over too."

Ladd Marsh Wildlife Area offers protection for a variety of wild animals, but also allows visitors a chance to see the wildlife up close.

The Ladd Marsh auto tour route is a little over a mile long but there are also six miles of hiking trails that take you into the wetlands for close up views to more than 225 different bird and other wildlife species—perhaps deer, elk, even antelope. Speaking of watching wildlife—don't leave home without the binoculars; they make a big difference for enjoying the show. In the spring, you can also enjoy a unique event called the Ladd Marsh Birdathon. All of the trails are open with experts: artists, teachers, and biologists on hand to teach you more about what you are seeing—plus, many exhibits and children's activities that are set up too. Cathy added that it is a fun and educational weekend outdoor experience: "It is not competitive, it's a celebration—a celebration of the birds, bird-watching, and the out of doors. So, it is an exciting time of the year with migrating species moving through, plus the young are hatching everywhere across the wildlife area. You can see something new every day."

For More Information

Where: 59116 Pierce Road, La Grande, OR 97850

Web: www.dfw.state.or.us

Phone: 541-963-4954

Watch the Episode: www.traveloregon.com/laddmarsh

Easy to Reach Outdoors
Wild in the City

GETAWAY #94 – GREATER PORTLAND

If you have an appetite for outdoor adventure, consider a getaway that satisfies your hunger for the great Oregon outdoors and teaches you more about your community too. Discover the new "Intertwine" where it's easy to connect with nearby nature. Time in the outdoors can refresh the eye and lift the spirit and the beauty of Oregon is that you won't travel far to find it! *Wild in the City* is a new book copublished by the Portland Audubon Society and Oregon State University Press. Mike Houck, M. J. Cody, and Bob Sallinger coedited and wrote essays for the impressive collection of writings and practical nature-finding "ramblings."

"The book is really educational for people who enjoy our parks," noted M. J. "But if they lack a sense for the Northwest—that lifelong depth—that's what we also provide in the book."

More than one hundred writers contributed to finding the wild in the city, authors who wrote the text, prepared the maps, sketched wildlife drawings, and really provided the nuts and bolts of locating the Portland area's parks, trails, and refuges. From Washington County's Fernhill Wetlands near Forest Grove where flocks of geese fill the sky to the region's eastern edge at Oxbow Park on the Sandy River that seems more wilderness than campground.

There are also well-known wildlife areas—like Sauvie Island—that continue to fill us with "wonder and surprise," noted the Audubon Society's Bob Sallinger—a dedicated naturalist who enjoyed one particular essay. "A piece called 'Raptor Road Trip' is all about the different places you can visit on the island—whether you hike, bike, or drive or paddle—around the island. It's simply phenomenal wildlife viewing and winter is really a spectacular time of year to get out and see wildlife." Whether you are a longtime resident, a newcomer, or just passing through Portland, you will fall in love with *Wild in the City.*

It's far more than a guide book, for the text also presents a call to action and a new way to look at the expanding network of connections between the wild places that we prize: a network that is called the Intertwine. "The Intertwine is a name for the region's network of trails, parks, and natural areas," noted Metro's Dan Moeller. Dan is Metro's natural area land manager, the agency that manages much of the fourteen-thousand-plus acres of parks, trails, and natural areas acquired through two voter-approved bond measures. "You can find everything from beautiful wetlands to oak woodlands to prairies and upland forests," added Dan. "You can find a little bit of everything and it's really magnificent land."

The Intertwine is growing all of the time too. In fact, recent additions include Cooper Mountain Nature Park near Beaverton, Graham Oaks Nature Park near Wilsonville, and Mount Talbert Nature Park in Clackamas County. Each site is distinct, each offers special features, and each is connected as natural space and outdoor environmental classrooms. "That's exactly what the Intertwine is," said Dan. "It goes beyond bureaucracies and boundaries and it works among varied agencies, communities, and cities to bring all of these parks and natural spaces together. Citizens can go out and enjoy them as seamlessly and easily as possible."

Mike Wetter is director of the Intertwine Alliance, a group of more than fifty public and nonprofit agencies plus many private businesses. The Alliance has created a new Intertwine website that provides maps, directions, and tips so you can explore the wild places. "You don't have to drive an hour to get to nature," said Mike. "It's right here where we live and we can enjoy it as a part of our everyday lives."

For More Information

Portland Audubon Society
Where: 5151 NW Cornell Road, Portland, OR 97210
Web: www.audubonportland.org
Phone: 503-292-6855

The Intertwine
Where: 111 SW Oak Street, Suite 300A, Portland, OR 97204
Web: www.theintertwine.org
Phone: 503-445-0991

Watch the Episode: www.traveloregon.com/intertwine

Northwest Nature Guide
Smith and Bybee Wetlands Natural Area

There's quite an outdoor show for those in the know at a place where you set your own pace for a walk on the wild side. Smith and Bybee Wetlands Natural Area is a wildlife refuge that's as grass roots as it gets where you can stroll paths marked with amazing wildlife moments at a time of year brimming with wild critters. It's hard to believe how special a place we have in this wildlife area in North Portland. Framed by industrial parks and development on all sides, it is two thousand acres of cottonwood forest and wetlands, the largest urban lake and marsh in the country.

Metro's urban park naturalist, James Davis, recently told me that it's also a premier site for hiking and watching wildlife. "It's big enough—at two thousand acres—a big solid chunk and not divided up into pieces by roads and such—so it's not fragmented and that's great for wildlife." While human activity occurs all around, all the time, along an easy paved trail, the city hubbub seemed a million miles away. "It is nature in the city," remarked the exuberant James. "Nature in your neighborhood and you don't have to go out to the wilderness to live with wildlife."

As Canada geese winged by—a red-tailed hawk soared past on its hunting foray—it was easy to see that waterfowl and raptors provide the best shows that you can watch in winter. "It is pretty unbelievable to most people," added James. "We have two pairs of bald eagles nesting here, we've got a nesting colony of great blue herons, we've even had tundra swans hanging out here in the winter . . . really, any bird that comes through the Portland area can show up here." But what doesn't show up much are people! I wondered aloud, "Could Smith and Bybee be a well-kept secret?"

"Perhaps," nodded James. Although as Metro's point man of sorts and the park's naturalist for the past dozen years, he insisted that the word is getting out and more folks are discovering the many pleasures that the wetlands offered—either on the easy hiking trail—or—in a canoe with a paddle.

In fact, James does all he can to spread the word about Smith and Bybee, and other local places too, through his book *The Northwest Nature Guide*, a month-by-month, comprehensive wildlife-watching guide with seventy-five color photos and extensive maps and directions. Top of his local list for newcomers: Crystal Springs Park in Southeast Portland. "It is the best beginner's bird-watching place in Portland," said James. "I've been there on a bird walk in February—and we saw thirteen different species of waterfowl without binoculars. There may not be a lot there, but the diversity is just spectacular."

Fast on the wings of Crystal Springs comes the relatively new Tualatin River National Wildlife Refuge in Sherwood: "Ah, they really planned the trail across the refuge right," said James. "It's in such an excellent location so that you can get out there, see them, and yet there are many other areas closed to the public. So, the birds actually have a refuge on the refuge." Part of the wonder of Smith and Bybee Wetlands Natural Area is that it's not on the way to anywhere; you must go there to explore it for yourself on a journey of discovery. "It's one of the things that makes Portland such a great place to live. The idea is that nature doesn't have to be way away from people. We can have nature in the city, nature in the neighborhoods—we can have urban wildlife."

For More Information

Where: Off I-5 at exit 307, then drive west on North Marine Drive for 2.2 miles to the parking area.

Phone: 503-797-1700

Watch the Episode: www.traveloregon.com/baldeagles

Lewis and Clark Slept Here
Fort Clatsop National Memorial

I f your family yearns for a holiday getaway that teaches unique Oregon history about a group of explorers who found themselves stranded in Oregon over two hundred years ago, then head to Fort Clatsop National Memorial at Lewis and Clark National Historical Park, where their story of survival is alive and well.

Chances are you will spy retired schoolteacher Tom Wilson covered head to toe in buckskins and history. He relishes the role of Captain William Clark—one of the coleaders of the famous Lewis and Clark Corps of Discovery—and is on duty this time of year at Fort Clatsop. He explained to nearby visitors: "This fort wasn't really in their plans—they had hoped to get downriver, see a ship, get reprovisioned, get back over the mountains before winter and home. Well, it is winter so things didn't go as planned."

Tom is part of a small group of volunteers who bring the Lewis and Clark story to life through living history experiences that you can enjoy on your visit. "Oh, it was a miserable, cold, wet winter. They were low on provisions, their clothes had rotted, military uniforms had rotted away, and so the ship was going to reprovision them. Unfortunately, they arrived much later than they thought—the trading season was over." So, they were forced to stay and they chose a small area on the Oregon side of the river to build a log fort. When you visit at this time of year, you get a feel for what the explorers experienced in December 1805.

The Corps also stayed in Oregon because abundant deer and elk made the hunting easier—especially for the elk. "Yes," added Tom, "the reason this fort is here is because of more word of elk and deer than anywhere else and so they were out hunting the entire time." Elk provided the explorers with many things: food, hides for clothing, elk fat for tallow candles, and the antlers could be made into buttons. Nothing was wasted.

The replica Fort Clatsop transports you to Oregon's earliest days of exploration and discovery.

Indoors at the nearby Fort Clatsop Museum, you can learn more about the Corp of Discovery's remarkable journey across America through exhibits, drawings, and equipment that also put you in touch with history. You can also do the same on the recently completed Fort to Sea Trail that stretches from Fort Clatsop nearly seven miles to the ocean. And it can be joined at many locations along the way.

If you travel this way, you may also consider a longer stay at nearby Fort Stevens State Park. The trails and campgrounds at Fort Stevens are quiet at this time of year. The summer crowds have disappeared and the beaches, Coffenbury Lake, and the wetland areas are all yours to explore. Fort Stevens Park Manager Mike Stein explained: "People are looking to get away from the larger crowds and we specialize in that at this time of year. We've got over four thousand acres to spread across, plus miles of beachfront and nine miles of paved trail, plus another seven miles of nature trail."

If you lack a trailer or an RV, no need to worry, Fort Stevens boasts fifteen yurts that make the camping easy: "Yurts are wonderful camping opportunities," explained Mike. "They offer a domed platform with canvas sides and top. They have furniture in them: a futon sofa and a bunk bed. They've proven to be very popular because they reach out to the visiting public that's unable or lacks the time to invest in a tent or RV."

Back at Fort Clatsop, Superintendent David Szymanski said that folks should consider Fort Clatsop a launching point to make their own trail of discovery in the region: "It is a way to give a lot of people the experience of what the expedition would have faced. It's a place where you can spend a day or two exploring and get to know more about our national history." Tom Wilson agreed: "What they endured and how they persevered to make this place their temporary home for nearly four months—and the story behind it—it wasn't just a camping trip—this wasn't just a bunch of guys looking for an adventure. This had so many purposes and was well laid out and executed. It truly was the best of any expedition ever."

For More Information

Fort Clatsop National Memorial /
Lewis and Clark National Historical Park
Where: 92343 Fort Clatsop Road, Astoria, OR 97103
Phone: 503-861-2471

Fort Stevens State Park
Where: 100 Peter Iredale Road, Hammond, OR 97121
Web: www.oregonstateparks.org
Phone: For information only, call 503-861-1671 or 800-551-6949. To make reservations, call 800-452-5687.

Watch the Episode: www.traveloregon.com/lewisclark

Fort to Sea Trail

You'll want to allow yourself plenty of time to walk in the footsteps of legendary American explorers Lewis and Clark and the Corps of Discovery as you connect with a different time but the same place along the Fort to Sea Trail in Clatsop County. "This trail allows people to walk in the expedition's footsteps!" said David Szymanski, National Park superintendent at Fort Clatsop. "You're out in the woods and you're feeling it in a way that's not too different from the way the expedition would have known it. Don't be surprised if you see deer or elk and then you cross under US Highway 101 and suddenly reach sand dunes with freshwater lakes and soon the coastline. It's all rather remarkable. It's also a quiet place this time of year, more serene and it feels wonderful to get away from it all. This is the place to do that."

Keep in mind the trail is more than six miles long, so allow plenty of time for the easy to moderate hike; a portion of it is even wheelchair accessible. Bring water, snacks, and dress for the ever-changing Oregon coastal weather pattern of sun, then showers, and back to sunshine again.

A Home for Eagles
Twilight Eagle Sanctuary

How can you miss on a day like this when the endless drizzle that blankets the land or the buckets of drenching wet that fall from above have oh-so-briefly disappeared? It's a day that's given way to indigo blue skies and fine, wide-angle views along a less traveled byway called US 30. This route between Portland and Astoria may be among Oregon's oldest, albeit not the fastest, along the Columbia River. This green-bordered asphalt roadway skirts the southern shore of the mighty waterway and forces you to slow down to explore intersecting back roads where you may be surprised by what you see and hear.

For example, near Scappoose Bay, be on the lookout for flocks of sandhill cranes. They're hard to miss, for they are an imposing sight, standing nearly four feet tall and sporting striking red feather masks. Crane courtship is in full swing at this time of year, so if you spot a flock, watch as the males dance with their broad wings spread to reach sky-high. They will jump and lunge and prance about all day long, putting on quite a comical show. And they will bend

Neal Maine is an Oregon "photographer for all seasons" in the great outdoors, especially at Wolf Bay Wetlands near Astoria.

low and pick up sticks and small branches with their long, leathery-like beaks and then toss the woody debris into the air. All of this, biologists say, is how male cranes charm the nearby females—actions by which the lonesome boys hope to win a mate. Romance aside, it's an interesting way for you to spend a bit of time.

On these unusually warm winter days—when the thermometer peaks at 50°F— the surrounding hills along this drive seem to shake off their wetness for a time to form fog wisps that float above the hilly rims. Near Rainier, Oregon, at the famous site of the Trojan Nuclear Plant, a former power station, pull off the highway to the inviting view of tundra swans—sometimes numbering as many as two hundred— lounging across adjacent wetlands and ponds. This power-generation site turned parkland is home to the swans from November through March. Sometimes called the "B-52s of the waterfowl world," the swans fill the air in swarms on six-foot wingspans, then glide to ground for a well-deserved break. Many of these huge birds will make a two-thousand-mile one-way journey from their arctic breeding and nesting grounds to this site in Oregon. Although swans are not hunted in the Pacific Northwest, they remain a cautious bird, so don't expect to get too close. To ensure a close-up view, bring binoculars or a spotting scope and admire the snow-white plumage against the otherwise drab winter background.

Clatsop County draws you farther west along US 30 to the Wolf Bay Wetlands, in the midst of the Twilight Eagle Sanctuary, where you can step up to a wooden deck and gaze out across the broad breadth of the Columbia River. Don't be surprised if some awesome sights are much closer at hand—for if you are lucky and gaze overhead at just the right moment, you may see our national symbol slowly cruise by. The sanctuary testifies to a community's efforts to protect wildlife habitat while providing an educational opportunity.

Nearly twenty-five years ago, the Twilight Sanctuary was but a dream to a group of local Clatsop County folks who seized upon an opportunity to save a 15.3-acre parcel. The site was offered for sale by Cavenham Forest Industries, Inc., who had planned to log the last of the parcel's old-growth Sitka spruce and western hemlock trees. But the site also contained a nesting pair of bald eagles and served as a winter roosting site for many more. Cavenham agreed to sell the land to the Lower Columbia River Eagle Task Force, a local group. However, the first order of business for the citizen-based nonprofit organization was the challenging task of raising the money for the purchase—a princely $50,000.

Lest you doubt that "everyday people" can protect wildlife, you need to spend a few moments with Neal Maine, an energetic, innovative educator from nearby Seaside. I first met Neal when I was working on various news stories about the Twilight refuge purchase in the late 1980s. He was a member of the task force that spearheaded the fund-raising efforts to save the critical eagle habitat. He's also a big believer that folks of all ages can make a difference in helping wild critters. To that end, Neal told me that more than $68,000 was raised in little under two years in donations ranging from a few dollars to $5,000 from corporations, foundations, conservation groups, governments, local garden clubs, and individuals. He was especially proud of the role that local schoolchildren played in raising more than $3,000 for the purchase.

"Those kids—and there were hundreds from throughout Clatsop County, Grant," he smiled and softly noted, "did everything from bake sales to bottle drives to arm twisting their parents, and these children really embodied our hope for the purchase. That is, each of us can make a difference saving wildlife habitat."

The Twilight Eagle Sanctuary is one of the few remaining sites adjacent to the Columbia River affording the roosting, feeding, and territorial requirements of bald eagles. A thick canopy provides shelter and moderates the otherwise cold winter temperatures. The eagles also prefer the area because of its riverine habitat since their winter feed consists mostly of ducks, geese, and swans. According to Neal, up to fifty bald eagles roost in or near the sanctuary during the winter and that's nearly half of the remaining eagle population along both sides of the Columbia River.

The viewing platform is located about three-eighths of a mile from the sanctuary proper so visitors won't disturb the wildlife. The broad wooden deck overlooks a peaceful riverscape of wetlands, islands of grass, and sloughs. Interpretive signs at the platform explain facts about eagles and their habitat and also how people affect the birds' world. There are good chances to see bald eagles hunting or perching at or near the sanctuary at nearly any time of year, but as Neal likes to say, there's an almost "money-back guarantee" that you will see eagles in the winter months.

For More Information

Where: Eleven miles east of Astoria off US Highway 30 between mile markers 87 and 88 at Burnside Road.

Contacts: 503-325-9306

Watch the Episode: www.traveloregon.com/waterfallwanderings

Snow Play
Mount Hood National Forest

On a sunlit day without a cloud in the sky, the crowds at Ski Bowl East near Mount Hood were eager for action on the groomed tubing hill. Ski Bowl Manager Sean Maloy noted with a smile, "It's more fun than any one person deserves, so they usually bring lots of friends!" Judging by the line-up of enthusiastic visitors, Sean seemed to be right! Winter tubing has become popular recreation at Ski Bowl and other snow park sites around Mount Hood. In fact, Ski Bowl draws as many tubing enthusiasts as skiers to the nearby slopes. "Snow play has taken off," said Sean. "You don't need lessons or pieces of sophisticated equipment to ride a tube. You just come out and have fun and now the secret's out!"

At Ski Bowl East, you not only ride a comfy cushioned seat atop a vinyl-wrapped inner tube, complete with handles and a towrope, but you can enjoy an easy tow up the hill or try the new escalator style, stand-up ride back to the top. "Helps take the trudging out of tubing," noted Troy Fisher, Ski Bowl operations manager. "From small kids up to adults, tubing is a good family-oriented activity where everyone can hang out, socialize, and spend the day together."

At the nearby snow park hillside Snow Bunny, managed by the Summit Ski Area, you will find less grooming and a rental shack where you pick up an old-fashioned inner tire tube. "It's a great place for large groups," added Troy. "They have their own space and it is more affordable. We get a lot of church groups that come out to Snow Bunny and play all day long."

If you wish to "freelance" and find a hill to call your own in the Mount Hood Forest, be cautious of the site you choose. Hillsides are usually heavily wooded and not groomed at all. One exception is the Littlejohn Sno-Park in the Mount Hood National Forest that's located along Highway 35 less than ten miles from Government

The downhill ride on the tubing hill at Ski Bowl East is an absolute blast measured by the mile-wide smiles on the visitors who come to play.

Camp. Adjacent to the parking lot look for a "sled at your own risk" sign that marks important rules should you choose to slide down the site's steep slope.

Climb the highway back up to White River West Sno-Park and enjoy a spacious and popular play area. It's a great site for snow play and it is where Devan Schwartz, a guide with Adventures Without Limits, brings newcomers for a hike along the eastern approach to Mount Hood. "It's one of the more popular destinations and just a few miles past Government Camp," noted Devan. "Everything from inner tubing to snowshoeing to backcountry skiing happens up this way." You'll also find plenty of elbow room and a stunning view to the mountain that makes the snowshoe effort so worth your time. And that is the point—get out there and explore the Mount Hood National Forest in winter. "When we get fresh snow—and we will," added Ski Bowl's Troy Fisher, "it's a good getaway and feels a world away."

A Sno-Park permit is required in most snow play areas. The money from the sale of the permits offsets the cost of snow removal along roadways and parking areas. Something else to keep in mind: Winter is "weather fickle!" and the snow level can rise and falls thousands of feet each week, so check snow conditions and the weather forecast before you head for the hills.

For More Information

Where: Mount Hood Ski Bowl, 87000 East US Highway 26, Government Camp, OR 97028

Web: www.skibowl.com

Phone: 503-272-3206

Watch the Episode: www.traveloregon.com/tubingmthood

Snow Survival

Under the warm, brilliant sun, Oregon's winter weather may fool you into thinking all is well in the great outdoors but as it turns out, that's not always true: Jim Peters is a survival pro—a search and rescue volunteer for nearly twenty-five years who said that the folks he's found had one thing in common: They forgot to ask, "What if?"

"What if I twist my ankle? What if I have to stay out overnight?" noted the longtime search and rescue volunteer. "What if I should need a shelter or a way of making a warming fire—would I know how to do it in the cold?" Jim added that the answers demand preparation for the worst that Mother Nature serves up, even if it's just a day of family fun in the snow.

For example, would you know how to seek simple shelter? Jim acted quickly when I put him to the test—he scanned the trees—specifically, the tree wells that the deep snow had created. "There—see that natural little cave in there," he said as he pointed to a nearby spruce tree with its branches bowed low from the weight of fresh snow. "You can crawl right in there and could probably rest in there just the way it is." Jim said that a tree well with branches bent low keeps out overhead snow and protects you from energy-sapping winds. "Plus—there's a lot of needles down here on the ground—really thick and spongy—excellent to sleep on. I won't be sleeping on the snow."

He pulled a lightweight tarp from inside his daypack, unfolded it, and laid it across the ground. "This will keep me from getting wet and if there's little bit of wind that does come through here, this will help block it too." Jim said that the "right" clothing is critical for staying warm too. He insisted that you should never wear cotton—it won't wick moisture away—but you rely on a base layer of polypropylene or other synthetic wear. "It has a wicking property about it that pulls moisture away from the skin into your insulating layer of clothing—and for that I use thick fleece."

Jim wears a waterproof shell over the fleece because it also blocks the wind. He added that you not forget a hat too, for if your head's left uncovered, up to half your body heat can escape. "Keeping your ears covered is as important as fingers and toes because when they get cold, it starts to affect your attitude. You want to have a positive mental attitude." Attitude means attention to preparation and that equals energy conservation. "You don't want to spend a lot of time building something that takes a lot of effort and energy," said Jim. "You want to save your energy as much as possible, find something Mother Nature already started. That's the way to go."

Sharon Ward is another search and rescue volunteer who partners with her dog, Seeker, to find people who get lost in the outdoors. She said that when people head for snow country, anything can happen: "Often we'll get someone who has gone out for a fun day in the woods and a foot or two of snow comes down and they can't drive out. They're stuck!"

And when the sun goes down—getting stuck takes on a whole new dimension. "If it's dark," said Sharon, "there are many dangers—you could fall in a creek, fall off a ledge; we've had people who walked straight off ridges at night—so at night it's very dangerous to travel in the woods."

Sharon strongly advocates carrying essentials to help you make it through a night or two—items that are packed away in your rig, like water . . . in a shatterproof lightweight container of plastic or aluminum. She added that you should carry food, even as simple as nuts and raisins or other high-energy food. Don't forget a whistle

Sharon Ward is a big believer that "the simpler and smaller the better" when it comes to winter survival gear that can be stowed away in a small pack.

to signal for help, a lamp or flashlight with spare batteries, a knife, and some source of heat. "I always bring hand warmers in the winter," added Sharon. "They are wonderful and inexpensive and you can put them in your boots or mittens to warm you up."

She always carries a small first aid kit and keeps everything in a small daypack or fanny pack—stored away in the vehicle. If you leave the car on a hike, you can take your essentials with you. "If you do these small things, you'll be well on your way toward surviving your time should conditions change and you get stuck in the snow." Search and rescue experts agree it's the little things added together that could make a big difference in your ability to survive an unexpected turn of events.

You should also check the weather and be sure of the forecast, leave a note with someone—a friend or family member—that says where you're going and when you expect to return, and pack some survival essentials and keep them in your vehicle—either in a daypack or fanny pack. All of this may just help you through an emergency in the great Oregon outdoors.

Wintertime Wapiti
Jewell Meadows Wildlife Area

Oregon's natural beauty is easy to come by when you spend days afield and sometimes incidental moments become valuable lessons on wildlife that stay with you for years to come. It can be like that any December morning at Jewell Meadows Wildlife Area when the hillsides are cloaked in a slate gray mist and one sound above all signals the season in the Oregon Coast Range.

On a recent December daybreak, cold and crisp and quiet conditions greeted the visitor across the seven-hundred-acre Jewell Meadows, one part of the expansive Wildlife Area. But the otherwise silent morning perked up when the hay wagon came into view. Even though the mercury registered at just 7°F, when the hay wagon showed up, the two hundred elk that live here quickly responded.

Refuge manager Brian Swearingen says the morning feeding is a regular winter event across Jewell Meadows—the feeding keeps the elk here rather than foraging across nearby private agricultural lands. "Okay, folks," whispered Swearingen. "This hay comes off in little flakes and if we could drop a flake off every ten feet or so that would be perfect—the tractor will tow the wagon slowly across the field and we'll feed two bales of the hay to the elk this morning."

We were on the western fringe of the refuge, an area where approximately twenty-five bull elk spend their time together. Brian noted that this group is referred to as the "bachelor herd."

"The bulls use so much energy during the breeding season from September through early October that they can go into winter in real poor condition. So, they're trying to regain that energy and fat reserves to make it through the wintertime." Some of the bulls in the Jewell herd are massive animals that tip the scales at more than eight hundred pounds—with antler spans of five or even six feet.

292

Roosevelt bull elk are majestic and can tip the scales at eight hundred pounds, so being this close to such a large wild animal is awesome.

On this particular day, there was another sound on board the feeding wagon— as Dean Crouser's camera made the tell-tale "click-click-click" of auto mode as he snapped shots with his digital camera that had a 200mm zoom lens attached to it. Dean sported a mile-wide smile on his face and beamed, "I'm a native Oregonian and I've always been proud to be an Oregonian—this is one more thing that makes it such a cool place to be. This is just another little gem."

Dean is a wildlife artist who searches for Oregon wildlife in "everyday moments"— the times that many of us take for granted. This day marked his first wintertime trip to Jewell Meadows Wildlife Area and he was a bit like a kid in a candy store—so many photo opportunities were presented in front of him from the cozy confines of the feeding wagon, because the elk were feeding just twenty yards away. "I am looking for just the right light," he noted. "The contrast of the dark and the light with a bull's head turned to where it's in the shadow, a real dark tone but his back is all lit up and a nice yellowish orange. Like that one right there."

It's the sort of material that has long stirred Dean's imagination: "It really is the stuff that I've seen and done nearly all my life in the Northwest. Elk are kind of the cherry on top of our big game animals in Oregon. Yet, across the country there aren't a lot of places that have them. They're pretty special." Dean travels across Oregon— often corner to corner—and his work reflects the adventure and inspiration and wild moments that he has seen.

While his work begins with a camera (on this day he will take more than four hundred photos, but only a handful will be used as reference models), all too soon, paintbrushes and watercolors take over in his Gresham, Oregon, studio. "I do not strive to replicate the animals. It doesn't have to be accurate from the standpoint of what an elk really looks like. Now, a lot of people really like to paint that way, almost photo-realism, but I have no interest in doing that. I appreciate people who can, but I have no interest in doing that."

Dean has had many interests in his life and he has set many records too. Like the NCAA Track and Field Championships that he won back in the early '80s at the University of Oregon. A few years ago he was inducted into the University's Hall of Fame. Despite his athletic successes, he said that he's been painting since he was ten years old. It has grown into a passion for his home state that he likes to share with others. "Elk and deer are obviously intelligent animals and it's pretty neat to watch their mannerisms and feeding activities and then—especially with elk—how the bulls and younger bulls determine their hierarchy. That's what makes Jewell pretty cool. Anyone would love to go out and see it—even for an hour. How could you not? It's incredible."

For More Information

Where: 79878 State Highway 202, Seaside, OR 97138
Phone: 503-755-2264
Watch the Episode: www.traveloregon.com/jewellelk

Making Tracks in Deep Powder

Mount Bachelor

Bring your toes all the way forward, Grant, up to the clip of this binding, and then pull the strap across the top of your foot as tight as you can." So advised my guide, Jack Newkirk. But when it's 20°F with a windchill making it much colder, and the snowflakes are buzzing circles around your head like an angry hive of hornets, stepping into and strapping on a pair of two-foot-long snowshoes isn't the easiest of winter activities.

Yet with Jack's patient tone and simple instructions, it was but a matter of minutes before my companions and I were set and ready to follow his lead into the snow-covered hills of the Deschutes National Forest near Bend, Oregon. Jack is a guide who works for Wanderlust Tours in Bend, and leads varied year-round recreational outings across the region, but in wintertime when the snow is waist deep, the specialty is snowshoe hiking. It's the powder that folks live to play in near central Oregon's Mount Bachelor—High Cascade powder that is lighter and fluffier than the snow that falls across most of Western Oregon.

It draws folks from all over who yearn to ski or board the mountain's slopes. "These are going to be your friends," chuckled Jack. "When we're climbing uphill in the snow and the ice they will give you traction and you will learn to love them." Jack said that snowshoes have come a long way from the old days of heavy wood, leather laces, and beaver pelts. "When you think back to the people who would have used them the most—what kind of peoples were they? Eskimos and fur trappers! They needed a shoe large enough to support their weight plus hundreds of pounds of equipment, traps, and gear that they had to carry around."

Today, the shoes are made of aluminum alloys and other high-tech materials that are so lightweight, you hardly know that you're wearing them. "Okay, troops, let's go up this way." With that said, Jack herded his largely inexperienced charges into a semicircle around him to receive more helpful tips: "When you go uphill make sure you dig your toes into the hill, dig the balls of the feet in, and just start moving."

Dan and Shelly Coe chased down Wanderlust Tours all the way from Ohio and they were surviving their very first snowshoe venture just fine. Shelly laughed as she toppled into the powder after stepping onto the back of her left shoe with the front of the right. In between her giggles she told me, "The walking isn't the hard part. It's getting up after you fall down, and I discovered that if you put your hand down on the snow for balance, you keep falling deeper and deeper into it."

There is a blissful feeling of nearly floating across the snow on the broad, lightweight shoes. It isn't anything like the desperate plodding you often see in movies, or read about in Jack London's tales of the far north. "The coolest part of snowshoeing is that what must go up—doesn't have to come down but gets to come down—and going downhill in snowshoes is fantastic!"

With that, he invited each of us to run or jog downhill— he called it "snow surfing."

"Big steps, gang! The trick is to not stop running—whatever you do, just keep moving."

"It's a blast," shouted Dan. "I love the really light, fluffy powder—I mean it's amazing—like what they call 'champagne snow'— just don't find it on the East Coast or frankly very much on the West Coast—it spoils you!" Rather, despite the six-foot snow depth, there's a certain rhythm to the walking, and it takes only minutes to get the hang of it. Then you begin to look up, take stock of your surroundings and the magnificence of the snow on the trees, burdened with the heavy overcoat of fresh snowfall. And then there is the quiet of the forest. It seems to whisper to you, "This is Mother Nature at her finest."

For More Information

Where: 61535 South Highway 97, Suite 13, Bend, OR 97702
Web: www.wanderlusttours.com
Phone: 541-389-8359 or 800-962-2862; Fax: 541-383-4317
Watch the Episode: www.traveloregon.com/makingtracks

Higher Education
High Desert Museum

It's funny how some of the best surprises are often found right in your own back-yard. So it is from the eastern Cascades point of view where elbow room is mea-sured by the wide-open vistas of snow-shrouded landscapes; the kinds of scenes that capture your heart and may lead you to wonder aloud: "Why have I never traveled this way before?" It is a question on many visitors' minds at a place where the answer is easy to find and higher education is center stage at the High Desert Museum near Bend. You'll agree with the staff's adage that this remarkable complex of displays, demonstrations, and hands-on events make the museum "more like an expedition than an exhibition."

According to museum spokesperson Dana Whitelaw, the museum examines and explains the natural history and the special qualities of high desert life: "They may have seen the sign on the highway for years and finally stopped in and people on a regular basis are blown away by how much is here. They experience so much of the West through art, cultural and natural history, and the wildlife. We are proud that we can be that relevant."

From birds of prey, such as hawks and eagles, to river otters and porcupines, this is a place where you can see and learn about the arid Intermountain West, which includes portions of eight western states and the Canadian province of British Columbia. The museum spreads across 150 acres filled with exhibits and demonstra-tions. A mile-long trail goes through twenty-five acres of trailside exhibits, includ-ing a trout stream, otter ponds, porcupine dens, and historic interpretive displays of frontier life and industry.

A favorite part for me is the Earl A. Chiles Center and a walking tour through vignettes of life called Spirit of the West. This timeline stroll covers thousands of years in the span of a few hundred feet. Along the way, you are invited into a Native American campsite to learn how hardy vegetation, abundant wildlife, and a mineral-rich terrain sustained generations of natives. Then come the explorers and the fur trappers, the miners and sheepherders and sodbusters, and finally the immigrants, fresh off the Oregon Trail. All of this is explained through sights and sounds that put you in scenes from the Stone Age to rustic dirt roads in a Western frontier town.

Few places convey the story of humans in the desert as well as this experience, including how the mines, then the ranches, and then the railroads brought more and more people to the desert, so that by the 1880s, small cottage industries began to

Drop in at the High Desert Museum near Bend and learn about the natural and cultural history east of the Cascade Mountains.

sprout and, in many ways, forever change the face of the desert. A new large-scale exhibit called Sin in the Sagebrush serves up sights and sounds and role players in costumes to put you into a scene from Oregon's most recent past. Museum curator Bob Boyd told me that cowhands, buckaroos, trappers, and miners enjoyed a brief escape from the drudgery of daily routines inside the Frontier Saloon: "For many thousands of people, going west in itself was taking a chance—and if the weather killed your sheep or if your mining claim wasn't paying off—you were a risk taker just showing up. So, perhaps one more turn of the card or spin of that roulette wheel and things might turn around for you."

Other risk takers of the same era included countless homesteaders like Mrs. Blair, portrayed in full costume by local volunteer Linda Evans, who helps you to see and understand how tough life was in the high desert as you stroll through her replica farmstead from the 1880s. She admitted that the hardest part of all was "loneliness, because we're forty miles from Prineville and it takes two days to get there. I go maybe four or five times a year. So, we do get lonely and the children keep us busy, but I dearly love to have visitors."

You'll love seeing the many wildlife species on display at the museum too. Hawks, eagles, and turkey vultures are frequently seen soaring over the wide expanse of the desert, but at the museum you can see them all close at hand and learn about their special adaptations for survival. "When it's behind a screen or behind glass, you're so removed," noted wildlife curator Nolan Harvey. "But when you're up close you can see the feathers move, you see the bird move and pay attention to you—that captures your heart and hopefully makes you want to know more about the animal and gives you that bond."

The close connection with wildlife is a lasting legacy from the museum's founder, Donald Kerr, who owned a passion for wildlife. He was a big believer that animals can connect with newcomers and perhaps change attitudes about the high desert. "We're very proud that all the animals you see here were either captive born or they have been through rehabilitation and cannot be released," added Nolan. "Our wildlife get a second chance at life to educate the rest of us."

Whether education or recreation, the High Desert Museum will capture your heart and bring you back time and again. "It's a real jewel," noted Dana. "A true treasure of Central Oregon!"

For More Information

Where: 59800 US Highway 97, Bend, OR 97702

Web: www.highdesertmuseum.org

Phone: 541-382-4754

Watch the Episode: www.traveloregon.com/highdesertmuseum

Recommended Reading

Bishop, Ellen. *Hiking Oregon's Geology*. Seattle: The Mountaineers Books, 2004.

Bjornstad, Bruce, and Eugene Kiver. *On the Trail of the Ice Age Floods*. Sandpoint, ID: Keokee Co. Publishing Inc., 2012.

Blair, Seabury. *The Creaky Knees Guide to Oregon*. Seattle: Sasquatch Books, 2010.

Bloom, Barbara, and Garry Cohen. *Romance of Waterfalls: Northwest Oregon and Southwest Washington*. Portland, OR: Outdoor Romance Publishing, 1998.

Brown, Clint, and Cheryl McLean. *Oregon's Quiet Waters*. Corvallis, OR: Jackson Creek Press, 2003.

Campbell, Robert. *Illustrated Rigging: For Salmon Steelhead Trout*. Portland, OR: Frank Amato Publications, 2007.

Contreras, Alan, and Hendrik G. Herlyn. *Handbook of Oregon Birds*. Corvallis: Oregon State University Press, 2009.

Davis, James. *The Northwest Nature Guide*. Portland, OR: Timber Press, 2009.

Fletcher, Roger. *Drift Boats and River Dories: Their History, Design, Construction, and Use*. Mechanicsburg, PA: Stackpole Books, 2007.

Frank, Gerry. *Gerry Frank's Oregon*. Salem, OR: Gerrys Frankly Speaking, 2012.

Friedman, Ralph. *Oregon for the Curious*, 3rd rev. ed. Caldwell, ID: The Caxton Printers, Ltd., 1972.

Giordano, Pete. *Soggy Sneakers: A Paddler's Guide to Oregon Rivers*. Seattle: The Mountaineers Books, 2004.

Houck, Michael C., and M. J. Cody, editors. *Wild in the City*. Corvallis: Oregon State University Press, 2011.

Jones, Phillip. *Canoe and Kayak Routes of NW Oregon*. Seattle: The Mountaineers Books, 2007.

Lichatowich, Jim. *Salmon Without Rivers: A History of the Salmon Crisis*. Washington, D.C.: Island Press, 2001.

Nehls, Harry. *Birds of the Willamette Valley*. Olympia, WA: R.W. Morse Company, 2004.

Seideman, David. *Showdown at Opal Creek: The Battle for America's Last Wilderness*. New York City: Carroll & Graf Publishing, 1993.

Sheehan, Madelynne Diness. *Fishing in Oregon, revised and updated*. Portland, OR: Flying Pencil Publications, 2005.

Steinhauser, Karla. *I Am Karla's Smokehouse*. Rockaway Beach, OR: Karla Steinhauser, 2010.

Sullivan, William L. *100 Hikes in the Central Oregon Cascades, 4th edition*. Eugene, OR: Navillus Press, 2012.

Whitehill, Karen, and Terry Whitehill. *Nature Walks in and around Portland: All-Season Exploring in Parks, Forests, and Wetlands*. Seattle: The Mountaineers Books, 1998.

Williams, Travis. *The Willamette River Field Guide*. Portland, OR: Timber Press, 2009.

Index

Deschutes River Scenic Byway, 234

Deschutes River steelhead, 232–35, *233*

Diamond Craters Outstanding Natural Area, 112

Diamond Lake, 154–55

Diamond Mill, off-roading, 51

Dickison, Paul, 255–56

Dickison, Wes, 255–56

Dickson, Irene, 26

Dickson, Jim, 248–49

Dierckx, Steve, 22, 24

Dietz, Steve, 240

disc golf, 185–87, *185, 186*

Discovery Museum, World Forestry Center, 62–63

Doc Hay, 108–9

dog sledding, Mount Bachelor, 34–36, *35–36*

Dolphin, Glenn, 70–71

Don Best's Clam Fritters, 104

Dotson, Holly, 91

Dotson, Sean, 91

Dotson, Shannon, 91

Doug fir trees: Oregon Heritage Trees, 23–24; Valley of the Giants, 24, 124–25

Dovre Campground, 120

Dovre Creek Waterfall, 120, *121*

Doyle, Marissa, 92–93

Drawson, Maynard, 22–23

Dreiling, Randy, 127, 128

drift boats, 33, 271–73, *272*

Drift Boats and River Dories (Fletcher), 272

Drift Creek, 72–74, *73, 74*

Driggs, Jeremiah, 130

Ducks Unlimited, 162

Duncan, Valerie, 162

Dungeness crab, 224, *224*, 247–50

Eagle Cap Wilderness, 207, 208

East Lake, Newberry National Volcanic Monument, 146, 147

eco-pub, Hopworks Urban Brewery (HUB), 19–21

Edwards, Deborah, 55

E. E. Wilson Wildlife Area, Youth Outdoor Day, 161–64, *162*

Elkhorn Wildlife Area, 37–39, *38–39*

elk, Roosevelt elk, 144–45, 292–94, *293*

Empems, Laura, 181

Epperson, Chester, 41

Erickson, Jennifer, 247–48

Erickson, Steve, 247

Erratic Rock State Natural Site, 45–47

Ettinger, Christian, 19–20

Ettinger, Roy, 19

Evans, Linda, 298–99

E. Z. Orchards, 240–41

Fan Creek Campground, 120–21

farm tools, Three Mile Museum, 64–65

Fernhill Wetlands, 259–61

Fick Crab Cakes, 250

Fick, Steve, 101–2, 248–50

Fields Bridge Park, 46–47

field trips, 257

Firefighter's Guide Service, 217

Firsthand Oregon, 139–41, *139*

Fisher, Troy, 288, 289

Fish Hawk Adventures, 218–20, 222

fishing: crawfish, 188–90; Deschutes River steelhead, 232–35, *233*; Diamond Lake, 154–55; Green Peter Reservoir, 129–31, *129*; Klamath River rainbow trout fishing, 134–35, *134*; Lost Lake, 100; Metolius River, 148–50, *149*; Tillamook Bay Chinook fishing, 214–17, *214*; West Linn fishing dock, 140; White River, 76

flamingos, Wildlife Safari, 85

Fletcher, Roger, 33, 272–73

floats, glass floats, 274–75, *274*

flooding, Ice Age flooding and glacial erratics, 45–47

Flowers, Dale, 69

The Fly Fisher's Place, 148

fly fishing: Klamath River rainbow trout fishing, 134–35, *134*; Metolius River, 148–50, *149*

flying, Willamette Valley Soaring Club (WVSC), 90–91

Folkema, Jeff, 103–4

Ford, Brandon, 247–48

Forest Grove, Fernhill Wetlands, 259–61

Fort Clatsop National Memorial, 282–84, *283*

Fort Stevens State Park, 283, 284

Fort to Sea Trail, 283, 284

Fort Yamhill State Heritage Area, 29–30, *29*

Fossil, Oregon, 200–201

fossils, 200–201

Fox, Rachel, 238

Frame, Dennis, 26–27

Frank, Gerry, 240–42

Frederick, Morgan, 161

Frederick, Sydney, 161

"free riding," Black Rock Mountain, 165–66

Frenchglen Hotel, 111

French, Peter, 111

French, Rod, 233

fritters, Don Best's Clam Fritters, 104

Gable, Clark, 226

"gaper" clams, 103

Garibaldi Marina, 103

Gartzke, Jeff, 175–76

Gaskill, Tom, 230–31

"Gas Tank Getaways," 211–13

Geier, Joel, 253, 254

Geisendorfer, George M., 144

gemstones, Rice Northwest Museum of Rocks and Minerals, 40–41, *41*

Gentry, Sallie, 253–54

George Roger's Park, 240

Gerry Frank's Oregon (Frank), 241

giant sequoias, Washington County Courthouse, 22, 24

Giles, Marty, 158, 197–98

Gill, Gayle, 197

Gill, Kuri, 238–39, 240

giraffes, Wildlife Safari, 82

glacial erratics, Erratic Rock State Natural Site, 45–47

Gladish, Sandy, 180, 181

Glascow, Todd, 166

glassblowing, 274–75

glass floats, 274–75, *274*

Goldberg, Alan, 12, 13

golden eagle, *27*

"Golden Flower of Prosperity," Kam Wah Chung State Heritage Site, 108–9

Printed in the USA
CPSIA information can be obtained
at www.ICGtesting.com
JSHW012020140824
68134JS00033B/2790